Published by Applied Research and Design Publishing, an imprint of ORO Editions.
Gordon Goff: Publisher

www.appliedresearchanddesign.com
info@appliedresearchanddesign.com

USA, EUROPE, ASIA, MIDDLE EAST, SOUTH AMERICA

Graphic Design: Stefano Perrotta
Production Assistance: Valentina Marcarini
Research and Design Assistance: Aida Afsari, Venkataram Padmanabhan

This book has been subject to peer-review

10 9 8 7 6 5 4 3 2 1 First Edition

Library of Congress data available upon request. World Rights: Available

ISBN: 978-1-954081-21-5

Color Separations and Printing: ORO Group Ltd.
Printed in China.

International Distribution: www.appliedresearchanddesign.com/distribution

ORO Editions makes a continuous effort to minimize the overall carbon footprint of its publications. As part of this goal, ORO Editions, in association with Global ReLeaf, arranges to plant trees to replace those used in the manufacturing of the paper produced for its books. Global ReLeaf is an international campaign run by American Forests, one of the world's oldest nonprofit conservation organizations. Global ReLeaf is American Forests' education and action program that helps individuals, organizations, agencies, and corporations improve the local and global environment by planting and caring for trees.

AMERICAN FORESTS
- SINCE 1875 -

Posthuman Architectures

A Catalogue of Archetypes

Jacopo Leveratto

Contents

Preface

"Every era has had its own iconic architectural typology. The dream commission was once the church, Modernism had the factory and then the house; in the past decade we celebrated the decadent museum and the gallery. [...] The most significant architectural spaces in the world are now [...] empty of people."

Liam Young, *Machine Landscapes: Architectures of the Post Anthropocene* (London: Wiley, 2019), 9; 8.

At first sight, the expression posthuman architecture can be read as an oxymoron, there is no doubt about it. A real contradiction in terms. Because for too long a time design has been seen as an exclusive human prerogative. Especially spatial one. As it always represented an action that could be performed by people and for people only, with no exceptions. No need to imagine a possible one. Recently, however, things seem to be gradually changing, as different researches have started to challenge this idea. Quite a large number of scholars, for instance, has already highlighted how some animals actually design and not only build their dwellings. Intentionally responding, so to say, to symbolic needs besides functional ones. Far fewer, by contrast, have focused their attention on how humans have conceived spaces and objects also for other kinds of subjects. Even though relevant references in this regard are not entirely missing. Whether datacenters or natural reserves, third landscapes or biospheres, some of the most innovative and meaningful projects of our times in fact seem to fall into this category, since they all feature a subject that is not only human, either in terms of fruition or agency, and they all materialize diverse interpretations of a larger project of living that involves different and interconnected entities. Nevertheless, the ability of design to spatially mediate this relationship has often been overlooked, as they have mostly been considered simple infrastructures. And this probably explains why qualitative researches in this regard are still partially lacking.

This is why this book collects and discusses archetypal models of posthuman design, in its broader sense. To identify its features beyond the limit of a functional determinism, within which it seems to be relegated. Even when it is barely aware of its role. Not all archetypes presented here can in fact be considered entirely paradigmatic. Some of them, for instance, may appear inadequate in dealing with complex interspecies relationships only in figurative terms. Moreover, almost none of them represent a conscious and explicit attempt of realizing a true posthuman habitat, considering all the philosophical complexity that the term entails today. This however is not a real problem. Even pre-modern church builders were not aware of creating archetypal spaces for the earliest industrial buildings. As well as Renaissance architects could not know that palaces would have been considered a model for the typological development of museums and universities. The purpose of this book is in fact not the development of a new architectural typology, but to offer some possible references for its ideation. Spatial ones, of course, but mainly methodological. Since the specific focus of this catalogue is design, both as a product and as a process. And its objective is therefore showing how architectural, but also landscape, and industrial designers, whether professional practitioners or not, have redefined their tools and strategies in order to meet the needs of new and different kinds of subjects. Or rather to show how they have turned this redefinition into a source of poetic expression and created a novel understanding of conventional categories through their work.

More than a historical research, therefore, this book represents a collection of stories of posthuman architectures, structured in a way to cover the topic both from a vertical and a horizontal perspective. At first, through an in-depth analysis of how some specific projects have reacted to the presence of different and extended subjectivities, in terms both of design process and form of expression. And then, through a visual atlas of multiple references that traces their possible genealogy. All this is comprised in ten chapters, one aimed at clarifying the features of the posthuman condition, and nine organized in a chronological order, conceived like single architectural tales. Each one is dedicated to a different archetype and its design, in order to trace the evolution of a certain idea of coexistence between humans and other subjects. And each one is complemented by technical drawings, to translate that idea into an operational set of instructions. As the book was meant not only as an iconographic repository of case studies, but also as an operating manual for designing spaces like those illustrated. From the cabin of Henry David Thoreau, for instance, to the Korean Demilitarized Zone. Considering projects like the Svalbard Global Seed Vault and designers like Cedric Price, Diller and Scofidio, or Junya Ishigami. To show how a different way of looking at the world is not only desirable and imaginable, but also actually realizable.

Spaces for new alliances

"Designers are always understood as solving a problem. Artists, intellectuals, and writers are expected to ask questions, to make us hesitate, to see our world and ourselves differently for a moment, and therefore to think. Why not design as a way of asking question? Why not design that produces thought-provoking hesitations in the routines of everyday life rather than simply servicing those routines? Why not design that encourages us think? Design as an urgent call to reflect on what we and our companion species have become?"

Beatriz Colomina and Mark Wigley, *Are We Human?* (Zürich: Lars Müller, 2016), 162-163.

Earth rising

All the questions mentioned on the previous spread are obviously rhetorical. Since any architectural project, from a certain point of view, can be seen as a sort of critical theory, albeit extremely local and punctual. As a critical theory, a project in fact suggests and prefigures a concrete and feasible alternative to the existing reality. It is its constitutional invariant. What varies, on the contrary, is its instrumentality, or the objective for which it is aimed. Because, if one wants a project to be also a critical tool, it is not enough for it to indicate the direction of a change. It is also necessary for this direction to emerge as a response to the internal contradictions of society, not from their acceptance.[1] A critical project, in other words, must be capable of questioning the order of things and the principle of development that are increasingly given as natural, instead of replicating them. And today there is no greater contradiction for our common condition than that concerning the role of humankind in its constructive relationship with the world. The one that is interesting, so to say, the world habitability in an ecologically profound sense,[2] as well as the way in which humanity can or cannot be part of its possible future scenarios.

Michel Serres already explained this contradiction very well some years ago, using as a metaphor the characters of an 1820 painting by Francisco Goya called *Fight with Cudgels*, which depicts two armed men, one against the other, immersed to the knees in a swamp, when a storm is approaching. He compared the unawareness of their own condition to that of western society towards the changes in the relations of dependence and control characterizing the bond between humankind and nature over the last few centuries.[3] In antiquity, in fact, according to Serres, a clear distinction was marked between things that were depending on human will and the natural ones. Those, in other words, against which it was absurd even to think of being able to intervene. Then, the modern progress in science and technology prompted an idea of extensive control over the world that consolidated over the years, following the Cartesian precept of exponentially increasing the things that depended on human will, in order to proportionally decrease the others. To such an extent that today, at the height of this project of domination over nature, it has become evident that people have no long-term control over the effects of their actions. And, in fact, they depend on the things that were supposed to depend on them.

From this point of view, it is no coincidence, therefore, that this awareness emerged for the first time after the end of the first Industrial Revolution, with the earliest geological studies on the "anthropozoic era."[4] Nor is it a coincidence that this awareness spread after the nuclear devastation of the Second World War, with a first recognition of the role played by humanity "in changing the face of the Earth."[5] But it was only during the early seventies, along with a worldwide economic recession, that the definitive acknowledgement of the inherent limits to the current model of growth began to make clear both the responsibilities for and the consequences of such a lack of control.[6] And it was only at the beginning of the following millennium that the human transformative activity was to be definitively identified as the cause of the main territorial, structural and climatic changes of the last few years.[7] From the development of extensive agriculture to the consequent deforestation, from the extraction of fossil resources to the emission of greenhouse gases, from the acidification of oceans to the degradation of soil, up to an extinction rate thousands of times higher than it had ever been over the last five hundred million years.[8] All of this in such a clear attribution of fault that, today, the International Commission on Stratigraphy and the International Union of Geological Sciences are considering whether to declare the Holocene definitively concluded, promoting the Anthropocene as a new geological era.

The consequence, of course, is that the constructive role of humankind has never been so questioned. The awareness of its impact on the natural balance of the planet has in fact opened a global debate on the legitimacy and the future sustainability of this position. It is not surprising, therefore, that in

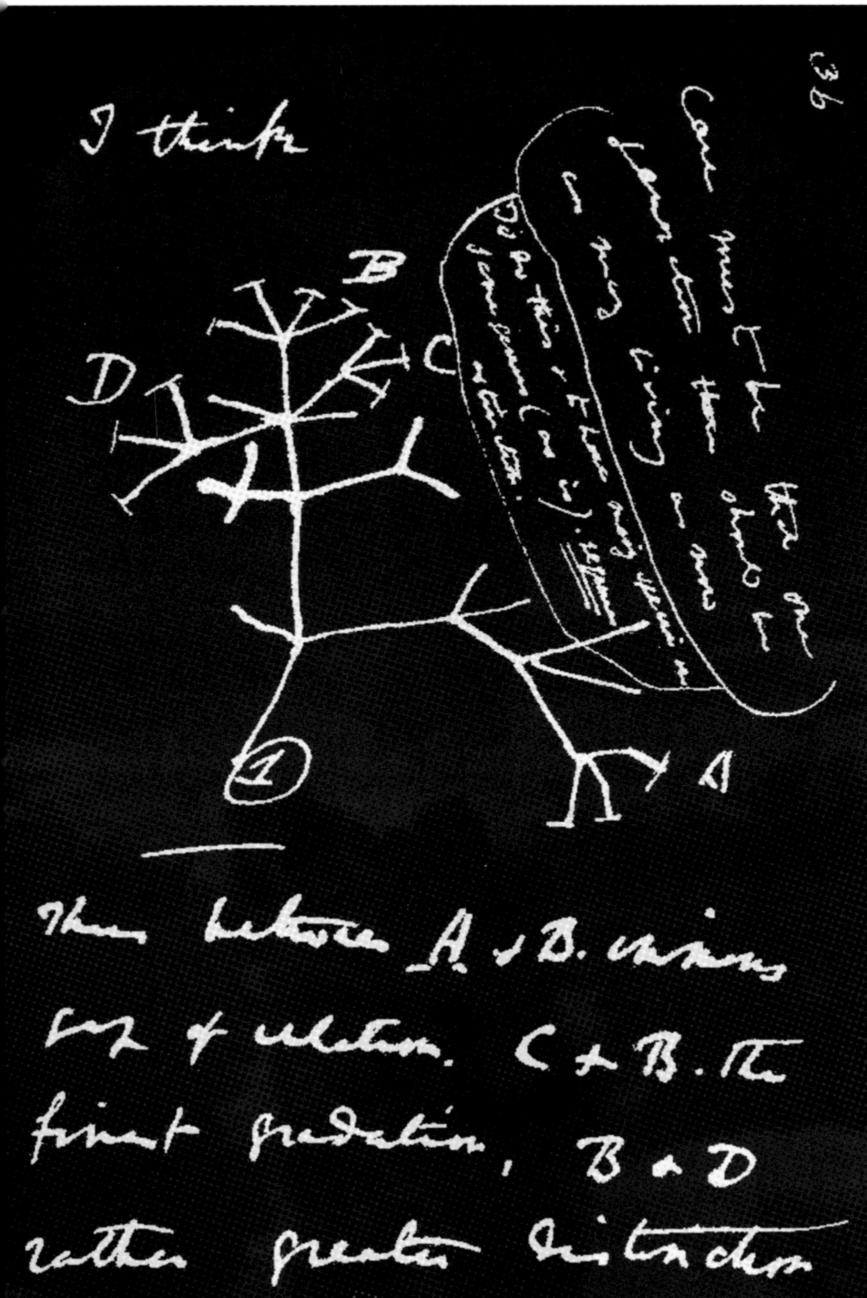

Posthuman roots. Charles Darwin and the atomic bomb

the same period in which nature has progressively shown itself to be increasingly anthropized, the cultural horizon of human sciences has moved towards a theoretical position that, today, entails a substantial overcoming of its own category of reference or, in other words, the human itself.[9] An idea that, in comparison with the last decades of the twentieth century, does not imply the abandonment to radical claims of self-extinction. Nor the construction of a transhumanist imaginary marked by the fusion between man and machine. On the contrary, it requires a reconsideration of human subjectivity within new limits. The same limits that define the field of critical experimentation that today is simply called "posthuman," and that has taken shape in the last twenty years from the progressive convergence of a post-humanistic ontology and a non-anthropocentric ethics.[10]

Today, in summary, the responsibility for a possible sixth mass extinction is orienting human sciences in the same direction in which the aftermath of the Second World War had pushed the first critical theory. Hence precisely towards the abandonment of the modern ideology of "man" as the subjective origin and interpretative limit of reality, coming from the classical ideal formulated by Protagoras as "the measure of all things." A detachment that first emerged with Martin Heidegger's opposition to the concept that existentialism was a form of humanism.[11] But which was already present in Karl Marx's discourse, when he first described all that previously seemed to belong to the depth of the human as determined by current relations of production.[12] It is not surprising, therefore, that owing to the structuralist radicalization of his work, in the mid-sixties, the necessity of a true "overcoming" of the subject was first decreed.[13] Nor that, after a few years, thanks to the Deleuzian interpretation and its ramification within gender studies,[14] this form of theoretical anti-humanism evolved into the critique of the traditional ideal of "man," male, white and European, as the sole universal representative of the human subjectivity. The same that, by introjecting the refusal of a hierarchy of species, over the last two decades has finally focused on a fundamentally biocentric perspective, according to which all living organisms have equal importance.[15]

In this regard, the tradition is even longer, as it can be traced back to that conceptual space that Linnaeus opened by classifying humankind among other *Anthropomorpha*, such as apes, thus describing *Homo* as constitutively nonhuman.[16] The same space further scrutinized by Jeremy Bentham when he ascribed to their capacity for suffering the essential criterion entitling animals to equal consideration of moral interests than human beings[17]. These are in fact the bases on which, for example, Jakob von Uexküll moved life sciences towards the radical dehumanization of the image of nature that unfolded almost fifty years later.[18] But also those that pushed "deep ecologists," after the publication of the first pictures of the Earth from space,[19] to try to overcome the inconsistencies of anthropocentric environmentalism, by advocating a transformation of consciousness.[20] All of this consistently with the development of the Gaia hypothesis,[21] and in consonance with the contemporary rise of radical movements in defense of the planet. In the belief, in other words, that the whole living environment had to be considered as having some basic legal and moral rights to flourish, regardless of its instrumentality for human purposes. As though it were part of a technologically mediated continuum between nature and culture, which today also extends to the articulated relationship between humans and intelligent machines.

From this point of view, therefore, the rise of a posthuman condition does not concern the end of humanity or its replacement by something else, but its definitive extension. It concerns the opening of subjectivity to an "extended nature-cultural self,"[22] animal and artificial, alternative to the classical humanist subject, but still profoundly human. The same subject which Donna Haraway referred to, for example, when using the metaphor of the "cyborg" to oppose her refusal to identities based on binary categories.[23] Or again, that subject emerging from the recovery of the animality proposed by Jacques Derrida and Giorgio Agamben.[24] As anthropologist Eduardo Kohn in fact wrote, one just needs to read the riddle that the Sphinx asked Oedipus to understand the polyvalence inherent in this condition.[25] Since a human being, four legs in the morning, two at noon and three at sunset, has never been just a man, but also an animal and a technologically increased organism. For this reason, the construction of the habitat of a posthuman subject cannot be limited to the standardized needs of an idealized man, but must open up to an extended creative subjectivity, which is simultaneously multiform and interconnected, situated and culturally differentiated. It must be capable, in other terms, of thinking the world through connections rather than divisions, and welcoming different species and technologies, in a perspective of coexistence and collaboration among different parts of an expanded self.[26] Moreover, there is no need to mention imaginary Einsteinian prophecies about bees to justify this need. Because the goal, after all, is simply to try to live well together "on a vulnerable planet."[27]

To tell the truth, it cannot be said that environmental design has been insensitive to the subject, at least since the first studies on the subject by Ian McHarg.[28] From the beginning of the new millennium, however, the vast majority of proposals in this regard moved along the line of a utilitarian principle of environmentalist nature, which was based only on the acknowledgement of human needs. In fact, while partially opening up to the inclusion of other species and technologies, design researches on the subject almost never extended the principle of habitability, understood as the possibility of appropriation and construction of one's own living environment, to non-human subjects. What was missing, in other words, was a critical perspective of the design theory, able to imagine a reality that was alternative to the internal contradictions of the current principles of development and its accompanying exploitation of nature. Thus, even over the last twenty years, with the exception of some systematic but very sectorial studies,[29] the debate has gradually coagulated around specific proposals, alternatively centered on large urban utopias without any feasibility and sim-

Designs for Earth

ple design solutions for immediate commercial exploitation.[30] While, from the outside, the model most often invoked is the one that envisages a progressive withdrawal of all design attempts.

Today, therefore, rather than formalizing another single solution, it seems more important to construct a different critical and theoretical framework within which to articulate a design thought that could unfold proactively as well as retroactively. Able, in other words, to recognize its roots to make innovative proposals. Because what is missing, after all, is still the definition of that *Operating Manual for Spaceship Earth* to which Richard Buckminster Fuller, in 1969, addressed architects, planners and engineers.[31] And if one still wants to ascribe to architectural design its critical role even in front of a new subjectivity of reference, probably the best way to construct this picture is to consider the criteria according to which the critical theory has already renewed its own methodological principles in light of the posthuman emergency.[32] In this way, one could thus compose an analogical system of operational references, to review some criteria and design paradigms that have never changed in recent years, even when confronted with a different sensitivity.

The first principle, of course, refers to an analytical approach and concerns cartographic accuracy. Or better, the need to construct a theoretically founded reading of the present that is capable of tracing the locations of power and, from there onwards, detecting the reciprocal position of the subjects to whom one addresses. This means, more simply, that every critical activity must start from a situated knowledge of the context in which it intervenes, in order to identify its contradictions. At the same time, however, these critiques concerning the locations of power are not sufficient in themselves. They only work if they are accompanied by the search for new figurations or conceptual characters that express alternative representations of the subject as a dynamic and connected entity. Like Haraway's "cyborg," for example, or the Deleuzian "nomad."[33] All counter-cultural subjects through which overcoming those differences of gender, race and species on which the oppressive mechanisms that were previously thought as natural and substantially unavoidable were based. Each one represents a complex singularity in its development, whose research is not accomplished by a simple action of recognition, but by a true affirmative project that is opposed to the dominant vision of the subject. All of this through a creative practice that, by starting from a process of "defamiliarization" from the usual normative categories, is articulated in an exercise of memory intended as an active reinvention of the subject, along the axes of non-linearity and interdisciplinarity.[34]

Likewise, if one adopts an inter-scalar perspective and keeps a certain distance from the classic typological catalog to which the project of dwelling is normally reduced, it does not seem difficult to imagine alternative spatial figurations for the extended and relational subject represented by the posthuman, even by simply looking at how the history of architecture has produced spaces of defamiliarization. Because building a posthuman habitat does not mean so much to find a new space for a new subject, as to reconsider the subjectivity that is at its center, in its affirmative, evolving and interconnected consistency. And if one attempts to interpret a project as being an apparatus,[35] it is not difficult to find some real and situated architectures that, instead of merely serving some needs or solving some problems, have represented multiform sites of resistance to the assimilation into dominant discourses about how to be in the world as humans, both functionally and symbolically. All of this by building an extended dimension in which humans and their companion species, be they animal or technological, have found a space for new alliances in order to live better together. And transforming a world of houses, gardens, and factories into a new one, which could ultimately question the inevitability of the existing reality.

Notes

1 As Herbert Marcuse wrote in 1937, critical theory is not limited to a description of reality, but it is aimed at proposing an alternative to its contradictions, through an approach that is different both from political economy and from the philosophical one. "Like philosophy, it opposes making reality into a criterion in the manner of complacent positivism. But unlike philosophy, it always derives its goals only from present tendencies of the social process. [...] The discussion leads back to the question: In what way is the theory more than economics? [...] The difference lies in the decisive factor, precisely the one that makes the society rational – the subordination of the economy to the individuals' needs." Herbert Marcuse, "Philosophy and Critical Theory (1937)," in *Negations: Essays in Critical Theory*, trans. Jeremy J. Shapiro (London: MayFlyBooks, 2009), 105-106.

2 The word ecology, introduced in 1866 by the German scientist Ernst Haeckel, uses the prefix *oikos* (dwelling) to define the study of the systemic relationships between an animal and the environment it inhabits. Ernst Haeckel, *Generelle Morphologie der Organismen* (Berlin, 1866).

3 Michel Serres, *Le Contrat naturel* (Paris: Flammarion, 1992).

4 The term was used by Italian geologist Antonio Stoppani to describe the telluric impact of the human activity of that age. Antonio Stoppani, *Corso di geologia: Geologia stratigrafica, Vol. 2* (Milan, 1873).

5 The title was that of the second international symposium sponsored by the Wenner-Gren Foundation (1956), which brought together seventy international scholars to discuss the changes to human habitat. William L. Thomas, ed., *Man's Role in Changing the Face of the Earth* (Chicago: University of Chicago Press, 1956).

6 Donella H. Meadows, et al., *The Limits to Growth* (New York: Universe Books, 1972).

7 Paul J. Crutzen, "Geology of Mankind," *Nature* 415, no. 23 (2002): 23.

8 Erle Ellis, *Anthropocene: A Very Short Introduction* (Oxford: Oxford UP, 2018). For a complete overview of the philosophical consequences of such a recognition, see the latest works of Timothy Morton, and in particular *Dark Ecology: For a Logic of Future Coexistence* (New York: Columbia University Press, 2016); and *Being Ecological* (Cambridge MA: The MIT Press, 2018).

9 As an example of the breadth and interdisciplinarity of the debate, see Lambros Malafouris and Carl Knappett, eds., *Material Agency: Towards a Non-Anthropocentric Approach* (New York: Springer, 2008); Eduardo Kohn, *How Forests Think: Toward an Anthropology Beyond the Human* (Berkeley: University of California Press, 2013); Heather Davis and Etienne Turpin, eds., *Art in the Anthropocene* (London: Open Humanities Press, 2015); Donna J. Haraway, *Staying with the Trouble: Making Kin in the Chthulucene* (Chicago: Duke University Press Books, 2016); Mariano Gomez-Luque and Ghazal Jafari, eds., *New Geographies 09: Posthuman* (Cambridge MA: Harvard GSD, 2018).

10 Rosi Braidotti and Maria Hlavajova, eds., *Posthuman Glossary* (London: Bloomsbury, 2018), 1.

11 Martin Heidegger, *Brief über den Humanismus* (Frankfurt am Main: Klostermann, 1947).

12 Louis Althusser, *Pour Marx* (Paris: Maspero, 1965).

13 Michel Foucault, *Les mots e les choses* (Paris: Gallimard, 1966).

14 Gilles Deleuze and Felix Guattari, *Mille Plateaux: Capitalisme et Schizophrénie* (Paris: Minuit, 1980); Luce Irigaray, *This Sex Which Is Not One* (Ithaca NY: Cornell University Press, 1985). In this regard, see also Judith Butler, *Gender Trouble: Feminism and the Subversion of Identity* (New York: Routledge, 1990); and Raewyn Connell, *Gender: In World Perspective* (Cambridge-Malden: Polity Press, 2002).

15 Emanuele Coccia, *The Life of Plants: A Metaphysics of Mixture* (Cambridge-Malden: Polity Press, 2018).

16 Carolus Linnaeus, *Systema naturae, sive, Regna tria naturae systematice proposita per classes, ordines, genera, & species* (Haak: Lugduni Batavorum, 1735).

17 Jeremy Bentham, *An Introduction to the Principles of Morals and Legislation* (London, 1780), chapter XVII.

18 Jakob von Uexküll and Georg Kriszat, *Streifzüge durch die Umwelten von Tieren und Menschen: Ein Bilderbuch unsichtbarer Welten* (Berlin: Springer, 1934). About the following developments, see Umberto Maturana and Francisco J. Varela, *Autopoiesis and Cognition* (Dordrecht: Reidel, 1980).

19 Frank White, *The Overview Effect: Space Exploration and Human Evolution* (Boston: Houghton-Mifflin, 1987).

20 Arne Næss, *Ecology, Community and Lifestyle* (Cambridge: Cambridge University Press, 1989).

21 James E. Lovelock, "Gaia as Seen through the Atmosphere," *Atmospheric Environment* 6, no. 8 (1972): 579-580.

22 Rosi Braidotti, *The Posthuman* (Cambridge: Polity, 2013), 103.

23 Donna J. Haraway, "A Cyborg Manifesto: Science, Technology, and Socialist-Feminism in the Late Twentieth Century (1985)," in *Simians, Cyborgs and Women: The Reinvention of Nature* (New York: Routledge, 1991), 150.

24 Jacques Derrida, "The Animal That Therefore I Am (More to Follow)," *Critical Inquiry* 28, no. 2 (2002), 369-418; Giorgio Agamben, *L'aperto: L'uomo e l'animale* (Milan: Bollati Borighieri, 2002).

25 Kohn, How Forests Think, 5.

26 Anna Lowenhaupt Tsing, *The Mushroom at the End of the World: On the Possibility of Life in Capitalist Ruins* (Princeton: Princeton University Press, 2015).

27 Donna J. Haraway, "Sowing Worlds: A Seed Bag for Terraforming with Earth Others," in *Beyond the Cyborg: Adventures with Donna Haraway*, eds. Margret Grebowicz and Helen Merrick (New York: Columbia University Press, 2013), 137.

28 Ian McHarg, *Design with Nature* (New York: Doubleday, 1969).

29 See for instance, Debra Benita Shaw, *Posthuman Urbanism: Mapping Bodies in Contemporary City Space* (London: Rowman & Littlefield, 2018); Paola Antonelli and Ala Tannir, eds., *Broken Nature: Design Takes on Human Survival* (Milan: Electa, 2019); Liam Young, *Machine Landscapes: Architectures of the Post Anthropocene* (London: Wiley, 2019).

30 See, for example, the project by Andrea Branzi for the Grand Paris in 2008 and the IKEA production entitled *Wildhomes for Wildlife*.

31 Richard Buckminster Fuller, *Operating Manual for Spaceship Earth* (New York: Simon & Schuster, 1969).

32 Braidotti, *The Posthuman*, 163-169.

33 Haraway, *A Cyborg Manifesto*; Deleuze and Guattari, *Mille Plateaux*.

34 Braidotti, *The Posthuman*, 163.

35 "What I'm trying to single out with this term is [...] a thoroughly heterogeneous set consisting of discourses, institutions, architectural forms, regulatory decisions, laws, administrative measures, scientific statements, philosophical, moral ... propositions [...] [aimed at] a certain manipulation of relations of forces, [...] either so as to develop them in a particular direction, or to block them." Michel Foucault, *Power/Knowledge*, ed. Colin Gordon (New York: Pantheon Books, 1980), 194-96.

A nest

Henry David Thoreau
Concord, Massachusetts, USA
42.442104, -71.342524
1844-1854

"Henry often reminded me of an animal in human form. He had the eye of a bird, the scent of a dog, the most acute, delicate intelligence – but no soul. No … Henry could not have had a human soul."

Ralph Waldo Emerson, quoted in Rebecca Harding Davis, *Bits of Gossip* (Boston: Houghton Mifflin, 1904), 44.

In the beginning, before and beyond the human, was the forest, no mystery in this regard. No gardens of Eden could challenge this role. For it was in a forest that humanity took its shape, by literally clearing a space in the midst of it. And forests, in turn, have always defined their limits by difference, like a cast, representing a space of inherent otherness to the human. A place that has been of profanity, lawlessness and insecurity, but also of sacredness, abandon and enchantment. It all depended on how different cultures in different times have decided to interpret its alterity.[1] It was only, however, at the beginning of what the Enlightenment called "civilization,"[2] when the sciences of "man" were attempting to delineate "his" normative features, that forests emerged also as spatial figurations for imagining alternative visions of the human. And particularly in opposition to the new apparatuses of power that were being planned, namely schools, hospitals and prisons.[3] As though they were representing sites of resistance to the idea that civilization was the only true "natural" form of life for those who wanted to be called "men."[4] And that humanity, by consequence, could only find space within its normative limits.

It was not a coincidence, for instance, that Italo Calvino set in 1767 his *conte philosophique* about the adventures of a boy who escaped the rules of society by spending his life on the trees.[5] For in the mid-eighteenth century, the *enfants sauvages* who appeared more and more often in the forests around the villages of Europe began to silently question this supposed "naturalness" and its physical location.[6] To such an extent that when Jean-Jacques Rousseau had to picture his "natural man," he placed him, in opposition to the corruption of civilization, wandering alone through the primeval forests of the Earth, living a simpler, more innocent, and happier life.[7] Nevertheless, it took almost a century for this ideal of resistance to current social standards of civilization to leave the philosophical dimension and finally unfold in a true model of dwelling. And precisely the time that passed from the publication of Rousseau's treatise to the two years, two months, and two days that

Henry David Thoreau spent in solitude in a cabin he built by himself amidst the woods of Concord, Massachusetts, as part of an original experiment through which he materially realized a sort of personal utopia. An experiment that, over the years, has brought generations of followers into the wild, in order to put into practice their refusal to conform to the identity that society projected onto them.

The story is well known, also because most of it was published in 1854 with the title of *Walden*, one of the most influential books of American literature. It all began in 1844, when the magazine *The Dial* ceased publication and Thoreau, as a former contributor, needed to find not only another occupation, but also another way to express his thoughts. It was at that point that, before turning thirty, he decided to take a sabbatical from the daily duties of the family business, to become a writer in earnest and take his role in society as he truly imagined. Something that, in his consideration, demanded much more introspection and, at the same time, openness than all he had experienced until that moment by living a normal life. Through, so to say, a temporary detachment from civilization and its normative categories, to return to a state of nature in which he could really find himself. For this reason, he accepted the offer of his mentor Ralph Waldo Emerson, with whom he had been living since 1841, to take care, in exchange for a stay, of a woodland of his, near Walden Pond. And here he went to live alone, without any kind of support, with the intention of understanding what he was really living for and writing about it, in a fresh and renewed relation with the world.[8]

This, in few words, was the starting point of the extraordinary flight from society to a state of nature through which Thoreau completed his process of personal definition. A process realized not by reduction, or by simply testing his own survival abilities, but through immersion and communion with the "Universal Being" that Emerson saw permeating each thing, whether animate or not.[9] Through a phenomenological study, so to say, of nature's native tongue, which gradually brought him, obser-

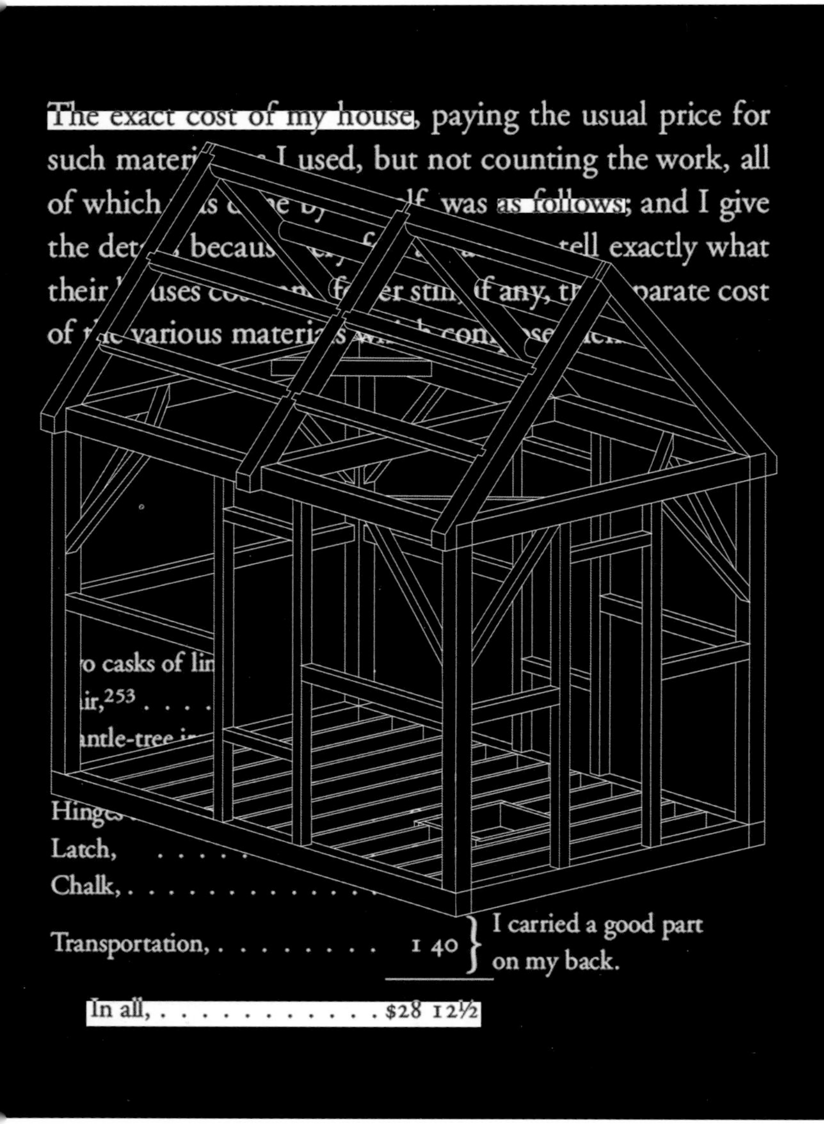

DIY home. Henry David Thoreau's instructions to live deliberately

vation after observation, to prioritize "nature's interest over the human [one]," in one of the first philosophical progressions, in Western culture, "from homocentrism to biocentrism."[10] All of this narrated, in a sometimes ironic and sometimes redundant manner, as an amused "experience of microcosmic and cosmic travel of the self,"[11] in which ethical and ontological reflections were juxtaposed to practical instructions and blueprints "to live deliberately [and] to front only the essential facts of life."[12] Like the suggestions on how to plant a garden, for example, or those on how to build furniture with the materials that could be found in the woods. But especially like the advice on how to build a house, which ultimately represented the very apparatus that he used to realize his existential project of living, in all its complexity.[13]

As he himself recognized, Thoreau's philosophical progression in fact began with an architectural act, which was that of building his own shelter. For this purpose, he wrote, he first borrowed an axe and went to the woods by the lake to cut down some young white pines, from which he obtained, in a couple of weeks, a frame comprising main timbers, floor timbers, studs and rafters. Then, he bought a shanty on a land not far away from the lake to recover from it the boards and some nails. Finally, once he had all the materials, he moved to the south side of a hill, where a woodchuck had already made its burrow, and dug his cellar, leaving the sides shelving and not stoned. And some days later, with the help of some friends, he set up the frame of the house, which he later boarded, roofed, waterproofed and equipped with a "recycled" chimney. Thus, in the end, the result was a single-room, "tight shingled and plastered house, ten feet wide by fifteen long, and eight-feet posts, with a garret and a closet, a large window on each side, two trap doors, one door at the end, and a brick fireplace opposite."[14] Inside there was "a bed, a table, a desk [and] three chairs" that he essentially made by himself.[15] All of this arranged in the form of a simple "nest," as he repeatedly referred to, reflecting his belief that "architectural beauty [...] [had to] grow from within outward, out of the

A cabin's genealogy. William Chambers, Andrew Jackson Downing, Henry David Thoreau, Gottfried Semper, Eugène Viollet-le-Duc

necessities and character of the indweller, who is the only [true] builder."[16]

Obviously, from this point of view, the idea that the construction of his cabin was an actual architectural act can be legitimately questioned. Especially as Thoreau explicitly mocked the professional practice of his age[17] to such an extent that, in some points, *Walden* looked like a "parody of the house book pattern genre."[18] Yet, as any other architect, Thoreau considered his shelter not only as a structure for keeping out the cold and providing a place to store his belongings, but primarily as a bearer of meaning, capable of being conceptualized and signifying an idea.[19] For this reason, over years, his writing has attracted the attention of architectural historians in many different ways, which ultimately followed three main directions. The first, as Lewis Mumford did, is to retroactively see the book, in direct continuity with the following work by Frederick Law Olmsted, as a means by which Thoreau built the American notion of landscape, by focusing on the totality of the natural environment, forgotten by his contemporaries.[20] The second, of which it is possible to find trace in Joseph Rykwert's study on the theme, consists in understanding his house as a native and self-taught reflection on the theme of the "primitive hut" as introduced by Marc-Antoine Laugier and then developed, in the Anglo-Saxon area, by William Chambers.[21] And the third is to consider its construction in light of the American reform of domestic architecture put forth by the "villa books" published in that period by the likes of Andrew Jackson Downing, which proposed the rustic English cottage as a model of fitness, integrity and simplicity.[22] By contrast, little attention has been placed on the value of its design as an ideological and political device for proposing an alternative way of life, in relation to a different philosophical thought.

In this regard, however, Thoreau's words were quite clear about the fundamental role that architecture played in this attempt of building a theoretical manifesto. First of all, as in fact reflected by both the specific report he made of the process of its construction and the detailed list of the costs which complemented the account, the cabin, in its design, represented an essential device of self-reliance. A concept with which he translated into financial terms a principle of personal independence. For to him the possibility of defining deliberately his own subjectivity had to go beyond the limits of current social constraints. And this did not only mean the necessity of stepping away from all the petty things that society entailed, but also the refusal to be in "need" of others. It was probably for this reason, for example, that, after having fashioned the structural elements with his own hands, he used the traditional mortise and tenon framing system instead of the simpler balloon-frame, which would however have required the use of nails. And it was for the same reason that he composed the part related to the project of what he often compared to a "wigwam" as a sort of manual of self-construction, as he wanted to demonstrate, also to "urbanized" people, the technical and economic feasibility of such a life choice.[23]

Secondly, as underlined in a passage of the book where Thoreau described with pleasure his whole household effects "like a gypsy's pack,"[24] the design of the cabin, as a space of deliberation, also served as a device of liberation. Liberation from anything he felt as superfluous or imposed by a social norm and which could thus interfere with the introspection that he needed in order to discover who he really was. A fact reflected by the dimensions, the proportions and the furniture of his shelter, which were those typical of a modest single bedroom of that age,[25] and which were thought to oblige him, voluntarily or not, to get rid of anything that exceeded his very fundamental needs. Yet, again, not in a form of moralistic self-constraining, but in a desire for freedom that is well remarked by the recurrent comparison with a "nest" or a "burrow," both as a critique of the traditional way of building and as an attempt at an original mode of expression. An attempt that ignored the traditional separation of the functions of living in hierarchical categories and exclusive spatial contexts, to propose a non-stereotypical idea of dwelling capable of translating daily experience into structure. As though the house was shaped, in a projective process of definition, by the simplest gestures of living materialized in the furniture.

However, the most relevant instrumental role that the design of the shelter fulfilled, as part of the original exercise of self-determination that Thoreau undertook, was that of building a form of responsive interface connected with the natural world outside. For the cabin represented the interpretative tool whereby he was able to contemplate and live the natural world by immersion. And not only because of its location but also due to its very design, which opposed to the coarse look of the exterior an interior openness that went well beyond the narrowness of the room. Something that could be experienced only when inside the space.[26] The light structure, the facing windows located just over a foot from the floor, the lack of curtains or shutters, all made Thoreau feel always and unavoidably outside, whether he was standing, seated at the desk or lying on bed, in that from any point inside the house there was no way to escape the sight of the forest, as well as the aroma of pine trees and the sound of birds. As if the dimension of his house could not be limited to its perimeter but had to expand, by design, to the range within which the outside world was attracted into his sensory experience. For this reason, he wrote of the cabin comparing it to a garment,[27] for he meant it, in its spatial arrangement, as only the first layer of an extended habitat that he felt to be part of.

In summary, even though Thoreau sometimes referred to it in these terms, the structure that he built was not a house, because it was not conceived to "domesticate" the environment by adapting it to his life. Nor was it a simple shelter, as it was not merely aimed at making him survive in a hostile territory. On the contrary, in its being a bedroom abruptly thrown into a forest, it rather represented a device of "defamiliarization" from the usual normative categories, specifically designed to place Thoreau's most intimate dimension into direct contact with the unknown. And it is precisely here that lies the very reason of

N

0 0.45 0.90 1.80 2.70m

A porous interface. Henry David Thoreau's cabin from within

"What of architectural beauty I now see, I know has gradually grown from within outward."

Henry David Thoreau

its extraordinary architectural originality.[28] In the constructed belief that dwelling could be something different from the Kantian idea of raising a "rampart against the dread of nothingness, darkness, and the obscurity" of the exterior world.[29] And that a house could represent also a tool to "accommodate him to the natural order rather than seek to overwhelm and transform it."[30] A belief realized through both a whole series of specific design solutions, which ranged from the choice of the furniture to the height of the windows, and a particular design approach that would have been theorized only some years later by the likes of Gottfried Semper and August Schmarsow, and exemplified after a century by Gaston Bachelard with the metaphor of the nest.[31] The one going "from within" outwards, in a defining rather than confining process of construction, of the architecture as well as the self.[32]

With Thoreau, in other words, the identity between the architecture of a house and the feeling of domestic seclusion ceased to be univocal, in an early anticipation of the temporary decline of the bourgeois idea of dwelling that took place in the following century. First, for instance, with its identification by Wilhelm Reich with the main tool for training individuals committed to perpetuating the existing social order, and then through the categorical imperative of Theodor Adorno for whom it was moral never to feel at home.[33] However, it was only during the early seventies, when the long wave of the protest of the previous decade merged with a first awareness of the limits of growth, that Thoreau's experiment began to be considered as a tangible example for turning the definition of one own subjectivity into a truly self-directed existential project.[34] On the one hand, as a methodological reference for all the manuals of self-construction that, from Stewart Brand's to Johan van Lengen's,[35] provided an "access to tools" on self-sufficiency, ecology and alternative education. And on the other, as a conceptual guide for a whole series of "radical" design proposals that suddenly, as in the last scene of *Zabriskie Point*,[36] had to be confronted with the "explosion" of the house and with the idea that the

Metaphors. Ettore Sottsass' designs for the destinies of mankind

act of dwelling needed other models to survive.[37] No longer a shelter but rather, as Herbert Muschamp later wrote about another project, a "shelter from a shelter."[38]

In this regard, for example, to appreciate Thoreau's influence on design counterculture, one can look at the series of installations made from fabric, wood sticks and string, built and photographed into the wild by Ettore Sottsass during six years of nomadic life,[39] and presented in 1974 at the Cooper-Hewitt Museum with the title of *Metaphors*. Each one was in fact nothing more than a pretext to renew a bond between humankind and nature, by dematerializing the act of dwelling through the metaphors of the simplest architectural elements in their relation with the landscape. Like a skeleton of a window hanging from a trellis of sticks, purposely set to frame the sunset on a hill in August. Or a door through which, in certain times of the day, one could enter the shadow created by a mountain. But also floors made of cotton threads, arches that responded to the wind, monuments for worms and a whole series of virtual architectures that reflected a way of living that was never stereotypical. All of this in a form of design, in which fragility, precariousness and simplicity referred to the microscopic gestures and the elemental actions of dwelling that were capable of restoring the sense of the human position within the world, in a perfect integration among nature and its elements.

In his six sabbatical years, in other words, Sottsass, just like Thoreau, used architecture to create a place for his own subjectivity to expand, by participating in a totality that went beyond every social norm and every contrast between being and having to be. A subjectivity that was not given, imposed or inherited, but which had to represent the ongoing development of a process of self-determination that knew no limits of range, whether social or biological. For this reason, he designed, so to say, in interrogative form, as testified by the writings that complemented the photographs, to ask questions, just as Thoreau did, on how one wanted to be in the world. And for the same reason, their experiments remained partially unmatched, even in spite of the later growth of the number of people who have decided to go living off the grid.[40] Because their architectural acts were not meant to simply solve a problem, but were designed to produce hesitations in the routines of their everyday lives and call them to reflect on what they really were, by "re-establishing a physical connection with the cosmos [...] and the sense of [their] position,"[41] in a sort of real "expansion of consciousness." A process that, for both, started with the return to an original way of being and then ended with the surprise of being happy again, in a new and extended dimension of the self.

Notes

1 Robert Pogue Harrison, *Forests: The Shadow of Civilization* (Chicago: The University of Chicago Press, 1992).

2 Adam Ferguson, *Essay on the History of Civil Society* (1767) (Philadelphia: A. Finlay, 1819).

3 Michel Foucault, *Surveiller et punir: Naissance de la prison* (Paris: Alcan, 1975).

4 "Thrown onto the earth, without physical strength and without innate ideas, [...] only in society man can find the eminent place assigned to him by nature, and without civilization, he would be one of the weakest and less intelligent of the animals." Jean Marc Gaspard Itard, *De l'éducation d'un homme sauvage ou des premieres developpements physiques et moraux de jeune sauvage de l'Aveyron* (Paris: Goujon Imprimeur-Libraire, 1801), foreword [translation by the author].

5 Italo Calvino, *Il barone rampante* (Turin: Einaudi, 1957).

6 Giorgio Agamben, *The Open: Man and Animal* (Stanford: Stanford University Press, 2004), 30.

7 Jean-Jacques Rousseau, *Discours sur l'origine et les fondements de l'inégalité parmi les hommes* (Paris: Marc-Michel Rey, 1755). In this regard, by the same author, see also *Émile ou De l'éducation* (Paris: Jean Néaulme, 1762).

8 "I have lived some thirty years on this planet, and I have yet to hear the first syllable of valuable or even earnest advice from my seniors. [...] Here is life, an experiment to a great extent untried by me [...]. If I have any experience which I think valuable, I am sure to reflect that this my Mentors said nothing about." Henry David Thoreau, *Walden: Or Life in the Woods* (New Haven: Yale University Press, 2004), 9.

9 Ralph Waldo Emerson, *Nature* (Boston: James Munroe and Company, 1836), 13.

10 Lawrence Buell, *The Environmental Imagination: Thoreau Nature Writing and the Formation of American Culture* (Cambridge MA: Harvard University Press, 1995), 135; 138. About Thoreau's maturation from transcendental idealism to ecological materialism, see also Cristin Ellis, *Antebellum Posthuman: Race and Materiality in the Mid-Nineteenth Century* (New York: Fordham University, 2018), 61-95.

11 Sherman Paul, *The Shores of America: Thoreau's inward Exploration* (Urbana: University of Illinois Press, 1958), 282.

12 Thoreau, *Walden*, 88.

13 For an overview, see Jeanne M. Zimmer, "A History of Thoreau's Hut and Hut Site," *Concord Saunterer*, Supplement no. 3 (1973).

14 Thoreau, *Walden*, 47.

15 Ibid., 62.

16 Ibid., 44-45.

17 Ibid., 45. Particularly he referred to the work of Horatio Greenough (1805–1852) who was an early proponent of the idea of functional architectural decoration.

18 Richard N. Masteller and Jean Carwile Masteller, "Rural Architecture in Andrew Jackson Downing and Henry David Thoreau: Pattern Book Parody in Walden," *New England Quarterly* 57, no.4 (December 1984): 483-510.

19 "It would be worth the while to build still more deliberately than I did, considering, for instance, what foundation a door, a window, a cellar, a garret, have

in the nature of man, and perchance never raising any superstructure until we found a better reason for it than our temporal necessities even." Thoreau, *Walden*, 44.

20 Lewis Mumford, *Roots of Contemporary American Architecture* (New York: Dover Publications, 1972), 104-107.

21 Joseph Rykwert, *On Adam's House in Paradise: The Idea of Primitive Hut in Architectural History* (New York: The Museum of Modern Art, 1972), 17. See also Marc-Antoine Laugier, *Essai sur l'architecture* (Paris, 1753); William Chambers, *A Treatise on Civil Architecture* (London: J. Haberkorn, 1759).

22 Maynard W. Barksdale, "Thoreau's House at Walden," *The Art Bulletin* 81, no. 2 (1999): 303-325. See also Andrew Jackson Downing, *Architecture of Country Houses* (New York: Wiley and Putnam, 1841).

23 "I see young men, my townsmen, whose misfortune it is to have inherited farms, houses, barns, cattle, and farming tools; for these are more easily acquired than got rid of." Thoreau, *Walden*, 3.

24 Ibid., 110.

25 In this regard, see for instance the catalogue in Downing, *Architecture of Country Houses*.

26 Although Thoreau's cabin was dismantled shortly after he left Walden, a faithful replica still exists today, thanks to archaeologist Roland Robbins who, in 1945, discovered its original hearth stone along with a number of artifacts from Thoreau's stay, which allowed him to reconstruct the original plan in an extremely precise way. See Roland Wells Robbins, *Discovery at Walden* (Somerville MA: Thoreau Foundation, 1970). A good reconstruction can also be found in Urs Peter Flückiger, *How Much House: Thoreau, Le Corbusier and the Sustainable Cabin* (Basel: Birkhäuser, 2016).

27 Thoreau, *Walden*, 26.

28 See, for instance, the 2018 exhibition *Machines à penser*, curated by Dieter Roelstraete for Fondazione Prada in Venice, in which the huts of Martin Heidegger, Ludwig Wittgenstein, and Theodor W. Adorno were compared. In these cases, in fact, the structures represented simple means of personal and voluntary seclusion.

29 Bernard Edelman, *La maison de Kant* (Paris: Payot, 1984), 25-26.

30 Donald Worster, *Nature's Economy: A History of Ecological Ideas* (Cambridge: Cambridge University Press, 1995), 76.

31 Gottfried Semper, *Der Stil in den technischen und tektonischen Künsten oder praktische Aesthetik* (Frankfurt, 1860); August Schmarsow, *Das Wesen der architektonischen Schöpfung* (Leipzig: Hiersemann, 1894); Gaston Bachelard, *La poétique de l'espace* (Paris: Presses Universitaires de France, 1957). In this regard, see also Rudolf Arnheim, *The Dynamics of Architectural Form* (Berkeley: University of California Press, 1977), 97; and Sarah Robinson, *Nesting: Body, Dwelling, Mind* (San Francisco: William Stout Publishers, 2011).

32 Curiously, this approach had already been described quite well in a tale by E. T. A. Hoffmann, in which councilor Krespel built his own house by raising the walls as a solid mass and then removing part of them from within, to obtain windows that could really match the view he wanted. E. T. A. Hoffmann, "Rat Krespel," in *Die Serapionsbrüder* (Berlin: G. Reimer, 1819).

33 Wilhelm Reich, *Die Sexualität im Kulturkampf* (Copenhagen: Sexpol, 1936); Theodor W. Adorno, *Minima Moralia: Reflections on a Damaged Life*, trans. E.F.N. Jephcott (London-New York: Verso, 2005), 39.

34 The most extreme case was that of Theodore Kaczynski, the terrorist known as Unabomber, who in 1971 retired in a self-built cabin in the woods of Montana, to follow Thoreau's example. In this regard, see Mark Wigley, "Cabin Fever," *Perspecta* 30 (1999): 122-125; and Alessandro Rocca and Jacopo Leveratto, "Thoreau and Kaczynski, the Media Cabin: Building a Manifesto," *Vesper* 3 (2020): 36-48.

35 Stewart Brand, *Whole Earth Catalog* (Santa Cruz, 1968); Johan van Lengen, *Manual del Arquitecto Descalzo* (Mexico: Editorial Concepto, 1980).

36 *Zabriskie Point* is a movie directed by Michelangelo Antonioni, produced by Carlo Ponti and distributed by Metro-Goldwyn-Mayer in 1970.

37 See, for instance, the projects included in Emilio Ambasz, *Italy: The New Domestic Landscape* (New York: The Museum of Modern Art, 1972).

38 Herbert Muschamp, "Living Boldly on the Event Horizon," *The New York Times* (19 November 1998).

39 Milco Carboni and Barbara Radice, eds., *Ettore Sottsass, Metafore* (Milan: Skira, 2002).

40 For a complete review in this regard, see Lori Ryker, *Off the Grid Homes: Case Studies for Sustainable Living* (Layton UT: Gibbs Smith, 2007); and Phillip Vannini and Jonathan Taggart, *Off the Grid: Re-Assembling Domestic Life* (London-New York: Routledge, 2014).

41 Ettore Sottsass, quoted in Carboni and Radice, *Ettore Sottsass*, 9.

Visual atlas (following spread)

1 Retreat in Skjolden, Ludwig Wittgenstein, 1914
2 House in Todtnauberg, Martin Heidegger, 1922
3 Las Pozas, Edward James, 1947
4 Experimental House, Alvar Aalto, 1949
5 Cabanon, Le Corbusier, 1951
6 Little House in the Garden, Walter Segal, 1963
7 *Architecture Without Architects*, Bernard Rudofsky, 1964
8 Drop City, 1965
9 *Whole Earth Catalog*, Stewart Brand, 1968
10 *Zabriskie Point*, Michelangelo Antonioni, 1970
11 *Inflatocookbook*, Ant Farm, 1971
12 *Supersurface Life*, Superstudio, 1972
13 House in the Wood, Jan Szpakowicz, 1971
14 Can Lis, Jorn Utzon, 1973
15 Azuma House, Tadao Ando, 1976
16 Unabomber House, Ted Kaczynski, 1971
17 Autonomous House, Alexander Pike, 1974
18 *Into the Wild*, Jon Krakauer, 1996
19 De Markies, Eduard Bohtlingk, 1995
20 Autocrat, Atelier Van Lieshout, 1997
21 NhEW - PAD, OpenOffice, 2000
22 Chen House, C-Laboratory, 2008
23 *Scrublands*, Antoine Bruy, 2013
24 Forest Temple, Marco Casagrande, 2016

machinesàpenser

1 1A 2 2A 3 3A

architectural realizations

4 4A 5 5A 6 6A

non-pedigreed culture

7 7A 8 8A 9 9A

undomestic dwellings

10 10A 11 11A 12 12A

n e w relations

13 13A

14 14A

15 15A

countercultural homes

16 16A

17 17A

18 18A

mobile modules

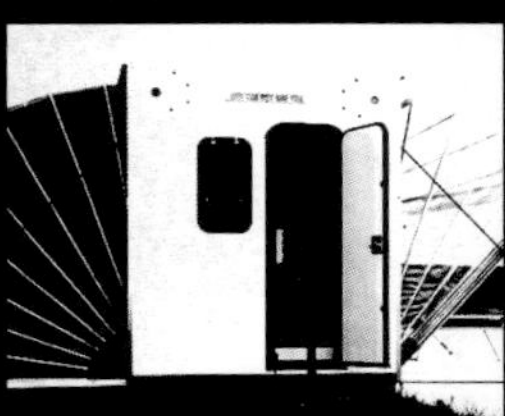

19 19A

20 20A

21 21A

new metabolisms

22 22A

23 23A

24 24A

A forest

Richard St. Barbe Baker
Kikuyu, KE
-1.245528, 36.660422
1920-1954

"For a human character to reveal truly exceptional qualities, one must have the good fortune to be able to observe its performance over many years. If this performance is devoid of all egoism, if its guiding motive is unparalleled generosity, if it is absolutely certain that there is no thought of recompense and that, in addition, it has left its visible mark upon the earth, then there can be no mistake."

Jean Giono, *The Man Who Planted Trees* (White River Junction: Chelsea Green Publishing, 1985), 5.

Sahara water

trees

plants

Challenge

juniper

Dangerous monoculture

Your
love of
your country will
extend to a feeling for
the **earth** beneath your feet
Like the ancients, you
will come to regard the
earth as a
sentient
being

I learned early to regard the **forest** as a society of living things, the greatest of which is the tree

You
will feel
your kinship
with the **earth**.
You will develop a
sense of the **one**
ness of
all
living
things and
realize your **dependence**
upon them. You will
learn the **art of**
leaving the earth
a little better for your
having lived on it

Montereycypress

Front plants

Green

trees

Nigeria

fungi

Groundnuts

There is continual decline as well as growth in the forest. There is no standing still

olive

trees

Although Thoreau was a very eloquent representative of an "arcadian" view of nature, it cannot be said that his position was the preeminent of the second half of the nineteenth century. And not even the longest, when seen in wider a historical perspective.[1] Only a decade after the publication of *Walden*, for example, the studies of natural sciences focusing on the relationship among organisms and their biophysical environment began to gain more and more credit, from Charles Darwin to Ernst Haeckel.[2] And the transcendentalist image of wilderness that had shone through Thoreau's pages as a figuration of nature soon started to be replaced with the more prosaic but also more manageable one of a dynamic system made of interdependent components.[3] Thus, in a few years, besides those who believed that people had to adapt themselves to the natural order instead of trying to transform it, a growing and predominant number of scholars began to glimpse the possibility to intervene in this system to improve its performances by means of the scientific method. And forests again represented the main field of experimentation for a multifaceted form of design that expanded the range of its subjects of reference. Not only to a whole new series of living organisms and nonliving components, but also to their mutual relationships.

In fact, it took a century for this scientific position to unfold also on a broader cultural level. And precisely the years that spanned from the publication of Thoreau's manifesto to 1954, when Jean Giono first published his allegorical tale titled *L'homme qui plantait des arbres*. The story is that of a shepherd named Elzéard Bouffier whom the narrator first encountered in 1913, when hiking across the wild lavender and the ruining buildings of a treeless and desolate valley on the French Alps. A man who, after being widowed, decided to restore the dilapidated landscape in which he lived, by planting alone a forest, tree by tree, thus causing a change that, in less than ten years, made the valley flourish again. For with trees growing, the harsh dry winds were transformed into a gentle breeze, the old streams, fed by the rains that the forest preserved, flowed again, and little by little the villages were rebuilt by the people coming from the plains, thus making a "land of Canaan ... spring from the wasteland."[4] And even though Bouffier was a fictional character, his life and endeavors were very similar to those of the British biologist and botanist Richard St. Barbe Baker who, in the same year, with the publication of *Sahara Challenge*, promoted one of the most impressive territorial projects of all times, for which he spent thirty years of his life. The "construction" of an eight thousand long and thirty miles wide "Green Front" of trees in the Sahel, from Senegal to Djibouti, to contain the advance of the Sahara.[5]

Obviously, the idea that forests could be the object of some form of design was not new at that age. For millennia, in fact, peoples dwelling in forests had deliberately changed them to ensure wood supplies, and the organized management of forestland was well developed in many parts of medieval Europe.[6] However, "forest rules were not intended to affect 'nature' and man's relation to it in any broad sense" at the time, in that forests were only considered a resource to be exploited.[7] Modern forestry, on the contrary, as developed during the Enlightenment, emerged in coincidence with a new form of caution about human modification of nature.[8] And even though at first its purpose was mainly limited to a strict economic approach,[9] with the institution of formal education in forestry, its focus progressively shifted on the relationship between human activity and climate change. In 1826, for example, an extensively discussed report detailed the role that the forest of Bialowieza played in water flow and climate.[10] And some years later, a broadly circulated book documented how deforestation, desiccation and drought were linked throughout the whole Mediterranean region.[11] All the studies that in 1855 brought Lord Dalhousie, Governor-General of British India, to issue the Forest Charter with which he initiated the first series of forest reservations in modern history, and that pushed the earliest generation of environmentalists to look at the protection and design of forests as the primary tool to manage climate changes.[12]

Nature as infrastructure. Atlantropa, the Prairie States Forestry Project, the Great Plan for the Transformation of Nature

This was precisely the background of St. Barbe Baker, who after having graduated from the School of Forestry at Cambridge began his professional life in 1920, as an Assistant Conservator of Forests under the British colonial office in Kenya. Here he could directly observe the stages of degradation from forest to desert, after which he recognized that colonial "conservatorship" could not work without an active regeneration. Once forests had been in fact cleared and burned for farming, the soil exposed to sun and rain made the humus rapidly degrade, leaving no space for other cultivations. For this reason, as part of his task, he simply proposed to plant more and more trees, by initiating the native people of Kikuyu to the first experiment of social forestry in history, for which he earned the name of "Man of the Trees."[13] And for the same reason, he also decided to establish with Chief Josiah Njonjo an international association dedicated to this purpose, with which he replicated the experiment over the following years from Nigeria to Palestine, as well as from New Zealand to California.[14] It was only in 1946, however, during The First World Forestry Charter Gathering that he first sought to tackle the reclamation of the Sahara Desert, proposing to redirect the energy that was internationally spent on armaments towards a battle against a common enemy. An aim that brought him to a twenty-six-thousand-mile exploratory trip across the desert to find the evidence that trees had once grown there and, once found,[15] to a relentless effort to persuade colonial administrations of the feasibility of the endeavor.[16]

Indeed, exemplar precedents were not lacking in this regard. In 1935, for instance, Franklin Delano Roosevelt, under the New Deal programs, initiated the Prairie States Forestry Project in response to the devastating storms of the Dust Bowl that had ravaged with erosion and drought the panhandles of Texas and Oklahoma. A plan that consisted in a system of green windbreaks planted on the perimeters of farms, and which by 1942 stretched almost nineteen thousand miles from Canada to the Brazos River, for a total of two hundred million of trees planted.[17] The same that, after the great famine of 1946, pushed Joseph Stalin to launch his Great Plan for the Transformation of Nature, which had to span the Urals to Ukraine with a gigantic network of irrigation canals and planted shelterbelts, to reduce wind velocity and lessen the evaporation of moisture from the soil.[18] Each one sharing the boundless trust in the human ability to improve nature that also marked the most ambitious engineering visions of the previous years. Like the one that Herman Sörgel presented in 1928, to create a new continent called Atlantropa, by building a hydroelectric dam across the Strait of Gibraltar, which besides providing enormous amounts of energy, would have led to the lowering of the Mediterranean Sea and the recovery of new lands for settlement.[19] Or also those published in 1931 by Walter de Haas about the infrastructures for alternative sources of energy in the post-carbon world.[20]

With any of them, however, St. Barbe only shared a grand and ambitious way of thinking, while their strict functionalistic approach remained substantially alien to him. For he never saw the forest as a simple infrastructure, or a facility for human needs. On the contrary, years before the seminal studies by Aldo Leopold and Rachel Carson,[21] he looked at it as an interrelated community of plants, animals, birds, insects, and fungi, linked together through nutrient cycles and energy flows. Or, in his words, as a self-regulating and life-sustaining "society of living things,"[22] maintained by the synergistic interrelationship of air, water, soil and organisms that develops in the body of trees. For this reason, his project for the Green Front in the arid savanna on the south border of the Sahara was not merely meant to create a barrier against the wind or a reservoir of fresh water, but mainly to recreate the complex conditions for any kind of life to flourish. Human, obviously, but first of all vegetal and animal. In that human livability represented just one of the effects and not the purpose of his plan, which was instead imagined to give shape to a real ecosystem, by taking care of the trees that he thought were its very biological fundament.[23] All of this realized through a global approach and a holistic perspective that made his project stand out among its predecessors also from a design point of view.

In this regard, in fact, although St. Barbe never left any sketch or general indication, no image would be more inappropriate to depict the Green Front than that represented by the geometric perfection of the linear forests dating back to Stalinist propaganda. For as a forester, he had a crystal-clear vision of the actual scale and the actual processes through which his project could be effectively realized. In his previous studies, for example, he was able to appreciate how in virgin forests the rhythm of growth and decay was harmoniously maintained by the interdependence of all its inhabitants.[24] But he also saw how the proliferation of certain species of trees relied on the local and specific interactions with other selected plants and animals.[25] And how, by contrast, monocultures planted all at the same time with single and sometimes non-native species proved more vulnerable to insects and diseases.[26] Then, he also noticed how traditional silvicultural practices often represented the best mechanic and biologic solutions to specific local conditions, and how agriculture could be an enrichment and not only a depletion for the ecosystem.[27] Without mentioning his continuous efforts to interrogate, involve and entrust local communities, without which no future sustainability could have been secured.

For this reason, if one tried to reconstruct the possible outcome of his project, this would not look like the extrusion of a typical section that characterizes any other infrastructure. On the contrary, exactly like St. Barbe's narrative style, it would recall a sort of mosaic that filled with a myriad of different tiles the "blank spots" lined along the irregular profile of the African semi-arid isoline. Each one featuring a different orientation, composition and pattern, according to the dominant winds, the interactions of diverse species and the presence of cultivated patches. But even a different size, density and duration, depend-

"I learned early to regard the forest as a society of living things, the greatest of which is the tree."

Richard St. Barbe Baker

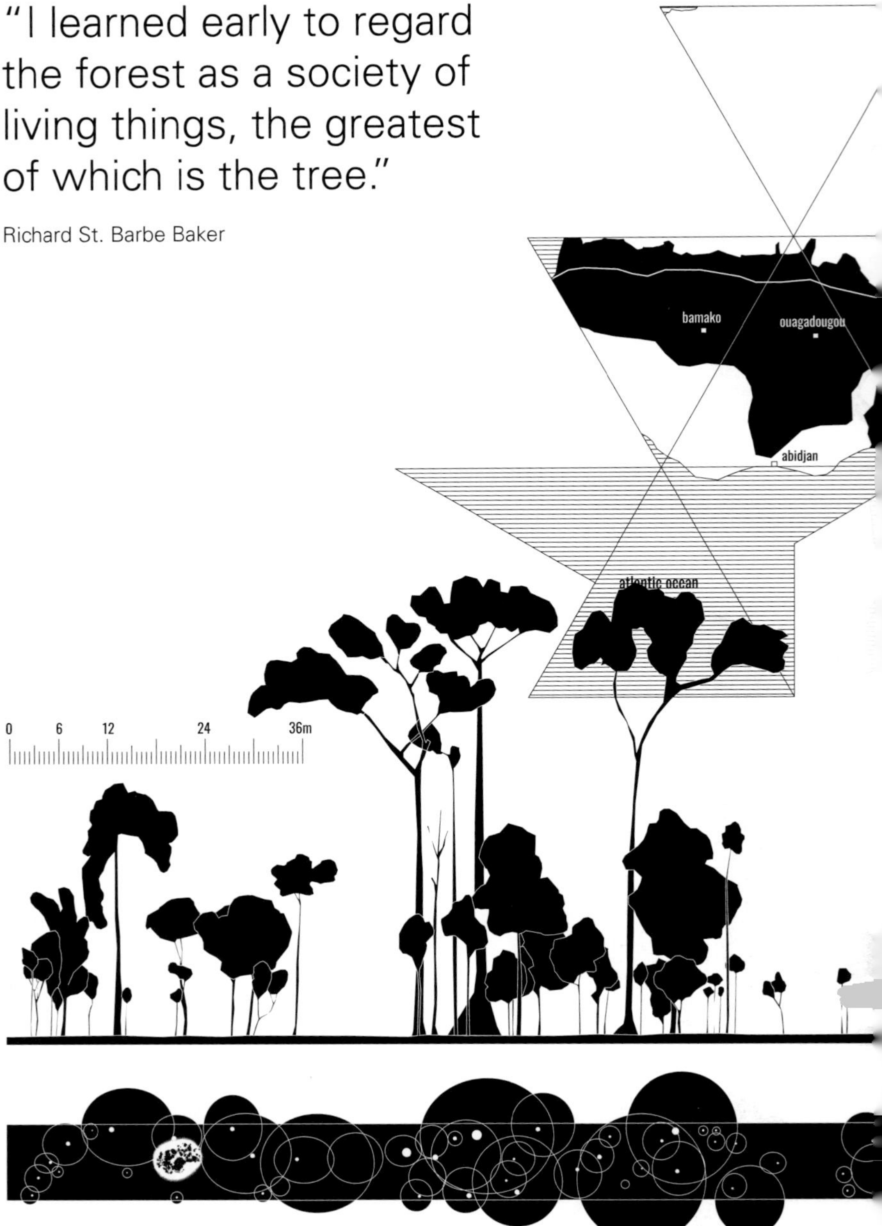

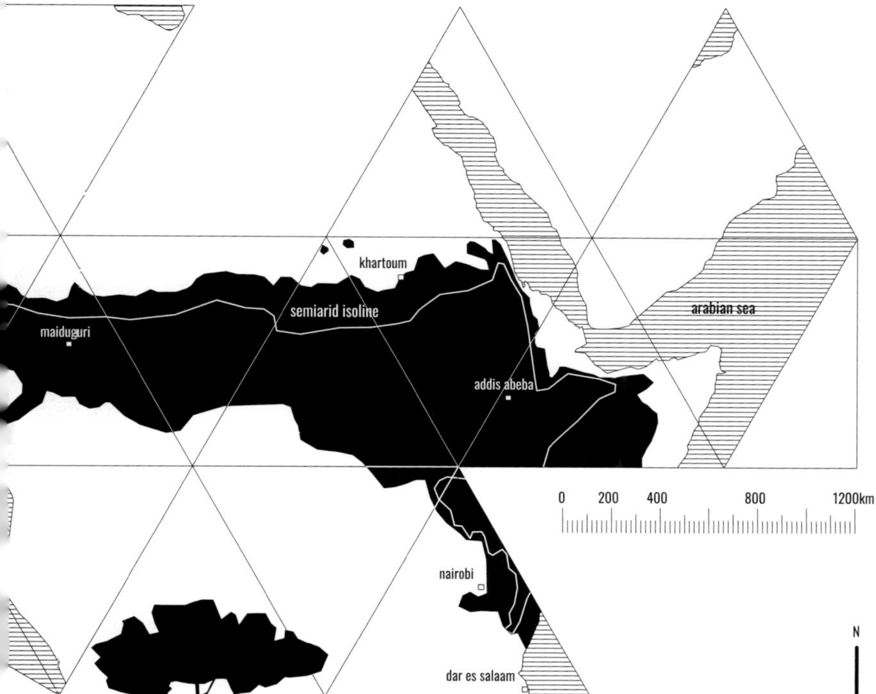

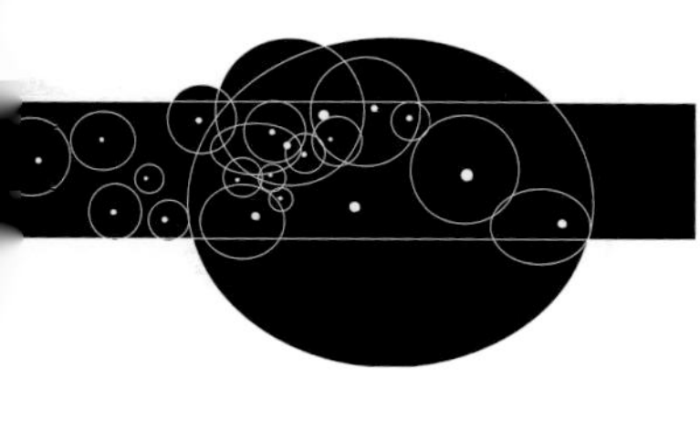

Speculative reconstruction of St. Barbe's Green Front

ing upon the extent of the local community, as well as its livelihoods and its stability. Any of them, however, kept together by a common guiding principle, which was that of planting trees in any available area, and by a design process, conducted in direct contact with its very inhabitants, which followed specific stages of development to reach the goal. First, for example, surveying all the biophysical, ecological and socioeconomic factors of an area to assess the direct and indirect causes of land degradation, through which choosing the most effective restoration strategy. And then, intervening by promoting diversity, interaction and the use of native species in the selection of the right plants for the place, by building a tree nursery that could produce high-quality material, and by preparing the site according to the carrying capacity of the environment, the species used and the traditional water harvesting techniques.[28] Everything with the purpose of triggering the spark of a self-regulating process of healing that could evolve and persist over time.

In summary, with the processual form, the situational strategy and the relational approach that characterized the Green Front project, St. Barbe defined an exemplary way to give shape by design to what he thought a forest had to be considered. An open-ended system of interdependence, in few words, among a multiplicity of subjects, be they animal, vegetal, or mineral, partaking in the same wholeness that embraces all beings. For no functions were mentioned in its description, nor specific conformations. By contrast, the focus was always on the construction of new and old forms of collaboration and interrelationship among different species over time through specific grafting. As though what mattered the most was the possibility of living and flourishing together in a world that had the size of a leaf as well as of a continent. Decades before the earth was photographed from space and understood as a unitary ecological reality, St. Barbe had in fact already seen the planet as the living organism that was later theorized by the Gaia hypothesis.[29] And his "program against the desert symbolized the potential to bring people and nations into cooperation with each other, and with the forces of growth and healing in nature itself," as much as his belief in "the capacity of humanity to transcend the separatist, non-synergistic tendencies of its nature."[30] A faith that he did not lose even when, as the years went by, twenty-five new African nations surrounded the Sahara struggling for political stability, and reforestation did not progress according to his view.

The story, however, did not end in 1982 with St. Barbe's death. Three years later, for example, after some severe droughts in the Sahel, the Marxist revolutionary leader of Burkina Faso, Thomas Sankara, inspired by the success of the Algerian Green Dam, revived the project as a tool for the continental development. And in 2007 eleven nations in the area founded a Pan-African agency to work on a harmonized regional strategy, which was finally adopted in 2012, under the name of Great Green Wall of the Sahara and the Sahel initiative.[31] A strategic plan to address food insecurity and poverty by creating a linear system of green productive landscapes across North Africa, Sahel and the Horn, which ultimately changed the original project of afforestation into a participative program of cooperation and development, centered on indigenous land use techniques and farmer-managed natural regeneration.[32] And which consequently redirected most of the resources initially dedicated to planting, to structuring a country-driven and collaborative process of capacity building, improving the governance and policy framework of the single areas, and creating the ideal conditions for investments from both public and private institutions.

In reality, elsewhere the idea of a physical wall of trees resisted, as demonstrated for instance by the Three-North Shelter Forest Program with which, in 1978, China began the attempt to curb the expansion of the Gobi Desert. Not to mention all the projects that, since then, have used nature-based solutions to secure, restore, or enhance the quality of a certain territory with new forms of soft infrastructure. However, it happened through

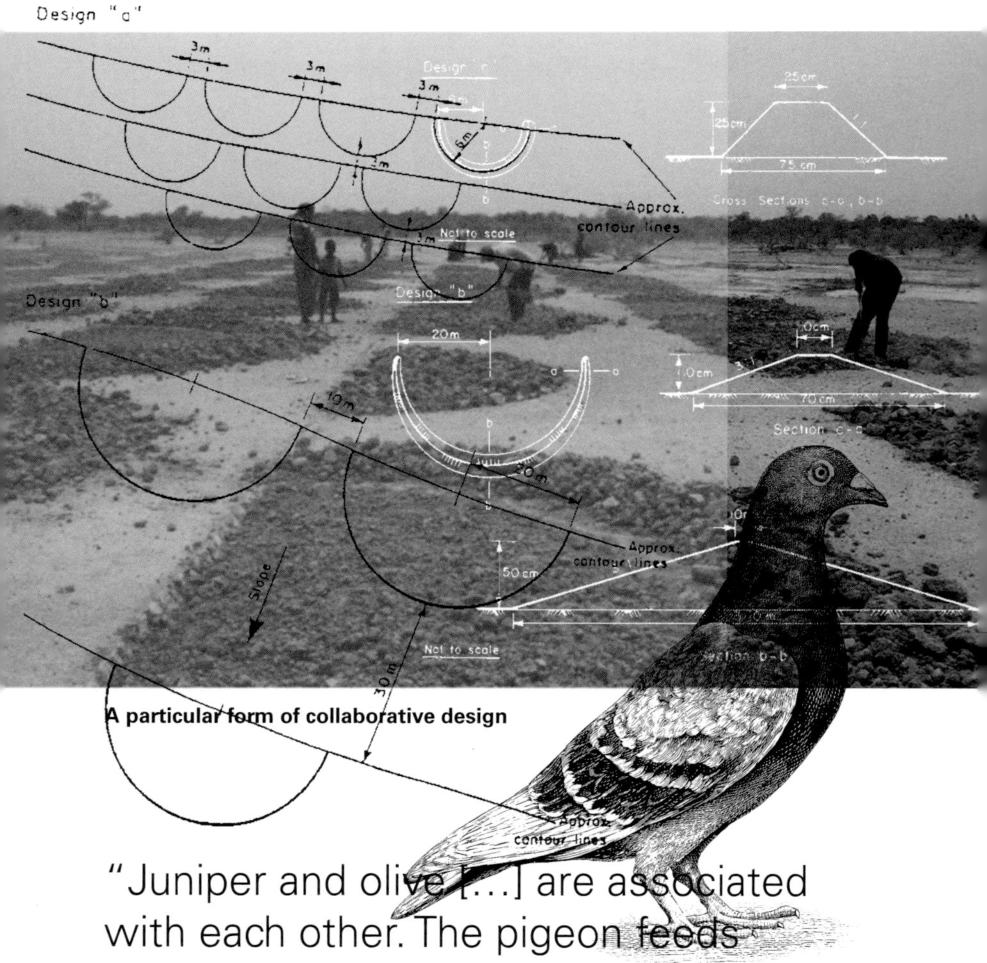

A particular form of collaborative design

"Juniper and olive [...] are associated with each other. The pigeon feeds on the juniper berries while perching on the olive branches; moreover, the juniper seed can only be germinated with the help of the gastric juices of this bird, who in discarding the seed in his droppings, lets it fall near the protecting olive."

Richard St. Barbe Baker

such an anthropocentric perspective and a functionalistic interpretation that definitely conflicted with St. Barbe's complex vision of forests.[33] Which, by contrast, anticipated by forty years the theoretical and technical direction of the most relevant change in landscape design of the second half of the twentieth century. And precisely that led by French gardener and designer Gilles Clément with the introduction of the concept of "Planetary Garden."[34] For Clément, since the mid-seventies, the project of the relationship between nature and humanity could no longer be expressed within the spatial boundaries of gardens. The ecological knowledge of the planet, he thought, would inevitably have led design to use the vocabulary of oceans and clouds, ecosystems and biotopes, pollution and remediation, as well as designers to answer different questions from those related to production and aesthetics. The garden of the ecological era, in his opinion, would have had a different shape from that enclosed by four walls, and a different purpose from preserving a selection of nature. And "gardeners" would have been called to take care of the whole planet, to protect and sustain life and diversity, through a design approach that would have taken into account, specificity, interconnectedness and temporal variability as bounding parameters.

Like St. Barbe, Clément in fact developed a particular way of gardening that has been quite indifferent to problems related to geometry and tidiness, having by contrast the objective of maintaining and increasing the biological diversity of an area.[35] And like him he believed and believes in a process that starts from a careful recognition of the species and the interactions at play, to intervene without altering their dynamics, by making a more efficient use of their natural capacities. However, even though for design culture his contribution has proven much more influential than his predecessor's, there are many aspects of St. Barbe's work that are still unparalleled from a design point of view. Like the scale of his vision, for instance, which spanned the width of a continent to the depth of a planting pit, or the political effort with which he complemented it, ranging from the international to the community level. But most of all, the paternity of a holistic idea of environmental design, for which problems can be more easily understood by looking at their cause rather than at their effects, as well as they can be more easily solved by working on their interconnection rather than on their specificity. For this reason, the idea of a Green Front has resisted through time in spite of all the adversities and criticism. For it still represents a possible utopia of belonging to a greater wholeness that is not limited to a human community but is open to the planet itself.[36]

Notes

1 Donald Worster, *Nature's Economy: A History of Ecological Ideas* (Cambridge: Cambridge University Press, 1995), 2.
2 Charles Darwin, *On the Origin of Species by Means of Natural Selection, or the Preservation of Favoured Races in the Struggle for Life* (London: John Murray, 1859); Ernst Haeckel, *Generelle Morphologie der Organismen: Allgemeine Grundzüge der organischen Formen-Wissenschaft* (Berlin, 1866).
3 See, for instance, the term "ecosystem" in Arthur George Tansley, "The Use and Abuse of Vegetational Terms and Concepts," *Ecology* 16, no. 3 (1935): 284-307.
4 Jean Giono, *The Man Who Planted Trees* (White River Junction: Chelsea Green Publishing, 1985), 37.
5 Richard St. Barbe Baker, *Sahara Challenge* (London: Lutterworth Press, 1954).
6 Bernhard E. Fernow, *A Brief History of Forestry* (Toronto: Toronto University Press, 1907). In this regard, see also Joachim Radkau, *Wood: A History* (Cambridge: Polity, 2011).
7 Gregory A. Barton, *Empire Forestry and the Origins of Environmentalism* (Cambridge: Cambridge university Press, 2004), 11.
8 In this regard, see, for instance, John Evelyn's *Silva* and the French Forest Ordinance of 1669. John Evelyn, *Silva, or a Discourse of Forest-Trees and the Propagation of Timber in His Majesty's Dominions* (London: John Martin, 1664); John Croumbie Brown, *French Forest Ordinance of 1669 with Historical Sketch of Previous Treatment of Forests in France* (Edinburgh: Oliver and Boyd, 1883).
9 The first modern treatise of forestry is in fact focused on the economy of silviculture. Hans Carl von Carlowitz, *Sylvicultura Oeconomica, oder haußwirthliche Nachricht und Naturmäßige Anweisung zur wilden Baum-Zucht* (Leipzig: Johan Friedrich Braun, 1713).
10 Baron de Brincken, *Mémoire descriptif sur la foret impériale de Bialowieza en Lituanie* (Warsaw: Glucksberg, 1826).
11 Matthias Jacob Schleiden, *The Plant: A Biography*, trans. Arthur Henfrey (London, Hippolyte Bailliere, 1848).
12 Barton, *Empire Forestry*, 7.
13 Richard St. Barbe Baker, *Men of Trees: In the Mahogany Forests of Kenya and Nigeria* (New York: The Dial Press, 1931).
14 The association founded in 1922 with the name Men of the Trees was renamed as Trillion Trees in 2017.
15 St. Barbe Baker, *Sahara Challenge*, 53-54.
16 Karen Gridley, ed., *Man of the Trees: Selected Writings of Richard St. Barbe Baker* (Willits CA: Ecology Action, 1989), 13.
17 Sarah Thomas Karle and David Karle, *Conserving the Dust Bowl: The New Deal's Prairie States Forestry Project* (Baton Rouge: LSU Press, 2017).
18 Stephen Brain, "The Great Stalin Plan for the Transformation of Nature," *Environmental History* 15, no. 4 (2010): 670-700.
19 Herman Sörgel, *Atlantropa* (Zurich: Fretz & Wasmuth; Munich: Piloty & Loehle, 1932).
20 Hanns Günther (Walter de Haas), *In hundert Jahren: Die künftige Energieversorgung der Welt* (Stuttgart: Kosmos, 1931).

21 Aldo Leopold, *A Sand County Almanac: And Sketches Here and There* (Oxford: Oxford University Press, 1949); Rachel Carson, *Silent Spring* (Boston: Houghton Mifflin, 1962).

22 Richard St. Barbe Baker, *My Life, My Trees* (London: Lutterworth Press, 1970), 55.

23 "I learned early to regard the forest as a society of living things, the greatest of which is the tree. Its value depends upon its permanence, its capacity to renew itself, to store water; its many biological functions including that of providing nature's most valuable ground cover." Ibid.

24 "There is continual decline as well as growth in the forest. There is no standing still: as soon as a tree stops growing it begins to decline. Even before this, decay may have set in within its heart, and it is set upon by beetles and borers, its roots are attacked by fungi, [...] it becomes a home for woodlice and millions of other insects, which play their part in returning the fallen tree to the earth from which it sprang." Richard St. Barbe Baker, *Green Glory* (New York: A.A. Wyn, Inc., 1949), 21-22.

25 "Juniper and olive [for instance] [...] are associated with each other. The pigeon feeds on the juniper berries while perching on the olive branches; moreover, the juniper seed can only be germinated with the help of the gastric juices of this bird, who in discarding the seed in his droppings, lets it fall near the protecting olive." St. Barbe Baker, *Sahara Challenge*, 114.

26 "[An] example of dangerous monoculture has been the foundation of pure plantations of Monterey cypress [...] in the high rainfall areas [...]. Many of these trees have become infected with a fungus caused by water running down the stem and being caught in the niches ... where the branches come out [...]. The risk of infection is greatly reduced in a mixed plantation that includes a larger percentage of broad-leaf trees." Ibid., 112.

27 "In Nigeria, groundnuts ... have been grown successfully for a hundred years or more. The nuts are planted between trees and they provide their own water in a mysterious and wonderful way. [...] This wonderful plan of nature will only function when surrounding trees provide relatively cool conditions during the day in the upper air and give off enough moisture to produce a dew fall. When the British government launched their groundnut scheme this important fact was forgotten [...]. The scheme was a complete failure and in the space of a few years man produced a new desert." Richard St. Barbe Baker, *Dance of the Trees* (London: Oldbourne Press, 1956), 52-53.

28 St. Barbe Baker, *Men of Trees*.

29 James E. Lovelock, "Gaia as Seen through the Atmosphere," *Atmospheric Environment* 6, no. 8 (1972): 579-580.

30 Gridley, *Man of the Trees*, 15.

31 Deborah Goffner, Hannah Sinare, and Line J. Gordon, "The Great Green Wall for the Sahara and the Sahel Initiative as an Opportunity to Enhance Resilience in Sahelian Landscapes and Livelihoods," *Reg Environ Change* 19 (2019), 1417-1428.

32 Nora Berrahmouni, Pedro Regato, and Marc Parfondry, *Global Guidelines for the Restoration of Degraded Forests and Landscapes in Drylands: Building Resilience and Benefiting Livelihoods* (Rome: FAO, 2015).

33 "Nature-based solutions can be thought of as a design approach that considers and responds to the effects and problems of modern development. [...] The benefits of this [...] create a compelling case for action in the face of rising population numbers, ageing populations and increasing competi-

tion for resources." Andrew Tempany and Tom Armour, *Nature of the City: Green Infrastructures from the Ground Up* (London: RIBA-Taylor and Francis, 2020), 23.

34 Gilles Clément, *Thomas et le Voyageur* (Paris: Albin Michel, 1997).

35 This approach to gardening, which Clément called "Garden in Motion," has been first experimented in his garden at La Vallée and subsequently developed in dozens of landscape projects, articles and books. Gilles Clément, *Le Jardin en mouvement* (Paris: Pandora, 1991).

36 "Your love of your country will extend to a feeling for the earth beneath your feet; like the ancients, you will come to regard the earth as a sentient being. You will feel your kinship with the earth and wish to protect its waters from abuse. [...] You will develop a sense of the oneness of all living things and realize your dependence upon them. [...] You will learn the art of [...] leaving the earth a little better for your having lived on it." Richard St. Barbe Baker, *Land of Tane* (London: Lutterworth Press, 1956), 140-141.

Visual atlas (following spread)

1 Prairie States Forestry Project, 1935
2 Great Plan for the Transformation of Nature, 1946
3 *The Man Who Planted Trees*, Jean Giono, 1954
4 *Time Landscape*, Alan Sonfist, 1965
5 *The Unending Attraction of Nature*, Max Peintner, 1970
6 *Ash Dome*, David Nash, 1977
7 Algerian Green Dam, 1971
8 Dead Sea Power Project, 1975
9 Three-North Shelter Forest Program, 1978
10 Le jardin de la Creuse, Gilles Clément, 1979
11 Green wall, Patrick Blanc, 1988
12 Bibliothèque nationale de France, Dominique Perrault, 1995
13 *60 Minute Man*, Marco Casagrande, 2000
14 *Vegetal Cathedral*, Giuliano Mauri, 2001
15 Serpentine Pavilion, Peter Zumthor and Piet Oudolf, 2011
16 Tar Creek Supergrid, Clint Langevin and Amy Norris, 2011
17 Sahara Forest Project, Exploration Architecture, 2012
18 Sponge Mountain, Angelo Renna, 2018
19 Bosco Verticale, Stefano Boeri, 2014
20 High Line, Diller Scofidio + Renfro, 2014
21 Sydney Park Water Re-Use Project, Turf Design Studio, 2015
22 Forest Park, PLAT studio, 2016

living infrastructures

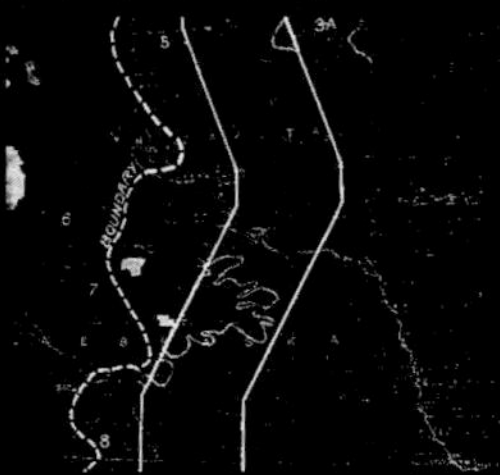

1 1A

2 2A

3 3A

landart experiments

4 4A

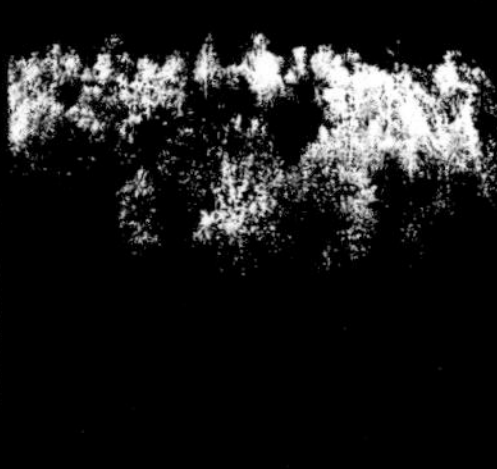

5 5A

6 6A

other infrastructures

7 7A

8 8A

9 9A

new gardening

10 10A

11 11A

12 12A

conceptual forests

13 13A

14 14A

15 15A

hybrid systems

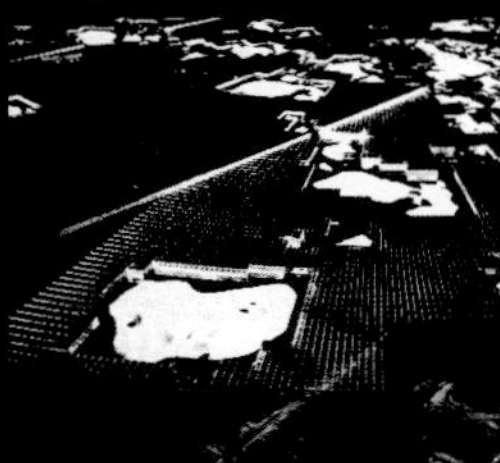

16 16A

17 17A

18 18A

urban forests

19 19A

20 20A

21 21A

22 22A

A garden

Cedric Price, Anthony Armstrong-Jones and Frank Newby
London, GB
51.536465, -0.157374
1960-1965

"The animals are divided into: (a) belonging to the emperor, (b) embalmed, (c) tame, (d) sucking pigs, (e) sirens, (f) fabulous, (g) stray dogs, (h) included in the present classification, (i) frenzied, (j) innumerable, (k) drawn with a very fine camelhair brush, (l) et cetera, (m) having just broken the water pitcher, (n) that from a long way off look like flies."

Jorge Luis Borges, "The Analytical Language of John Wilkins," in *Other inquisitions* 1937-1952, trans. Ruth L. C. Simms (Austin-London: University of Texas Press, 1964), 101-105.

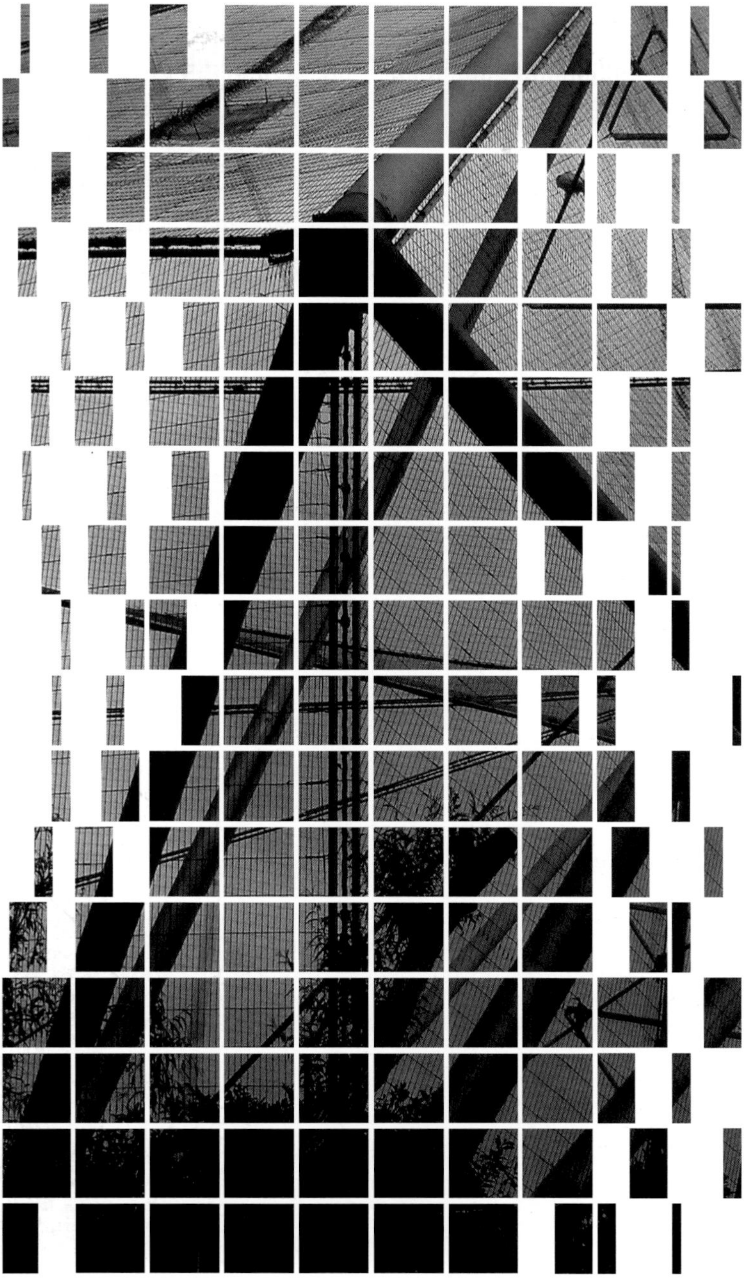

In the beginning of humanity, immediately after and out of the forest, was the garden, it is no mystery also in this case. And not only because it was in a garden that the earliest narratives of creation placed the first humans.[1] But also because, according to anthropologists, it was through gardening that humankind definitively became sedentary and started its millenary process of modification of the natural world. However not by clearing it, as one may think, but by distilling its essence within the physical boundaries of an enclosed system.[2] Historically, in fact, despite changes in terms of size, composition and characterization, gardens have always represented places in which a selection of the natural environment has been grown, accumulated and guarded. At first for alimentary reasons, as they were meant to collect and protect the livelihoods of a community, and then, over the centuries, according to the different ways in which different cultures have interpreted their relationship with nature. All of this with the only invariable feature of being a walled area, as also testified by the etymology of the term, and the sole constant principle of recalling as much as possible a sort of "paradise."[3] The same word that Greeks borrowed from Persians to indicate the closed "special parks, planted with palm trees, vines and flowers" in which they used to keep wild animals in captivity.[4] And which therefore served to indicate a first form of domesticated coexistence among different species.

From an architectural point of view, the story of this form of coexistence is the story of a particular spatial typology, which in the second half of the seventeenth century took the name of "menagerie," although its origins go back long before that date.[5] During the second millennium before Christ, for example, Queen Hatshepsut of Egypt founded in Thebes the first known zoological garden. But even Alexander the Great, Kublai Khan and Emperor Wen Wang of the Chou Dynasty in China were all founders of similar parks. Without mentioning, with regards to the Middle Ages, Charlemagne, Frederick II, or Henry III of England, who used to keep wild animals in the Tower of London.[6] It was only, however, after 1662, when Louis XIV of France created a garden for exotic animals at Versailles, that the term began to be commonly used, in its strictly domestic reference.[7] As it was a further evidence of the form of possess that characterized the relationship with the natural world, which was already materialized by the distinctive features of all the royal menageries. From the architectural shape of the cages to the panoptical plan of the compounds. And solely in 1828, with the opening in London Regent's Park of the first scientific zoo in the world, the perspective in this regard began to change. Both because of its urban location, which was opened to the public in 1847, and for its layout, which tried to recall a natural environment. Therefore, it was probably not a coincidence that the first attempt to create a form of architecture for animals that could be molded on their behavior was realized exactly in this venue. And precisely by the man who, according to Rem Koolhaas, more than anyone "changed architecture ... with fewer means."[8]

Everything began more than a century after the opening to the public of Regent's Park zoo, when the Royal Zoological Society, in 1960, informed the Duke of Edinburgh of their intention of building a new "birdcage" for the zoo, and he suggested to contact his brother-in-law, Anthony Armstrong-Jones, who studied architecture for a while, before failing his second-year exams.[9] And the latter, in turn, went for help to his old friend and contemporary at Cambridge, Cedric Price, who had just started his practice after a period at Erno Goldfinger's. Here, and previously at the Architectural Association, Price had already begun to develop an original and personal approach to architecture, which he saw more as a process than as a form.[10] And whereas his contemporary fellows, like Alison and Peter Smithson or the members of Archigram, had still shown "their own distinctive interests and individual tastes," he had manifested, by contrast, a strong "preference for dismantling architecture, and making it disappear into unconventional systems" of construction.[11] For this reason, in accordance with Lord Snowdon, he immediately dismissed the idea of designing a traditional birdcage, fashioned on the interpretation of domestic spatial typologies and clas-

Panoptic gardens. From Varro's aviary to Versailles

sical architectural elements, to work on something completely new. Thus, calling in the equally young engineer Frank Newby from Group Seven, the two began to work on a high-tech walk-through aviary, which could be made "for" and "by" the movements of its winged inhabitants.

In this regard, it must be said that, even though Snowdon Aviary was the first walk-through structure to be built in the United Kingdom, the idea was not totally new for that age, as in 1904 the Smithsonian Institute had already built an accessible flying cage for St. Louis World's Fair.[12] The true novelty, on the contrary, was bringing animals at the center of the formalization process, which made Price's project stand out from an architectural point of view, also from its most refined predecessors. Like the circular gorilla house, for example, designed in 1933 by Berthold Lubetkin for the same zoo, which gave the animals a sterile and harmoniously proportioned setting, through the balanced arrangement of curved and intersecting volumes. Or the spiraling shape of his renowned penguin pool, which served to showcase birds in a sort of grand choreography organized for the visitors.[13] Because each of them was based on the ethological principles formulated by the Swiss zoologist Heini Hediger, for whom animals' biological functions related to territoriality were not compromised in captivity, as long as the cage could guarantee a certain distance among its occupants.[14] But also on the common belief that the duty of artists was that of replacing the real world, spoiled by natural cycles of decay, with their own creations. For this reason, even in the best cases, the protagonists of this kind of design had always been the visitors, whereas animals had only been used to activate architecture by contrast, as they were actors on a stage.

Price and Snowdon's idea, on the contrary, could not be more distant.[15] After having chosen a rectangular lot on a steeply sloping canal bank of Regent's Park, they in fact began to sketch ideas for a sort of natural habitat covered by a curving tensile structure, the shape of which was meant "to accommodate the natural arcing flight patterns of birds."[16] Then, once satisfied

A veil over a flock. Snowdon Aviary's final shape

"The acceptance of the appropriateness of a finite container for the business of living [...] was a symptom of a particular half-century of artifactual history."

Cedric Price

with their basic concept, they asked Newby, who was studying Richard Buckminster Fuller's discontinuous compression systems, to design the technological solution that could guarantee the maximum volume for free flying, by providing a fifty meter cleared space, stretching some thirty meters high, with multi-level perches at both ends.[17] Obviously, while contemporarily ensuring the adequate transparency and permeability, which could both make the animals feel free and allow their view also from the outside. The solution was thus a diaphanous and netted enclosure made of a welded aluminum mesh, which had to be fixed to pretensioned steel cables, and draped across a composition of aluminum tubes, arranged into four different tetrahedral compression structures at the corners, all equipped with roosts.[18] And these would in turn have been anchored, by means of metallic legs, both on the ground near the canal and to a high retaining wall backwards, which, despite having been designed to simply reinforce the cliff, ultimately turned out to be the real spine of the project.

By crossing the whole site longitudinally and rectifying its topography, the wall would in fact have inevitably cut the space into two different levels. For this reason, Price decided to use it to separate the flows of people and water from that of birds, while still following the same direction, as defined by the position of the perches. On the one hand, by placing on top of its ridge a pedestrian path for visitors, which spanned the two opposing entrances with the broken line of a zigzagging cantilevered walkway. And on the other, by excavating at its base the bed of a stretched artificial lake, which had to be fed by two converging streams of water. The first springing from an indent of the cliff in the form of a continuous vertical cascade, and the other, slower and gentler, pouring from a small rectangular pool near one of the entries, and dropping through a series of shallow square platforms emerging from the wall like gigantic steps. All this while trying to keep the rest of the space as natural as possible, by simply integrating the existing vegetation with irregular patches of trees and bushes, in a layout that was substantially indifferent to the upper structure or the system of flows. As if he were simply not interested in achieving any sort of formal synthesis between the different elements of the whole, which ultimately took the shape of a strange, stranded vessel.

When in 1965 it was finally completed, the Aviary was thus unlike any other building that one could have seen. Nevertheless, its structure was almost immediately praised both by visitors, who could eventually enjoy an immersive view of forty-five different species of birds in a natural habitat, and by Price's colleagues, who appreciated his particular solution. If compared to the façadism of the Mappin Terraces or to the International Style of Lubetkin's pool, his project in fact represented a remarkable conceptual leap for that age.[19] And even though his friend Reyner Banham wrote about it as a "belated contribution to the Arcadian tradition" belonging to the unorthodox stream that dated back to Joseph Paxton,[20] Price's approach was so evidently alien to any arbitrary formal allegiances and technological determinism that the Aviary soon proved to challenge any possible form of traditional categorization.[21] And by contrast, as Charles Jencks wrote, it ended up representing the first declaration of independence from all the previous concepts of "enclosure, monumentality, stasis and even imagery," by which Price "put forward an idea of 'servicing' instead of architecture" that reflected his sense of "absolute freedom."[22] And along with that, of course, one of the most original architectural interpretations of the garden, meant as a system of relationships among different species.

For, despite being a zoological garden, and therefore little more than a cage, all the Aviary's distinctive features seem to be designed to contradict the fundamental principle of this spatial typology, which is its inherent anthropocentrism. Its distributive layout, for example, in a reversal of objects and subjects of the project, makes people look confined instead of animals. On the one hand, through the articulation of flows in section and not in a plan, which physically separates the path for visitors from the rest of the space and its actual inhabitants. And on the other, because of the material conformation of this element that immediately denounces its estrangement from both the stereotomic character of the landform and the light tectonic of Newby's canopy. Stretching from only two points of support, with a series of abrupt alternate right and left turns, the concrete ribbon of the walkway in fact crosses the volume of the building almost without touching its forest of trees and tubes, as to not to interfere with its life. An intention further underlined not only by its structure, which is independent from the upper one, but also by its formal matrix, which does not find confirmation in any other element of the building, as well as its width, which is not dissimilar from that of a corridor. As though it were meant to make people cross the Aviary, instead of staying there, in a sort of separate and suspended dimension that does not really belong to the whole space.

This is also because, unlike most of the gardens before it, the layout of the Aviary does not depend on the form of its enclosure, but it precedes it. Traditionally, in fact, the interior composition of enclosed gardens was based on a geometric process of partition that derived its logic from the formal configuration of the outer wall. And the division of the whole area in smaller fields, as well as the definition of paths, followed the same principle in a sequential progression that went from the outside inward, both in terms of formal and temporal priority.[23] In Price's project, on the contrary, the enclosure does not work as an ordering element, but it rather reflects the life inside its boundaries, in a process of formalization that followed the opposite direction, from the ideal movements of its inhabitants to the shape of their shelter. First, through its general conformation, which, recalling a veil spread over a flock, looks like being molded by the same birds while taking off. Then, for its consistence, which, besides providing transparency to this sort of crystalline cloud, gives the idea of a breathing layer capable of a quick change and response. And finally, because of its very structure, which, by following Buckminster Fuller's tensegrity principles, borrows from the natural world an adaptable mech-

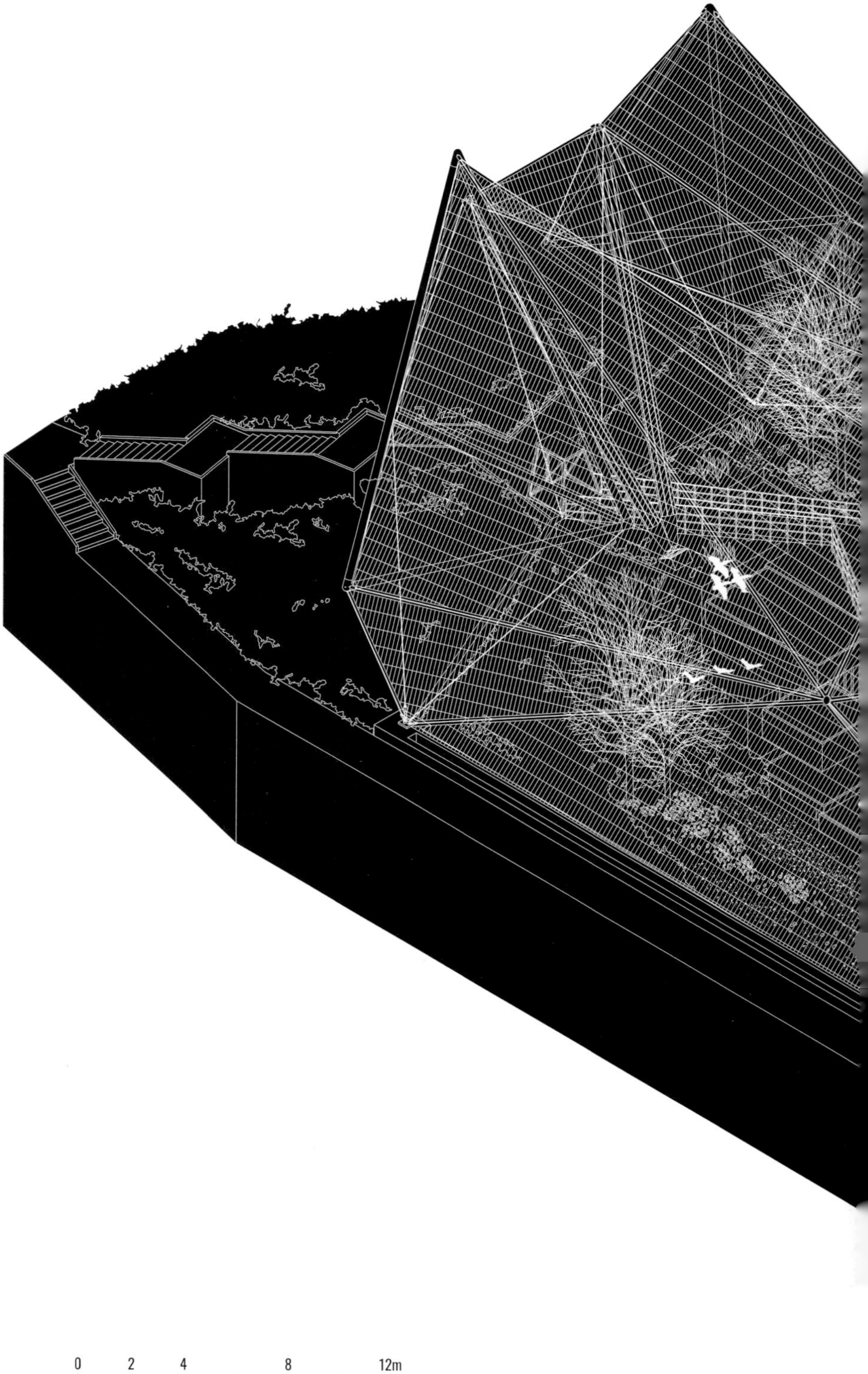
0
2
4
8
12m

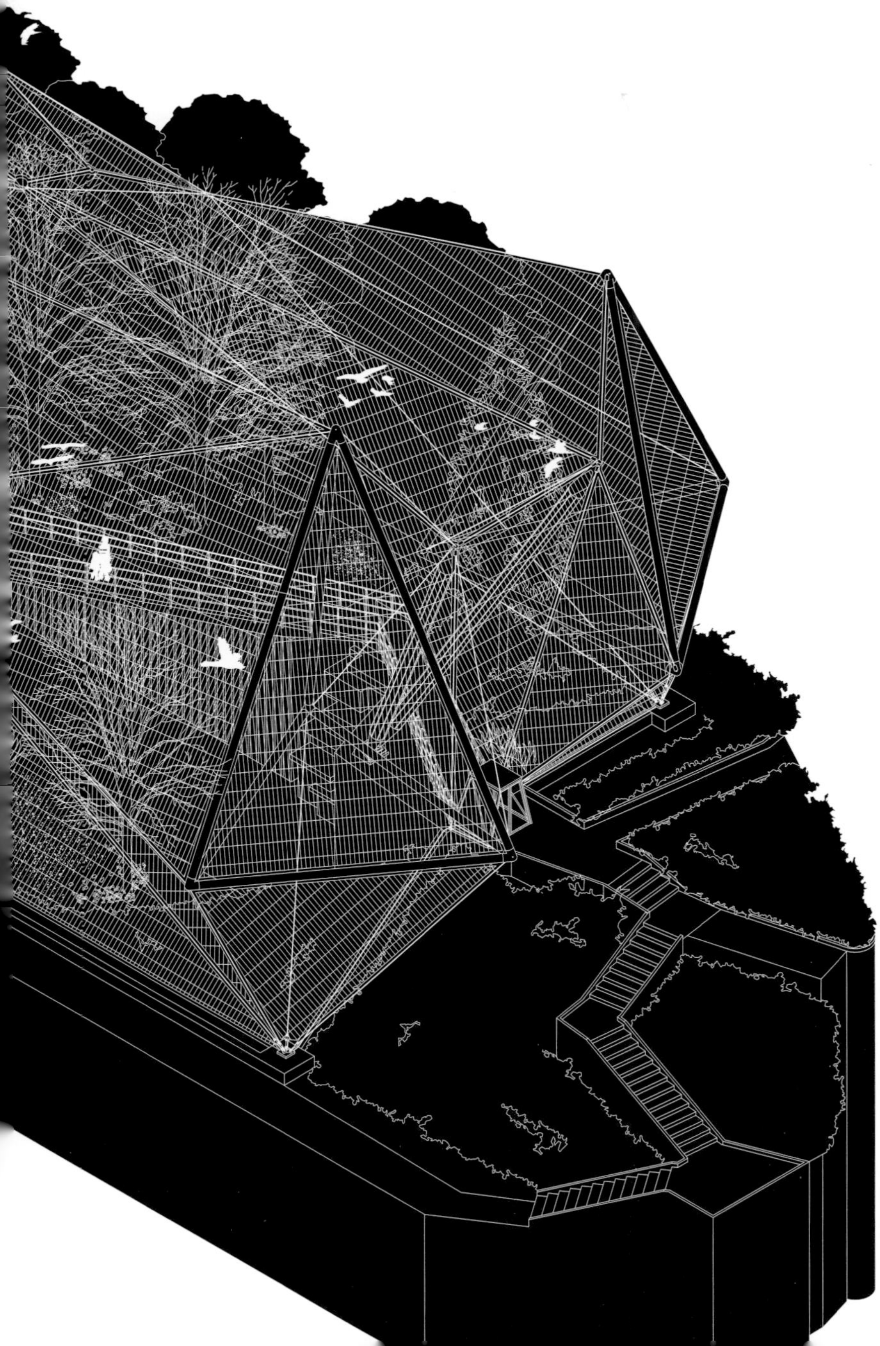

Designed for birds. Snowdon Aviary's conceptual core

anism for developing a lightweight frame that could in principle be dismantled and reassembled according to changing needs.[24] All this in a symbolic more than substantial way of prioritizing animals over humans, which Price pursued by using architecture as a figurative means to manifest the intention of enabling their possibilities rather than determining their expected behavior.[25]

In other words, as he did later by imagining a new kind of theater and a new type of university with his projects for the Fun Palace and Potteries Thinkbelt,[26] through the Aviary Price realized an idea of garden that was totally innovative for that age. And exactly as the former ones sprang from a new way of seeing the processes of learning and being educated, his first major project emerged from a novel way of interpreting the human relationship with nature, and not from the manipulation of traditional architectural typologies. In a vision that repeatedly recurred in his practice, through a sort of symbiotic form, across many of his later landscape projects.[27] Whereas, however, in all these following projects design developed in a programmatic dimension that was largely indifferent to formative characteristics, in the Aviary his poetic of indeterminacy still unfolded through a masterly work on the traditional constitutive elements of garden architecture, like the conformation of the "wall" and the composition of the layout. Thus, while the first ones had a considerable and broader conceptual influence over the years, the latter immediately opened the way for further concrete realizations, which followed the same direction. To such an extent that, when two years after its completion, Buckminster Fuller was entrusted with the design of the United States pavilion for the Montreal Expo, he looked back to his admirer's example and his design principles.

The story is well known also in this case. In summary, Fuller's idea for the World Fair was building a symbolic replica of what he liked to call "spaceship earth"[28] in order to bring visitors to experience what astronauts only one year later would have named "overview effect."[29] A cognitive shift, in few words,

Overview effect. Richard Buckminster Fuller's planetary garden

"Now there is one outstandingly important fact regarding Spaceship Earth, and that is that no instruction book came with it. [...] So, planners, architects, and engineers take the initiative. Go to work..."

Richard Buckminster Fuller

prompted by the possibility of looking at the Earth from space that, in his intention, would have pushed people to see it as a unique and fragile interdependent system to be protected beyond the limits of national boundaries. For this reason, to represent the whole biosphere in all its complexity and diversity, instead of a simple pavilion, he designed a sort of planetary garden, which was enclosed by the double layer of a huge geodesic dome, as a celestial body. And in addition, he fashioned its structure, made up of a composite system of tetrahedral cells, to emulate the homeostatic mechanisms of a natural system, as a permeable skin.[30] On the one hand, by covering the sphere with an outer layer of transparent acrylic panels, and on the other, by equipping about one third of its inner surface with modular roller shades, which were randomly spread across the dome like artificial clouds and were automatically operated by light sensors.[31] In this way, by adapting to changing sun conditions and shielding the space from a direct exposure, the structure would have maintained a constant temperature while reducing its energy consumption, like a real living organism. And although the system never worked properly and ultimately had to be dismantled, in its replication of the atmosphere's shape and functions, it definitively showed a whole generation of designers how a garden could materialize a different way to relate to the natural world, only by working on its constitutive features.[32]

What both Price and Fuller did, in other words, was not to change the essence of this space, which they still meant as an enclosed system to collect, grow and protect a selection of nature, be it a single class of animals or an extract of the biosphere itself. What they modified, by contrast, was the human role in this picture, which was symbolically removed from the center of the project and substituted with the end result of this selection, both as the subject and object of a design agency. As it was no longer the role of the owner nor of the spectator, but only that of one of the possible beneficiaries. And they did all this by essentially working on the material conformation of the enclosing element, which they transformed from a confining to a defining device. A responsive rather than an ordering element that had necessarily to emerge from a projective process of definition generated by the actions, the interactions, and the mechanisms of growth and exchange of its inhabitants, and not from an outer ruling gaze. For this reason, from an architectural standpoint, the project of the Snowdon Aviary had less to do with the subsequent typological development of zoological gardens, which progressively tended towards a closer imitation of natural environments.[33] Because, despite a deeper concern for animals' well-being, the great majority of zoological gardens however revolved around the visitors' experience as a main parameter. On the contrary, Price's project, as also Fuller's one, represented evolved forms of "arks," in which they sought to experiment new modalities of coexistence. All this, moreover, within an artificially mediated continuum between nature and culture that finally extended the range of design also to the articulated relationship between different species and technologies.

Notes

1 The story of Eden, for instance, as depicted in the second chapter of the Book of Genesis, recalls also a previous Mesopotamian myth about a primordial man who was placed in a divine garden to guard the Tree of Life. In this regard, see Robert Davidson, *Genesis 1-11: Commentary by R. Davidson* (Cambridge: Cambridge University Press, 1973).

2 Gilles Clément, *Une brève histoire du jardin* (Paris: Editions du 81, 2011). In this regard, see also Pierre Grimal, *L'art des jardins* (Paris: PUF, 1974).

3 The terms garden, paradise and enclosure are strictly interrelated. Garden, for instance, stemmed from the German *Garten*, which meant enclosure. And paradise, which comes from the Greek *paradeisos*, directly referred to the Persian *pairidaeza* that meant enclosure too. Ibid.

4 Gustave Loisel, *Histoire des Menageries: De l'antiquité à nos jours* (Paris: Doin et Fils, 1912), 45.

5 Eric Baratay and Elisabeth Hardouin-Fugier, *Zoo: A History of Zoological Gardens in the West* (London: Reaktion Books, 2002), 41-42.

6 William N. Mann, *Wild Animals In and Out of the Zoos* (Washington: Smithsonian Institution, 1930).

7 The term menagerie in fact derived from the French *ménage*, which was used to refer to housekeeping. Baratay and Hardouin-Fugier, *Zoo*, 42.

8 Rem Koolhaas, "Introduction," in *Re: CP*, ed. Hans Ulrich Obrist (Basel: Birkhäuser, 2003), 6.

9 Stephen Mullin, "Cedric Price: 1934-2003," *Arq* 7, no. 2 (2003): 113-118.

10 Stanley Mathews, *From Agit-Prop to Free Space: The Architecture of Cedric Price* (London: Black Dog Publishing, 2007), 30-34.

11 Arata Isozaki, "Erasing Architecture into the System," in *Re: CP*, ed. Hans Ulrich Obrist (Basel: Birkhäuser, 2003), 45.

12 National Zoological Park, *Records: 1887-1966* (Washington DC: Smithsonian Institution Archives, 1966).

13 Baratay and Hardouin-Fugier, *Zoo*, 254-262.

14 Heini Hediger, *Wild Animals in Captivity* (London: Butterworth, 1950).

15 Referring to another project, Price in fact significantly stated that the "acceptance of the appropriateness of a finite container for the business of living [...] was a symptom of a particular half-century of artifactual history, during which there appeared to be a recognizable equation between the compatibility of the dimensions of inventions [...] and the kinesthetic sensibilities displayed by their inventors." Quoted in Mathews, *From Agit-Prop to Free Space*, 38.

16 Ibid., 35. Flight patterns studied with the contribution of the eminent conservationist and ornithologist Peter Scott.

17 For background, see "Aviary at the London Zoo. Designed by the Earl of Snowdon and Cedric Price," *Architectural Review* 127 (1961), 417-418; "Northern Aviary, London Zoo. Designed by: Lord Snowdon, C. Price & F. Newby," *Architectural Design* 9 (1965): 451-459; and Samantha Hardingham, *Cedric Price Works 1952–2013: A Forward-Minded Retrospective* (London: AA Publications, 2016), 87-103. The structure was probably inspired by the extraordinary tensile aviary in steel and nylon, built by Vittoriano Viganò in 1954 for Milan's X Triennale, although the implied philosophical concept was completely different. Suffice it to say that Viganò made the birds' feathers be artificially painted in blue, for the architectural

structure to stand out. See Attilio Stocchi, *Vittoriano Vigano: Etica brutalista* (Turin: Testo & Immagine, 1999), 22-23.

18 Roy Landau, "Engineers and Architects: Newby + Price," *AA Files* 27 (1994): 25-32.

19 Hadas A. Steiner, "For the Birds," *Grey Room* 13 (2003): 5-31.

20 Reyner Banham, "Aviary, London Zoological Gardens," *Architectural Review* 138 (1965): 186.

21 "In Price's work, the connection between the complexities and potential of the question, and the physical (or nonphysical) end product, is very close, and because [...] his work is consciously problem-solving [...], the importance of seeing each product as a problem-understanding and question-asking process [...] is necessary if it is to be understood." Roy Landau, *New Directions in British Architecture* (London: Studio Vista, 1968), 76.

22 Charles Jencks, *Modern Movements in Architecture* (London: Penguin, 1985), 285.

23 For an extensive view of the history of this spatial typology, see Rob Aben and Saskia de Wit, *The Enclosed Garden: History and Development of the Hortus Conclusus and its Reintroduction into the Present-day Urban Landscape* (Rotterdam: 010 Publisher, 1999).

24 Richard Buckminster Fuller, "Tensegrity," *Portfolio and Art News Annual*, no.4 (1961).

25 An approach that Price, some years later, called "anticipatory architecture," to indicate a way of designing that is "concerned with reactions, not merely initial appetites." Cedric Price, *Building Design* 1071 (January 11, 1991): 19.

26 For an extensive view of these two projects, see Mathews, *From Agit-Prop to Free Space*.

27 Such as Mills, Serre II, Ducklands, and IFPRI. In this regard, see Robin Middleton, "To Earth," in *Cedric Price Opera*, ed. Samantha Hardingham (London: Wiley, 2003), 28-29.

28 Richard Buckminster Fuller, *Operating Manual for Spaceship Earth* (New York: Simon & Schuster, 1969).

29 Frank White, *The Overview Effect: Space Exploration and Human Evolution* (Boston: Houghton-Mifflin, 1987). Everything began in 1968, when the publication of Apollo 8's picture of *Earthrise* brought people, for the first time, to see the world as a finite place that had not to be taken for granted.

30 Timothy M. Rohan, "From Microcosm to Macrocosm: The Surface of Fuller and Sadao's US Pavilion at Montreal Expo 67," *Architectural Design* 73, no. 2 (2003): 50-56.

31 Jonathan Massey, "Buckminster Fuller's Reflexive Modernism," *Design and Culture* 4, no. 3 (2012): 325-344.

32 Eva Díaz, "Dome Culture in the Twenty-first Century," *Grey Room* 42 (2011): 80-105.

33 Baratay and Hardouin-Fugier, *Zoo*, 265-280.

Visual atlas (following spread)

1 London Tower Menagerie, Henry III of England, 1235

2 Garden of Eden, Athanasius Kircher, 1675

3 Ménagerie du Jardin des Plantes, Bernardin de Saint-Pierre, 1794

4 Hannover Zoo, Oskar Friedrich Schmidt, 1870

5 Flight Cage, Smithsonian Institution, 1904
6 Mappin Terraces, Peter Chalmers Mitchell, 1924.
7 Penguin Pool, Berthold Lubetkin, 1934
8 Voliera, Vittoriano Viganò, 1954
9 Elephant and Rhinoceros Pavilion, Casson Conder Partnership, 1965
10 Parc André-Citroën, Gilles Clément, 1992
11 *Thomas et le Voyageur*, Gilles Clément, 1997
12 Lurie Garden, Piet Oudolf, 2004
13 Eden project, Nicholas Grimshaw, 2000
14 Elephant House, Foster and Partners, 2007
15 Giant Panda Forest, Hassell, 2010
16 Smithsonian Conservation Biology Institute, 2010
17 Zoo360, CLR Design, 2011
18 Zootopia, Bjarke Ingels Group, 2014
19 Cancer City, Visiondivision, 2010
20 Garden by the Bay, Gran Associates and Wilkinson Eyre, 2012
21 Northerly Island, Studio Gang, 2012
22 Host and Nectar Garden Building, Husos Architects, 2010
23 Jiyan Healing Garden, ZRS Architekten Ingenieure, 2016
24 *The Planetary Garden*, Manifesta 12, 2018

historical menageries

1 1A 2 2A 3 3A

picturesque gardening

4 4A 5 5A 6 6A

modern zoos

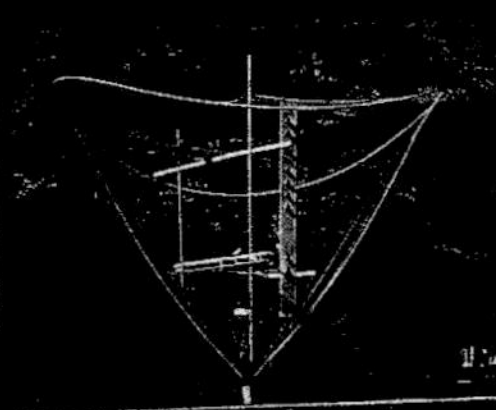

7 7A 8 8A 9 9A

wild enclosures

Gilles Clément
Thomas et le Voyageur

Dessiner le jardin planétaire ? Projet fou, démesuré, aux limites du possible. Telle est pourtant l'entreprise à laquelle Thomas, le peintre retiré dans sa propriété close de Saint Sauveur, et son ami le Voyageur ont décidé de s'atteler. Parcourant les terres australes, des Andes chiliennes à l'Australie, le Voyageur envoie à Thomas des données que celui-ci interprète. Observations des plantes, animaux, reliefs, horizons, ciels nourrissent leur relation épistolaire poétique et savante. Peu à peu se dessine une nouvelle vision, dans le surprenant chatoiement de leur évolution, de la nature et du monde dont l'homme ne serait plus le centre, mais le scribe et le gardien.

Avec ce récit lumineux et sensible devenu un livre-culte, Gilles Clément, paysagiste de renommée internationale, initiateur de la notion de « jardin en mouvement » qui réhabilitait la friche comme laboratoire et lieu de liberté.

10 10A 11 11A 12 12A

technological gardens

13 13A

14 14A

15 15A

open zoos

16 16A

17 17A

18 18A

urban metabolisms

19 19A

20 20A

21 21A

new relations

22 22A

23 23A

Manifesta 12
16.06–04.11.18
Palermo, Italy

24 24A

An ark

John Carl Warnecke
Manhattan, New York City, US
40.716557, -74.006009
1967-1974

"Then God said to Noah and to his sons with him: I now establish my covenant with you and with your descendants after you and with every living creature that was with you – the birds, the livestock and all the wild animals, all those that came out of the ark with you – every living creature on earth."

Genesis 9: 8-10 NIV.

Whereas the garden almost certainly represented one of the first archetypes of spatial coexistence among different species, it cannot be said that its preeminence was totally unquestioned, also during antiquity. On the contrary, it is almost striking to note how, even in the earliest narratives of creation, the garden was very soon replaced by another that emerged after an alleged catastrophic event. In the Mesopotamian myths from the second millennium before Christ, for example, there were nine different known versions of a story about a global flood that destroyed all life. And in each one, a chosen hero was commanded to build a boat and rescue life when the gods, for many reasons, decided to destroy it.[1] However, it is only in the Old Testament, and particularly through the comparison between the Garden of Eden and Noah's Ark, that it is possible to appreciate a first form of shift from an anthropocentric subjectivity to a biocentric one, even within the limits of a clear theocentric agency. Since in the tale of creation, animals were molded out of clay just to please Adam, who had in turn the faculty to name them, thus affirming his paternity over every form of life.[2] While in the flood, Noah and his family were kept alive only to preserve natural life and make it propagate, after human behavior had caused the destruction of the world.[3] For this reason, even after environmentalist culture underlined the inherent anthropocentrism of the biblical teaching,[4] the Ark has resisted as the clearest architectural archetype of an antithetical perspective.[5] As it embodied, unlike the garden did, the first device by which mankind was put at the service of non-human subjects, and not the opposite.

What is even more interesting, however, is that the Ark can also be seen as another form of architectural archetype, and precisely as a design archetype. At least, since the first attempt of mapping the system of human knowledge, which took shape, in 1751, with the publication of Denis Diderot and Jean d'Alembert's *Encyclopédie*. Because even though civil and naval architecture were treated in different articles, Jacques-François Blondel, who was commissioned to write the article "Architecture," clearly stated in his introduction that they belonged to the same discipline.[6] And the article "Ark," produced by the Abbé Edme-François Mallet, was distinctly structured as a sort of palaeoanthropological study on naval architecture.[7] But whereas Blondel, by writing almost exclusively about proportions, gave a rather classical definition of the art, demonstrated, so to say, *more geometrico*, Mallet introduced some considerations of another order, which took "a singularly 'modern' turn" in this regard.[8] Instead of trying to prove the tale's authenticity, he in fact treated the practical implications of the story of Noah, by assessing the technical and logistical efficacy of the design, construction and management of this "floating building" in relation to its function. And in so doing, for the first time, he focused on some specific aspects of design as found in the Scriptures, such as sizing, distribution and layout, which had never been particularly considered before.[9] As the Ark, in order to ensure the survival of a multiplicity of subjects in a limited space, had required a sort of initial "foray into what would [have been] called functionalist thought in architecture."[10] The same that was fully realized, at least in these terms, over two centuries after the publication of Mallet's essay, while dealing however with a very different set of subjects.

The story, in this case, involves a really unique skyscraper, built from 1967 to 1974 and located at 33 Thomas Street in New York, which represented one of the first architectures ever designed almost exclusively for automated machines. And whose stern or even hostile shape,[11] rising over a hundred and fifty meters without any kind of window, has often been explained, "in a Cold War fable, as a defense of important telephone equipment against nuclear attack."[12] Everything began after World War II, when AT&T, which was already retaining an almost complete monopoly on electronic communications in the United States, had additional justification in terms of national security needs for strengthening its role.[13] The idea was in fact that, if compared with the competitive market, a single phone company could have provided a more effective public service, while also

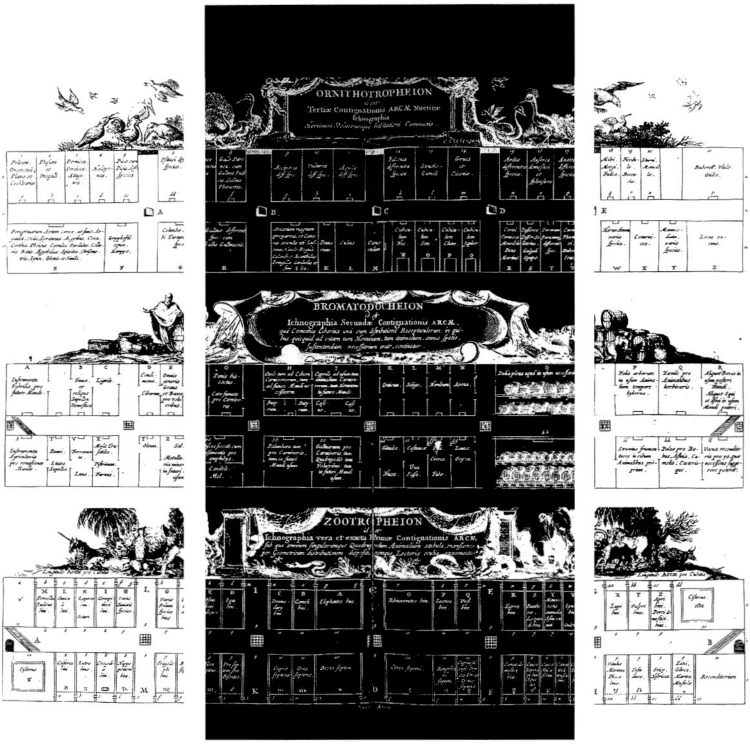

Arks and buildings. Athanasius Kircher and Jean-francois Blondel

granting the central government a full control over what was considered the most vital infrastructure of that age.[14] This, however, would have implied to secure the Long Lines Division, which enabled long-distance calls, in case of a fallout, by creating a centralized switching office that would have represented the largest and safest fully automated office in the world.[15] As if it were a sort of refined version of a nuclear shelter, however elevated and placed in the nation's most attractive bombing target, in order to show that its network was invulnerable to any possible risk. For this reason, the company chose a location very close to several established exchanges, whose nearness to Long Lines headquarters was likely to offer realistic opportunities to complement that building's capacity. And for the design, in line with the company's public relations program, they opted for the external firm led by John Carl Warnecke, "an early product of Walter Gropius's Harvard,"[16] who had to give the replicable layout implemented by AT&T's design team a civic symbolism that, on the contrary, was quite alien to its predecessors.[17]

33 Thomas, in fact, was not the first automated switching center in the United States, since already in the mid-fifties, most of AT&T's customers could dial local calls without an operator. And even in its being without windows it was not unique, as it was preceded by another one at 811 Tenth Avenue, and was contemporary with both 375 Pearl Street and few other lower structures located immediately outside Manhattan.[18] Therefore, it shared with any of them some common features established by the company's design team, given by the necessity to mediate between a massive switching device and a huge quantity of wiring passing underground. Like that, for example, of being tall and heavy prisms with deep floor plates packed with telephone frames, stacked one onto the other over the base of a cable vault. As though they were, for what concerned distribution, an almost literal cast of the diagrams by which tip cables were vertically articulated from the trunk lines to the main distribution frame, up to the system of switches.[19] Or also that of making cables run through the hollow concrete blocks of the

The project as an algorithm. Long Lines Building's consequential design

"Instead of forcing the functions of every sort of building into one general form [...] let us begin from the heart as the nucleus, and work outward."

Horatio Greenough

outer walls, thus maximizing free floor area for electronic devices while at the same time reducing the need for horizontal wiring.[20] Like the buildings themselves, in their being sort of mute and windowless boxes, were enlarged connection devices. All this, however, in the project for 33 Thomas was brought onto both a scale and to a level of expressive awareness that perfectly matched AT&T's will to transform a simple infrastructural facility into a real monument to public safety. And this was enabled by Warnecke's specific contribution, whose approach to public architecture had already been praised, quite ironically, for its "humanistic" touch.[21]

The Long Lines Building is in fact all but human, from any point of view. Save for the entrance placed on a corner of one of the long sides, the building, up to the tenth floor, which is just over a third of its total height, is nothing more than a fluted parallelepiped of granite, rising abruptly from the ground with no mediating plinth and no kind of opening, except for eighteen large mechanical grilles at its top, all a full story high. Then upwards, its section decreases, and while a smaller prism, finished exactly as the lower one, reaches the twenty-ninth floor with a second belt of ventilation grilles, six asymmetric shafts for vertical connection emerge from the base, like massive tubes of ductwork, and touch the summit with no vents or openings. All this by refusing any form of canonical tripartition and hiding the setback required by the 1916 Zoning Resolution behind the straight lines of the elevators,[22] as though the preeminence of its function was so strong to ignore any compositional rule or urban law. However, by reading into the technical documents and the rare declassified pictures, the space appears even less human. Although the building's loading limits, for example, are three times those of a typical office tower of that size, many of its stories can legally hold fewer than ten persons each, with a total occupation ratio of less than one fourth that of a similar building.[23] For despite having at the ground floor a lounge, a cafeteria and offices, all tastefully decorated, most of the rest of the space only contains tight stacks of automated machines and technical equipment. And each story, over five meters high and freed from the obstacle of the vertical connections, develops through a repetitive layout that has been sized to exploit the maximum capacity for technical devices, and organized to streamline their operation, through an unwonted scale, so to say, that prioritizes machines functions over human presence, and which is reflected not only by its eloquent shape, but also by a precise way of designing.

In this regard, the drawings and the pictures of the model presented in a 1969 issue of *Architectural Record* are quite revealing.[24] Plans and sections seem in fact to accept the schematic logic dictated by AT&T's design team without questioning it at all, but rather trying to retrace it in its purest form, by bringing stairs and elevators out in the shafts, for instance, which could otherwise have interfered with the horizontal distribution of the typical plan.[25] But even by adapting to a series of volumetric compositional studies realized to bypass the legal setback requirements, which would in turn have broken the continuity of the verticality, as well as that of the wiring system enclosed in the modular system of the walls.[26] As if the whole project represented a sequential progression of logical choices, obtained by reducing the building to its operating scheme, to then deduce by inference all the other solutions. All this by starting from its basic operational component, which through its size, its weight and its level of connection had to work as the constructive module of a system that could have indifferently ben replicated according to different side conditions.[27] Nonetheless, immediately after the construction of 33 Thomas, critics unanimously focused their attention on the urban character of the building and its impressive and massive power, almost overlooking all the other aspects. *Architectural Record*, for example, highlighted the architect's "concern for [its] impact on people and on the city itself," as well as his alleged attempt of creating "human-scaled streets."[28] While Paul Goldberger praised its ability in giving shape to "a powerful new form" of urban architecture.[29] Thus, even when time changed and, as the risk of a nuclear attack exponentially decreased, critiques became harsher, the arguments were always focused on its public appearance.[30]

But although there is no doubt that, from an architectural point of view, the greatest impact of the project lied in the urban dimension, what has often been forgotten is that this was not due to Warnecke's alleged humanistic touch, but to the fact that the building was explicitly nonhuman in all its aspects. In other words, it was not because he concealed its technical requirements behind a reassuring and rational face, as probably AT&T expected it to happen when they hired one of Gropius' pupils. On the contrary, the result was due to his ability to exploit the expressive features of the functional program, which were composed in a traditional and at the same time unseen form of construction. On the one hand, in the attempt to interpret its final purpose, by looking back at the architectures of urban water reservoirs and their massive and uncanny character.[31] And on the other, in a stricter adherence to its actual function, by making evident from outside the nature of its components, which were turned into both structural and symbolic elements.[32] Like the walls, for instance, which not only had to work like electric cables, by enclosing the main wires, but also recalled them, with their vertical flutings and their ventilation grills fashioned like gigantic sockets. Exactly as the whole building had to look like, and not just be, a massive mainframe. For not only it had to represent a form of ultimate "fortress" against fallout,[33] but it also had to work as a daily communication device, through an objectual dimension that, despite being indirect and intangible, had however to be displayed. And it was probably for this reason that Warnecke, instead of adapting traditional typologies, decided to work, for the first time, on both the content and the container of the building, as if they were a new and integrated system of operation, construction, and expression.

Through his project, in other words, Warnecke not only designed an architecture for automated machines, molded on their dimensions and their way of working, but transformed the building itself into an actual working machine, both from the

0
10
20
40
60m

An expressive containing machine. Louis Kahn's Richards Medical Center, Henri Labrouste's Bibliothèque nationale de France, and Croton Reservoir

functional and the symbolic standpoints. And he did all that by implementing a design methodology that aspired to be equally automated. As if the project were a sort of replicable algorithm, in which the operational diagram, the functional program, and the decision flowchart were perfectly superimposable. Not only in plan, of course, but also on its façade. Through a composition that, instead of simply revealing its interior mechanism, had to be defined by a process of scaling of its constitutive components and their way of operating, in a sort of unconventional interpretation of monumentality. For this reason, the design for 33 Thomas has little to do, from an architectural point of view, with the series of brutalist windowless fortresses of the same period to which it is usually compared.[34] Because they have typically been designed as standard offices, located in blast-resistant shelters, with no particular methodological implication in terms of process. Exactly as the later typological development of data centers and automated storages, in turn, despite following the same operational logic, has not shown a comparable interest in turning them into a form of architectural expression.[35]

What, on the contrary, appears to be closer to 33 Thomas' concept is the project for a totally different "ark," way more literal in its adherence to the metaphor and its posthuman character, but also more radical in terms of design. And it is precisely that for the construction of a global seed bank, built more than thirty years later, when the emergent awareness of the human impact on the main territorial and climatic changes of the previous decades suggested that there were other vital infrastructures to be secured in case of future disasters.[36] The idea, in reality, had already come to light in 1989, when the Norwegian government that had been storing duplicates of the Nordic countries' seed collection in an abandoned coal mine of Svalbard for five years, offered to construct an international repository for the most important plant genetic resources of the world.[37] The islands in fact had the perfect climate and geology for underground cold storage, as well as an international status that ensured equal rights to citizens from all States. And

Designed by excavation. Plan of the Svalbard Global Seed Vault

the plant genetic resources had been already recognized as the foundation of the global food security. However, it was only in 2004 that it was possible to resolve some of the most difficult political issues, and launch a new Norwegian initiative to secure duplicates of all the world's collections in a centralized global facility.[38] And it took other two years to finally assist to the cornerstone ceremony for a structure, then called Svalbard Global Seed Vault, which had to be dug into a mountainside near the village of Longyearbyen, on the island of Spitsbergen, and whose construction was eventually completed in 2008.

What is curious, after all these efforts, is that the bank, which was designed by Peter W. Søderman, from the outside is nothing more than an inclined concrete prow, jutting from the slope of a snowy and desolate mountain, with a short metallic drawbridge and a door. But the narrow opening actually introduces to an impressive tunnel, one hundred and twenty meters long, that goes straight deep into the permafrost. First through a sleeve of corrugated steel, aimed at protecting the passage from erosion and possible climate changes, and then directly into the rock, where the huge corridor, after meeting a small control room, gives access, by means of a transversal passage equipped with airlock barriers, to the three underground chambers reserved for the storage of the seeds. Three separate and rectangular excavated vaults, completely filled with metallic racks, going from the ground to the ceiling with narrow aisles among them. Each one stacked with plastic boxes, and packed by the seeds' aluminum bags. As though the whole building, once again, had been sized on the features of its content, through a projective process of definition. A process implemented, in this case, by a physical and conceptual act of excavation, through which all the environmental units acquired volumetric relevance, in a perfect reflection of its diagrammatic functional program.

For although they ended up representing two different types of monument to human vulnerability and resilience, what eventually characterized the design of an ark, both in Warnecke and Søderman's projects, was not the simple translation of an idea of protection, which was taken for granted. On the contrary, it was mainly the research of a possible architecture for non-human subjects, which could be different from a simple infrastructure, both from an organizational and from a formal point of view. For this reason, they both worked on an idea of expressive functionalism for which the architectural consistence of the building, despite being characterizing, was not given in advance, but represented a consequence of its interior mechanism and its essential features.[39] In other words, as if it were the outcome of the integration of content and container, projected onto the urban or territorial level. Thus, whereas the Long Lines Building ended up representing a sort of gigantic mainframe, the Svalbard Seed Vault works exactly as a global planting pit, both in terms of operation, construction, and expression. And if their spaces are avowedly nonhuman, and their undisputable resonance depends on that, their instrumentality is revealed by this precise process through which, by architectural means, they finally become objects. Or better, collective tools for a humanity that enjoys both the feeling of safeness and the sublime fascination of being excluded.

Notes

1 Helge Kvanvig, *Primeval History: Babylonian, Biblical, and Enochic: An Intertextual Reading* (Leiden: Brill, 2011).

2 Genesis 2: 19-20 NIV.

3 Genesis 6: 9-22 NIV.

4 Lynn White, "The Historical Roots of Our Ecological Crisis," *Science* 155 (1967): 1203-1207.

5 Richard Buckminster Fuller, *Your Private Sky: Discourse* (New York: Springer, 2001), 176.

6 Jacques-François Blondel, "Architecture," in *Encyclopédie, ou Dictionnaire raisonné des sciences, des arts et des métiers*, vol. 1, ed. Denis Diderot and Jean Le Rond d'Alembert (Paris, 1751), 617.

7 Abbé Edme-François Mallet, "Arche," in *Encyclopédie*, 607.

8 Hubert Damisch, *Noah's Ark: Essays on Architecture* (Cambridge MA: The MIT Press, 2016), 20.

9 In reality, the same features had already appeared over seventy years before in the drawings by the Jesuit scholar Athanasius Kircher, with which he tried to demonstrate how contemporary science supported the account of the Book of Genesis. Athanasius Kircher, *Arca Noë* (Amsterdam: Johannes van Waesbergen, 1675).

10 Damisch, *Noah's Ark*, 20. The relationship between functionalism and naval design had in reality already been highlighted by Horatio Greenough in the first half of the nineteenth century. "Observe a ship at sea," he wrote, "behold an organization second only to that of an animal [...] Could we carry into our civil architecture the responsibilities that weigh upon our shipbuilding, we should ere long have edifices as superior to the Parthenon, for the purposes that we require." Horatio Greenough, *Form and Function: Remarks on Art* (Berkeley: University of California Press, 1947), 60.

11 See for instance William Whyte's unflattering judgment in *City: Rediscovering the Center* (New York: Anchor Books, 1988), 224-225.

12 Addison Godel, "When Windows Were Wires: The Projection of Network Invulnerability and the Architecture of the AT&T Long Lines," *Grey Room* 61 (2015): 35. The essay represents the only critical study on the history of the building.

13 For a complete overview, see Richard D. John, *Network Nation: Inventing American Telecommunications* (Cambridge MA: Belknap Press, 2010).

14 David Nye, *Electrifying America: Social Meanings of a New Technology* (Cambridge MA: MIT Press, 1999), 175-181.

15 The necessity of critical-node redundancy, at that time, was of course very far from being discovered.

16 Godel, "When Windows Were Wires," 53.

17 "Designed for Machines but Mindful of People," *Architectural Record*, no. 146 (July 1969): 123-130.

18 "Windowless Skyscraper," *Architectural Forum*, no. 117 (December 1962): 17; "Windowless Phone Building," *Progressive Architecture*, no. 43 (August 1963): 56-58.

19 A. Michael Noll, *Introduction to Telephones and Telephone Systems, 3rd ed.* (Boston: Artech House, 1998), 133-134.

20 "Designed for Machines," 128.

21 Allan Temko, "The Humanist Architecture of John Carl Warnecke," *Architectural Forum* 113 (1960): 97-98.

22 The 1916 Zoning Resolution had established limits in building massing at certain heights, thus implicitly requiring the use of the traditional setback. In this regard, see, for instance Hugh Ferriss, *The Metropolis of Tomorrow* (New York: Princeton Architectural Press, 1929); or Keith D. Revell, "Law Makes Order: The Search for Ensemble in the Skyscraper City, 1890-1930," in *The American Skyscraper: Cultural Histories*, ed. R. Moudry (Cambridge MA-New York: Cambridge University Press, 2005), 38-59.

23 New York City Department of Buildings, Certificate of Occupancy for 33 Thomas Street, no. 74182 (January 1974).

24 "Designed for Machines."

25 Through a solution that clearly recalls Louis Kahn's project for Richards Medical Laboratories (1957-1960). See Vincent Scully, *Louis I. Kahn* (New York: George Braziller, 1962), 28.

26 Exactly as Ludwig Mies van der Rohe did, even though for different reasons, when he designed the Seagram Building (1954). Phyllis Lambert, *Building Seagram* (New Haven and London: Yale University Press, 2013), 49.

27 In this regard, it is in fact interesting to notice that the project was presented in an unusual "expandable" version, which could have been implemented in case AT&T had intended to increase its capacity by extending it to an adjacent lot.

28 "Designed for Machines," 126.

29 Paul Goldberger, "When Building for Future Means a Step Backwards," *New York Times* (6 December 1975): 33.

30 That by William Whyte, for example, who saw 33 Thomas as the epitome of the corporate "power and fear" architecture, or that by Robert Stern, who called it an "almost parodic" emulation of Kahn's design. Whyte, *City*, 226; Robert Stern, *New York 1960: Architecture and Urbanism between the Second World War and the Bicentennial* (New York: Monacelli Press, 1995), 163.

31 See, for instance, the Croton reservoir, which in the second half of the nineteenth century covered four acres on the Fifth Avenue with a gigantic mass of blank walled volume, and which undoubtedly was a reference for Warnecke. Sergey Kadinsky, *Hidden Waters of New York City: A History and Guide to 101 Forgotten Lakes, Ponds, Creeks, and Streams in the Five Boroughs* (Woodstock: Countryman Press, 2016).

32 A whole list of possible precedents in this regard can be found in Reyner Banham, *The Architecture of the Well-Tempered Environment* (London: The Architectural Press, 1969), 234-264. In summary, it can be considered the inversion of Peter Behrens' logic when, for the project of the AEG turbine factory (1909), he transformed the system of the overhead crane into a sort of classical architectural element. In this case, on the contrary, it was the whole architecture to be fashioned like a technical element.

33 James T. Ream in "Designed for Machines," 126.

34 Among the others, see, for example, the Buffalo City Court Building designed in 1971 by Theodore A. Biggie, whose precast concrete façade is almost without windows. Reyner Banham, *Buffalo Architecture: A Guide* (Cambridge MA: The MIT Press, 1981), 58.

35 About the two typologies, see respectively *Clog: Data Space* (New York: CLOG, 2012); and Liam Young, *Machine Landscapes: Architectures of the Post Anthropocene* (London: Wiley, 2019).

36 In this regard, see, for instance, Mike Davis, "Who Will Build the Ark," *New Left Review* 61, no. 1 (2010): 29-46.

37 Cary Fowler, *Seeds on Ice: Svalbard and the Global Seed Vault* (Westport CT: Easton Studio Press, 2016).

38 More precisely after the signature of the FAO International Treaty on Plant Genetic Resources for Food and Agriculture. Marte Qvenild, "Svalbard Global Seed Vault: a 'Noah's Ark' for the World's Seeds," *Development in Practice* 18, no. 1 (2008): 110-116.

39 Which is precisely the approach that, according to Horatio Greenough, architecture had to borrow from naval design. "Instead of forcing the functions of every sort of building into one general form, adopting an outward shape for the sake of the eye or of association, without reference to the inner distribution, let us begin from the heart as the nucleus, and work outward." Greenough, *Form and Function*, 60-61.

Visual atlas (following spread)

1 Great Pyramid of Giza, 2560 BC
2 Pozzo di San Patrizio, Antonio da Sangallo il Giovane, 1537
3 *Noah's Ark*, Athanasius Kircher, 1675
4 Fort Drum, United States Army Corps of Engineers, 1914
5 Cheyenne Mountain Complex, Army Corps of Engineers, 1965
6 Mount Weather Emergency Operations Center, FEMA, 1979
7 *Aircraft Carrier City in Landscape*, Hans Hollein, 1964
8 "The Story of the Pool," Rem Koolhaas, 1977
9 *Arca*, Massimo Scolari, 1986
10 Buffalo City Court Building, Pfohl, Roberts and Biggie Studio, 1974
11 Ricola Storage Building, Herzog & de Meuron, 1986
12 Public Safety Answering Center II, SOM, 2016
13 The Oppidum, Apocalypse bunker, 1994
14 Safe House, Robert Konieczny, 2011
15 Angebauter Tarnrucksack, Atelier F, 2012
16 Digital Beijing, Studio Zhu-Pei, 2007
17 Pionen (White mountain) Data Center, Albert France-Lanord Architects, 2008
18 Datacenter AM4, Benthem Crouwel Architects, 2017
19 *Dove riposa l'acqua*, Nexus!, 2017
20 Museum and Center for Biodiversity, Erkal Architects, 2018
21 Living Coral Biobank, Contreras Earl Architecture, 2020
22 *The Post Anthropocene: Envision Life in Hard Future*, JOA, 2019
23 Supercomputer for meteorological forecasting, Met office, 2019
24 Onkalo spent nuclear fuel repository, Posiva, 2023

h i s t o r i c a l a r k s

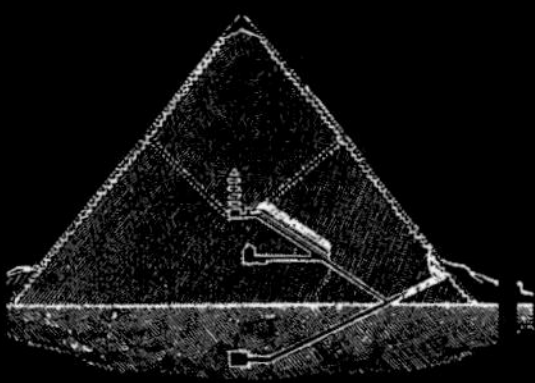

1 1A

2 2A

3 3A

m i l i t a r y f o r t r e s s e s

4 4A

5 5A

6 6A

c o n c e p t u a l a r k s

7 7A

8 8A

9 9A

w i n d o w l e s s b u i l d i n g s

10 10A

11 11A

12 12A

p o s t - a p o c a l y p t i c   s h e l t e r s

13 13A

14 14A

15 15A

d a t a   c e n t e r s

16 16A

17 17A

18 18A

b i o d i v e r s i t y   r e p o s i t o r i e s

19 19A

20 20A

21 21A

n e w   f u n c t i o n s

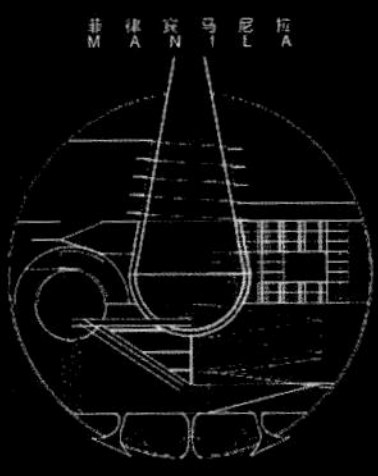

22 22A

23 23A

24 24A

A lab

Richard Rogers and Tony Hunt
Newport, GB
51.565890, -3.022337
1982-1987

"The most fruitful areas for the growth of the sciences [are] those which had been neglected as a no-man's land between the various established fields [...] It is these boundary regions which offer the richest opportunities to the qualified investigator. They are at the same time the most refractory to the accepted techniques of mass attack and the division of labor."

Norbert Wiener, *Cybernetics: Or Control and Communication in the Animal and the Machine* (Cambridge MA: The MIT Press, 1948), 2.

09

When looking at the relationship between humans and machines, it is quite odd to notice how there is no actual accordance, in the architectural debate, about the moment and the place in which they have finally been consolidated in a typologically consistent spatial dimension. Even in spite of the relative novelty of the fact, if compared with other forms of human relationships.[1] What is certain, in any case, is that this relationship was first spatially materialized in a factory, however embryonic. As certain as the fact that, at the same time, factories could never represent a spatial archetype of equal cohabitation of heterogeneous subjects. For once, however, at the expenses of their human inhabitants, who have usually been treated by design as interchangeable cogs of a larger productive machine. And very often, as the most expendable ones. Early in the nineteenth century, for instance, at the height of the First Industrial Revolution, Robert Owen had already denounced how the well-being of "inanimate machines" had outclassed, in the vision of manufacturers, that of the "living" ones.[2] And the subsequent application in the industrial production of Frederick Winslow Taylor's principles of scientific management only worsened this unbalance.[3] Thus, since the first decades of the twentieth century, the common image of the factory that resisted over time was that of an apparatus that explicitly excluded humanity in all its dimensions,[4] by means of labor division, individual specialization, and a "military type of organization."[5] Not as the agent or the beneficiary of its construction, obviously, but as one of the subjects of the project of its inhabitability.

Manufacturing processes, however, did not take place only in factories. And during the Second World War, other structures, like laboratories, started to materialize more equal forms of cohabitation. For even though scientists had been working almost alone for centuries, the extraordinary pressure of wardriven research and the consequential adoption of industrial modes of production pushed the organization of laboratories to change.[6] And expansion, centralization, and hierarchical articulation became the new principles of development for research facilities like Los Alamos, Oak Ridge, and Hanford, which not only had to work like factories, but were factories themselves. With the difference that, whereas in factories production was based on a mere act of reproduction, for which automated work was more important than human one, in these cases, given the experimental nature of the activities conducted, the situation required a different kind of relationship. For this reason, even when, thirty years later, centralization and vertical organization ceased to be a prerogative, laboratories continued to be studied as an original model of integration between people and machines, which slowly began to be paradigmatic also for some industrial manufactures requiring a high rate of innovation, both from an organizational and from spatial standpoints.[7] Like in the case of that which can be considered the first realized and successful attempt of applying cybernetics to architecture,[8] and which Reyner Banham rightly deemed as "the first really challenging building of the eighties."[9]

This was the case of the Inmos Microprocessor Factory, a strange and unorthodox building designed in 1982 by Richard Rogers for the plant of Newport, Wales, after Iann Barron, cofounder of the government-funded semiconductor company, asked him a project for a new manufacturing facility specialized in microchip wafer production, which could be characterized by rapid building methods and could adapt to different sites and sizes.[10] In 1979, in fact, the newly elected Thatcher administration had reluctantly inherited the control over Inmos and, despite an initial skepticism, it had decided to allocate new funding to turn the company into a driver to move Britain forward in electronics technology.[11] The problem, however, was that its representatives on the company's board knew very little about the semiconductor industry and its possible future development. The idea was therefore of creating a prototype, or a model factory, that could "be able to respond successfully to changes in the brief as the program evolved during construction," and "allow for maximum flexibility and potential growth ... in order to ... meet the needs of a new and fast-evolving in-

Communication and control. From Reliance Controls to Centre Pompidou

"The building should act both as a high-performance, precision production machine and as a friendly and stimulating environment [...] allow[ing] for maximum flexibility and potential growth and change."

Richard Rogers

dustry."[12] And no one better than Rogers, who was just realizing a similar concept with the construction of the Fleetguard plant in Quimper,[13] could be more suited to interpret the designer's role in that regard.

Since 1962, in fact, the year of his graduation at Yale, Rogers had already abandoned the idea of turning into "a conventional, corporate professional."[14] Thus, after a brief period at SOM, he went back to London, and with Norman Foster and their respective wives, he started a practice significantly named Team 4. As to assert "the idea of the designer not as a heroic formgiver, but as a disinterested professional working co-operatively with others engaged in a scientific endeavor."[15] And even though their main interests were initially focused on the housing problem, their first success, before the partnership was dissolved, was a new factory for Reliance Controls on the outskirts of Swindon. A building whose cross braced steel structure brought onto its façade had to ostensibly reflect the idea of both a modern place of production and a non-hierarchical workspace, characterized by the adequate flexibility to accommodate future changes.[16] Exactly the same structure and concept by which, ten years later, Rogers and his new partner Renzo Piano would have given shape to the first built attempt of realizing a new type of cultural institution, which could materialize the programmatic openness and the sense of absolute freedom of Cedric Price's Fun Palace.[17]

When Rogers accepted Barron' commission, therefore, not only he had already designed some of the most interesting industrial buildings of the previous decade, but he had also a certain experience in working with open and evolving programs. In the Inmos case, however, the design process had to be even more complex, because of the specific nature of the production activities. Microchip fabrication in fact, which was almost fully automated, required a highly controlled atmosphere, much more controlled than that of a surgical theater, since wafers were extremely sensitive to dust and to any other air impurity. Yet, Rogers wanted the factory to work not only as a highly performative "machine," but also "as a friendly and stimulating environment" for employees' daily lives.[18] The main problem was thus of articulating in one building two conflicting environmental settings, while also enabling communication and control between them. For this reason, his first idea was that of splitting the program into two identical opposing areas dedicated to different uses, with spaces for production on one side and ancillary ones on the other.[19] All this, however, while contextually providing the maximum flexibility both in terms of extension and arrangement. To ensure the possibility both of expanding linearly the layout and, in case of emergency, of switching instantly the distribution of the services, by assembling other rooms for manufacture on the other side of the building.

This would of course have entailed the definition of a totally column-free interior space, as well as a coherent system to accommodate the large volumes of a service plant needed for the environmental control.[20] Thus, Rogers also decided to split the section into two halves, by bringing all the structures and services out of the building envelope, into a sort of huge exoskeleton that could have left an adaptable closed space. And for the structural concept, he and engineer Tony Hunt worked on the idea of a sort of steel "umbrella," which would have hung a clear span and single story volume, through the combination of a loadbearing central core and a suspended roof structure.[21] The first, made of multilevel latticed columns, which would have allowed the building circulation while carrying the major loads of the air supply equipment. And the second, sustained by tension hangers and stabilized by means of composite bipods, which would have in turn cleared the space from any obstacle. In this way, the combination of the two elements would have formed a basic constructive module that could have been theoretically repeated without limits, bay after bay. And even though for Newport's site, only a small section of this expandable system could have been implemented, Rogers decided to develop his proposal according to this modular logic, presenting a first complex of eight bays that could eventually have been extended to twenty.

While being structurally open to any possible use, however, the building had also to respond to the very rigid functional specialization of the basic programmatic concept. For this reason, Rogers ultimately opted for a plan articulated by an ordered sequence of clearly defined spaces, which he organized in two wings along a central spine of circulation and service, thought as a real street for informal activities. In the northern one, which was facing a preexisting industrial area, he thus located a loading bay and the sealed "clean room" for microchip production, which occupied seven structural bays with a silent and aseptic setting. While in the southern, in front of a densely planted woodland, he lined up the service plant room, two testing laboratories, a restaurant, an open patio, and three bays for offices. And whereas he separated the first area from the corridor by means of a second closed longitudinal spine, which had to work both as a locker room and as an airlock barrier, he left the second one partially permeable, by making use of glazed and movable partitions and light furniture. All this while connecting them through an intricate mass of brightly colored pipes, which departed from the corridor to connect the different areas as a sort of pervasive vascular system. And by enclosing the whole space under the exoskeleton in a flat and simple mullioned box, which he cladded with opaque panels on one face, to suggest the location of the machines, and with partially transparent ones on the other, to show on the outside the presence of people. As if the façade were a reflection not only of the inner spatial articulation but also of the actual life that could be staged inside.

While the manufacture wing had in fact to be a substantially nonhuman environment, impassable to any external variation,[22] the ancillary one had to represent a free, joyful, and responsive environment, which could adapt to the employees' work, movements and habits. And Rogers worked on their definition, giving an entirely original interpretation of how two opposing ideas of inhabitability could be functionally and sym-

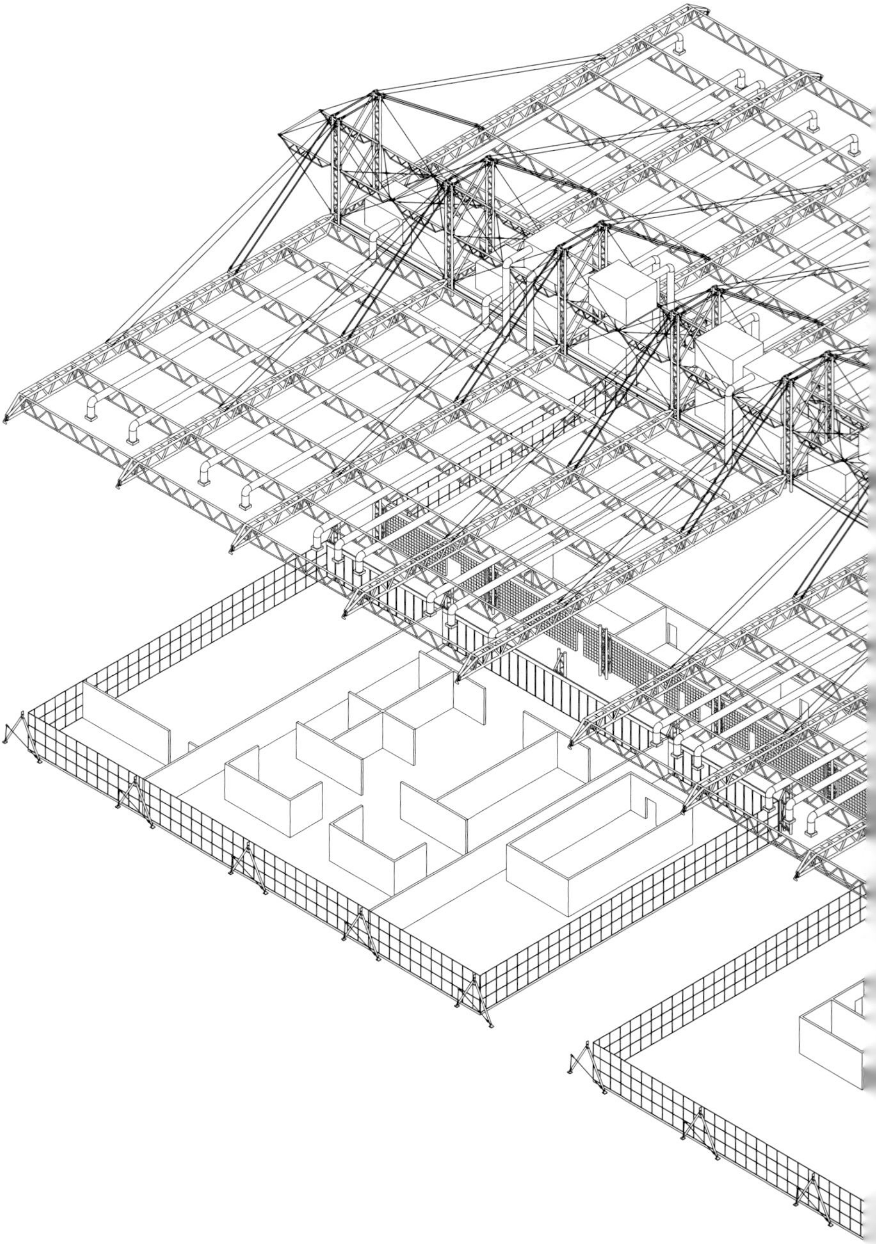

"The specificity of the design is concerned from the start with adaptability. […] What Inmos emphatically offers is that old Modern Movement dream of infinitely adaptable clear space between a floor plane below and a roof plane above."

Reyner Banham

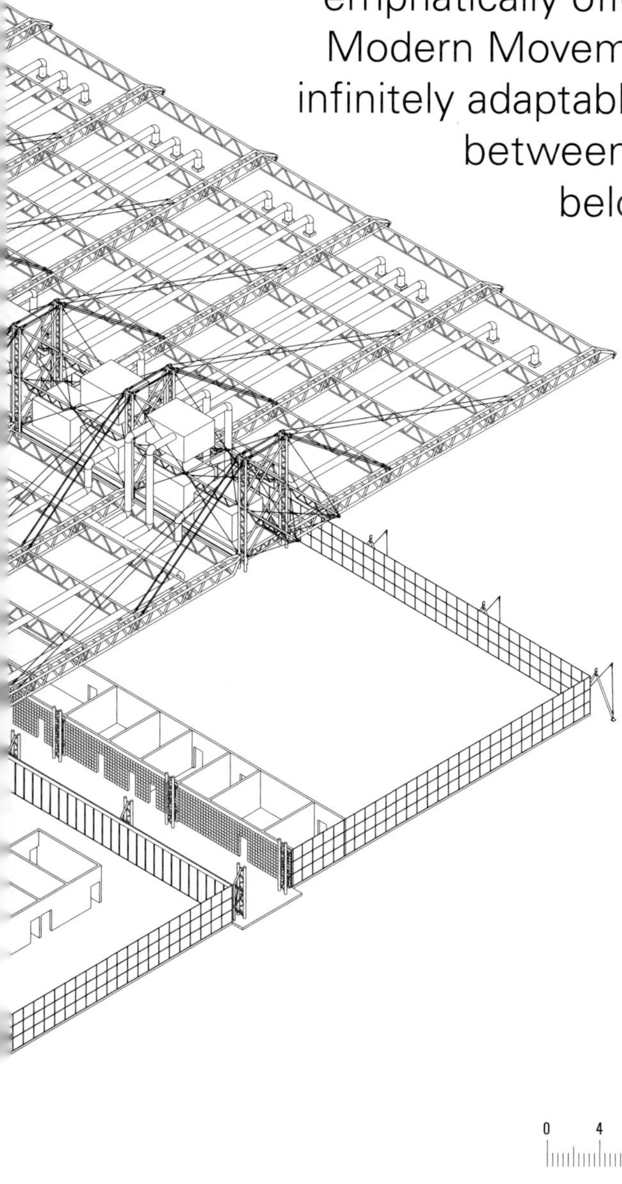

0
0.7
1.4
2.8
4.2m

bolically related, while being specifically individuated. As the building was a biological organism made of specialized and non-specialized cells. Yet, none of these features turned out to be crucial for its critical reception. On the one hand, because the authoritative voice of Reyner Banham, who first wrote extensively about the building, probably discouraged many others from attempting the venture.[23] And on the other, because the impressive masted structure, all painted blue and topped by a silver crown of plants and ductworks, was so powerful in its resemblance to an Archigram's fantasy, to fade any other aspect of the building's design. To such an extent that, even though Banham himself recognized that the structure was not the conceptual core of the project, but only the simple "device" to realize a perfectly "adaptable ... space," he could not help writing almost exclusively about it. [24] On how, for example, it interpreted the most genuine meaning of the term high-tech, which at the moment was turning into a purely stylistic category. Or about how it represented a technologically refined break from the "structural orthodoxy of rigid jointing."[25] But, most of all, on how it challenged traditional forms of categorization, by embodying what Banham called, in the absence of a better word, a "post-functionalist" example of "functionalism."[26]

If, however, the project for the Inmos factory transcended a strict functionalism, was not only due to the bright colors and the "starship" appearance of its structure.[27] On the contrary, it was mainly owing to Rogers' ability to design a building that, instead of being a static material object, could work as an active and responsive system among different subjects. A particular approach that the early studies in cybernetic architecture had already named "mutualism," to indicate the coevolutive nature of the relationship between an environment and its inhabitants, which had not been considered by functionalist studies before.[28] Whereas, in fact, the traditional functionalist comparison between the building and the machine entailed a bias towards the machine that worked as a serving tool for the inhabitants, mutualism intended it as a reactive and adaptive environment with which the inhabitants could cooperate. And Rogers, who had been acquainted with these studies since the early sixties,[29] seems to have followed this vision, treating the factory as a homeostatic system for heterogeneous uses and inhabitants. At first, by defining their relation as underspecified, so to allow unpredicted changes, and then by drafting a plan for adaptation and development, which could provide, instead of a fixed structure, a set of constraints "for certain [and] presumably desirable modes of evolution."[30] All this by identifying the single functional units, articulating them in a clear system, and leaving them a physical and conceptual space for communication and exchange as, more than a factory, he were really thinking to a particular kind of laboratory.[31] The same idea that, at the time, was taking shape also in the United States for an entirely different set of subjects and another exceptional kind of "spaceship."[32]

The story, in this regard, had already begun in 1978, when astrogeologist Jack McCauley showed the first pictures taken on Mars at the Institute of Ecotechnics' annual conference, and the members of the Institute realized that their studies on closed ecological systems could have a primary role in the space race of that time. [33] Since the sixties, NASA had in fact been debating different approaches to creating bioregenerative life support. But in a few years, it ended up focusing only on high-tech and super-controlled engineering ones. Previous works with open ecological microcosms and sealed ecospheres, by contrast, gave John Allen, co-founder and director of the Institute, the confidence that a biospheric approach could prove to be a useful scientific tool for living in space, on Mars and the moon.[34] His idea, in other terms, was that small models of natural ecosystems, having air exchange and replacing water lost through evapotranspiration, could provide more adequate ecological resilience than a mechanized system for growing hydroponic crops. Thus, in 1982, he assigned architect Phil Hawes the challenge of designing a spacecraft in which plants, animals, soil, and recycling systems could function as a life support sys-

"One consequence of functionalism and mutualism [...] is that architects are required to design dynamic rather than static entities."

Gordon Pask

tem. And two years later, getting the financial support from philanthropist Ed Bass and the benevolent blessing from Richard Buckminster Fuller, he launched the Biosphere 2 project to test the viability of his theories into a real laboratory.[35] A three-acre research facility opened in 1991 in Oracle, Arizona, which would have remained the largest closed system ever created and the second fully self-sufficient biosphere after the Earth itself.

The gigantic structure in fact included five natural biomes with different plants, animals and climates, complemented by two anthropogenic ones, and two technical facilities, all enclosed in a huge complex of different pavilions.[36] On the one hand, there were a dense rainforest, a mangrove wetland, a savannah grassland, a fog desert, and an oceanic coral reef. And on the other, a human habitat with living quarters for the scientist, an intermediate agricultural area to study the interactions between humans, farming and the rest of nature, and two variable volume "lungs," allowing for thermal contraction and expansion of air within the impermeable structure. All isolated and interconnected by a tightly sealed system capable of maintaining a wide range of interior environmental conditions through passive exchange among the different pavilions. Two ziggurats, two domes, some vaulted naves and a strange palace. Each of them fashioned as an independent structure made of steel tubing, glass, and pipes, and laid, with its own articulation and language, onto the desert landscape as a crystal concretion emerging from the ground. As if the whole complex was not planned, but rather represented a compound of extemporary shelters aimed at protecting a series of spontaneous biological processes that were already taking place and connecting them together. And as its flaunted indifference for a single synthetic shape reflected the lack of hierarchy and the singularity of each biome, in that which would have remained the most extreme and audacious experiment of interdependent coexistence ever built and, of course, ever failed.[37]

Like Inmos, in other words, the project for Biosphere 2 was not simply meant to define the shape of a particular building, but to materialize a homeostatic organism, partly natural and partly artificial, for making different subjects cohabit in the most suitable and equal way. Without claiming to create a new hybrid model, but only to identify the ideal habitats for each one and articulate them in a clear system of single yet interrelated spatial units. All this by replicating Rogers' logic on a territorial scale and working, on the contrary, by expansion, dispersion, and individuation, as well as through a strict form of functionalism. And therefore losing the perfect balance that Rogers had already achieved in defining the mutual relationship among different ideas of inhabitability through a new way of designing. By giving people and machines the same amount of space and relevance, for example, but also by distinguishing the two. Providing openness and flexibility on one side, to encourage people to "appropriate" their spaces, and rigidity and extreme control on the other, to offer machines the perfect environment for operating. And then, by reversing the approach, working the enclosed space by means of a perfect stereometry and the superstructure through a sort of functional expressionism. As to explicitly declare, with a specific form, what Biosphere 2 only implicitly did with its indifference towards it. That, in the end, architecture means servicing, and that its objective is the equal possibility of living comfortably together, no matter who or what the subjects are.

Notes

1 According to some, for example, this would date back to the end of fifteenth century and the appearance of the first printers' workshops, while for others, it would have taken place almost three centuries later, along with the earliest form of work automatization of American mills. To compare the two positions, see respectively Nikolaus Pevsner, *A History of Building Types* (Princeton: Princeton University Press, 1979), 273; and Sigfried Giedion, *Mechanization Takes Command: A Contribution to Anonymous History* (Minneapolis: University of Minnesota Press, 2013), 83.

2 Robert Owen, *A New View of Society* (London: Richard and Arthur Taylor, 1814), xi.

3 Frederick Winslow Taylor, *The Principles of Scientific Management* (New York: Harper & Brothers, 1911). Despite considering the factory as an organism, in fact, Taylor always believed that, in order to streamline its operations, the workers' body had to be transformed into a mechanism part of the assembly line, and not the opposite.

4 From Fritz Lang's *Metropolis* (1927) to Charlie Chaplin's *Modern Times* (1936).

5 Frank Barkley Copley, *Frederick W. Taylor, Father of Scientific Management*, vol. 2 (New York: Harper and Brothers, 1923), 213.

6 Peter Galison, *Image and Logic: The Material Culture of Twentieth Century Physics* (Chicago: University of Chicago Press, 1997). Born as a detailed study on the material culture of experimental microphysics, over the years Galison's book turned out to be an epistemological guide to technological innovation.

7 Peter Galison and Caroline A. Jones, "Factory, Laboratory, Studio: Dispersing Sites of Production," in *The Architecture of Science*, eds. Peter Galison and Emily Thompson (Cambridge MA: The MIT Press, 1999), 497-540.

8 Cybernetics emerged, during the early forties, as a highly interdisciplinary approach to deal with the transmission of information and feedback in self-regulatory systems. The term was first used in 1948 by the American mathematician Norbert Wiener to indicate the scientific study of how humans, animals and machines could control and communicate with each other. Norbert Wiener, *Cybernetics: Or Control and Communication in the Animal and the Machine* (Cambridge Ma: The MIT Press, 1948). About the architectural application, see Gordon Pask, "The Architectural Relevance of Cybernetics," *Architectural Design* 9 (1969): 494-496.

9 Reyner Banham, "Art and Necessity: Inmos and the Persistence of Functionalism," *The Architectural Review* 172, no. 1030 (1982): 34-38.

10 Richard Rogers, "Inmos in Gwent," *The Architectural Review* 172, no. 1030 (1982): 26-33; Id. "Una macchina leggera e flessibile," *Casabella* 61, no. 651/652 (1997/1998): 132-139.

11 Mick McLean and Tom Rowland, eds., *The Inmos Saga: A Triumph of National Enterprise?* (London: Pinter, 1985).

12 Ibid., 31.

13 Lance Knobel, "Rogers Quimper: factory," *The Architectural Review* 171, no. 1020 (1982) 23-30.

14 Deyan Sudjic, *The Architecture of Richard Rogers* (New York: Harry N. Abrams, 1995), 16. See also Richard Rogers, *A place for All People: Life, Architecture and the Fair Society* (Edinburgh: Canongate Books, 2017).

15 Sudjic, *The Architecture of Richard Rogers*, 16.

16 "La lógica de la industria: Reliance Controls," *Arquitectura y Vivienda* 78 (1999): 26-27.

17 The reference is of course to the Centre Pompidou, completed in Paris in 1977, which represented Rogers, Piano, and Peter Rice's first international success. About Rogers' role in this regard, see Samantha Hardingham and Kester Rattenbury, *Richard Rogers: The Pompidou Center* (Abingdon: Routledge, 2012).

18 Rogers, "Inmos in Gwent," 31.

19 For industrial buildings, the solution was quite innovative, since it had been experimented only once by Hawley and Peterson for the Qume Corporation Factory of San Jose (1978). By contrast, it was very common in laboratories buildings, at least since the publication of the already mentioned project by Louis Kahn for the Richards Medical Laboratories (1957-1960).

20 The problem was not uncommon for industrial buildings. See, for instance, Albert Kahn's project for Willow Run factory (1941). Roger Matuz, *Albert Kahn: Builder of Detroit* (Detroit: Wayne State University Press, 2002), 84-85.

21 Angus Macdonald ed., *Anthony Hunt* (London: Thomas Telford, 2000), 36.

22 The clean room could in fact be accessed only by a rigidly restricted number of people, and only after long cleansing "rituals," while non-dusting finished surfaces and a specialized equipment had to maintain the purest possible air quality, as well as constant hygrometric and temperature conditions. Rogers, "Inmos in Gwent," 33.

23 No other monographic critical essays have in fact been dedicated to the project, which however appears as a case study in many historical retrospectives about architecture in the eighties. See, for instance, Charles Jencks, *Post-Modernism: The New Classicism in Art and Architecture* (New York: Rizzoli, 1987), 144; and Colin Davies, *High Tech Architecture* (New York: Rizzoli, 1988), 26-31.

24 Banham, "Art and Necessity," 35.

25 Ibid.

26 "To read most of the architectural literature of the last 12 or 15 years [...] one would have to judge that Functionalism was [...] dead [...]. How then does it come about that many of the outstanding buildings of our time, [...] [like] Inmos, [...], seem to fall comfortably within the Functionalist tradition – if we are officially living in a Post-Functionalist epoch?" Ibid., 38.

27 Sudjic, *The Architecture of Richard Rogers*, 85.

28 Pask, "The Architectural Relevance of Cybernetics," 496.

29 In that period, Pask was in fact collaborating with Cedric Price to the project of Fun Palace.

30 Ibid.

31 The interior street can in fact be seen as the first architectural translation of Peter Galison's concept of "trading zone," a concrete or conceptual intermediate space that, since 1940, has characterized the organization of laboratories, by representing, in "an interesting disanalogy to Foucault's gloss of Jeremy Bentham's Panopticon," a "third" local context where different scientists could find a common ground of dialogue and exchange. Galison, *Image and Logic*, 781-844; 827.

32 *Spaceship Earth* is the title of a documentary directed and produced by Matt Wolf in 2020, about the first experiment implemented in the structure Biosphere 2.

33 Mark Nelson, *Pushing Our Limits: Insights from Biosphere 2* (Tucson: The

University of Arizona Press, 2018), 3. For background, see also John Allen, *Biosphere 2: The Human Experiment* (New York: Penguin Books, 1991).

34 This approach was firstly formulated by scientist Vladimir I. Vernadsky in his 1926 book *The Biosphere* (New York: Springer- Verlag, 1998). Vernadsky's ideas long preceded the Gaia hypothesis developed by James Lovelock about the role of life in maintaining a livable planet. In this regard, see James E. Lovelock, "Gaia as Seen through the Atmosphere," *Atmospheric Environment* 6, no. 8 (1972): 579-580.

35 Nelson, *Pushing Our Limits*, 12.

36 Bernd Zabel, et al., "Construction and Engineering of a Created Environment: Overview of the Biosphere 2 Closed System," *Ecological Engineering* 13 (1999): 43-63.

37 The story of the only two experiments conducted in Biosphere 2, as well as its destiny after the closure of the research facility, could appear in a dystopic novel by James G. Ballard. In this regard, besides the documentary directed by Matt Wolf, see also John Allen, *Me and the Biospheres: A Memoir by the Inventor of Biosphere 2* (Santa Fe: Synergetic Press, 2009).

Visual atlas (following spread)

1 Tesla Experimental Station, Nikola Tesla, 1899
2 MIT Radiation Laboratory, Alfred Lee Loomis, 1940
3 Willow Run factory, Albert Kahn, 1941
4 Fun Palace, Cedric Price, 1961
5 The Walking City, Ron Herron, 1964
6 Fermilab, Robert Wilson, 1967
7 Centre Pompidou, Richard Rogers and Renzo Piano, 1977
8 Fleetguard Factory, Richard Rogers Partnership, 1981
9 Patscentre, Richard Rogers Partnership, 1985
10 Škoda Modular Factory, HENN, 1996
11 Igus Headquarters and Factory, Nicholas Grimshaw, 2000
12 Volkswagen Transparent Factory, HENN, 2001
13 Facebook Prineville Data Center, Sheehan Partners, 2011
14 Googleplex, BIG and Heatherwick studio, 2015
15 Apple Park, Foster + Partners, 2017
16 Halley VI British Antarctic Research Station, Hugh Broughton Architects, 2013
17 Alpine Shelter Skuta, AKT II and Harvard GSD Students and OFIS Architects, 2015
18 Earth Station, Michele de Lucchi, 2018
19 Pasona Urban Farm, Kono Designs, 2013
20 Earthscape, On-iku, 2014
21 *Countryside: The Future*, OMA/ AMO, 2020
22 Amazon Spheres, NBBJ, 2017
23 Second Home Hollywood, SelgasCano, 2019

h i s t o r i c a l l a b s

1 1A

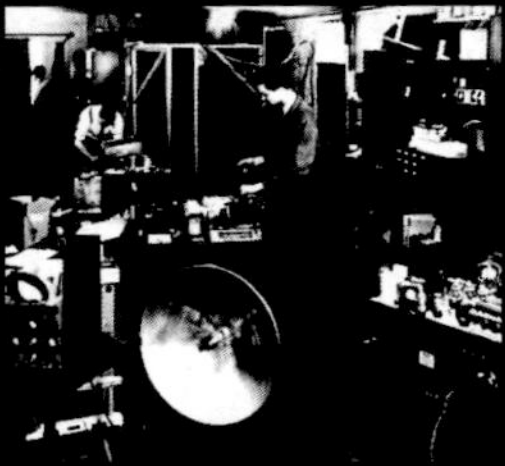

2 2A

3 3A

h e t e r o g e n e o u s r e f e r e n c e s

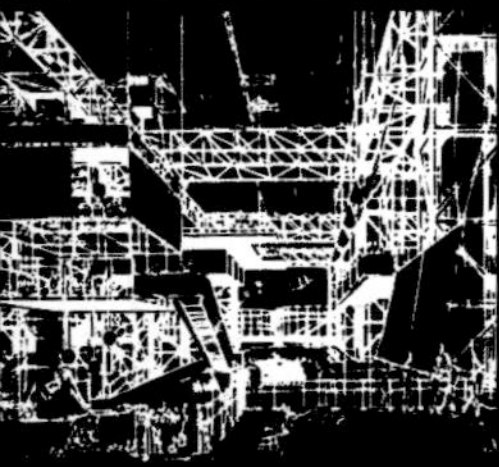

4 4A

5 5A

6 6A

h e t e r o d o x l a b s

7 7A

8 8A

9 9A

h y b r i d f a c t o r i e s

10 10A

11 11A

12 12A

bigtech labs

13 13A

14 14A

15 15A

moving structures

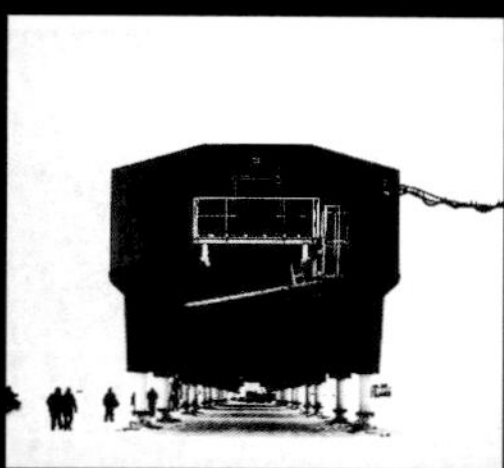

16 16A

17 17A

18 18A

biodiverse systems

19 19A

20 20A

21 21A

new workspaces

22 22A

23 23A

A starship

Elizabeth Diller and Ricardo Scofidio
Yverdon-les-Bains, CH
46.793682, 6.648848
1998-2002

"You can't build clouds. And that is why the future you dream of never comes true."

Ludwig Wittgenstein, *Culture and Value* (Chicago: University of Chicago Press, 1980), 41.

For one who looks at the architectural debate from an external perspective, it can be surprising to notice how the term "starship" has frequently been used with derogative connotations. For in the common discourse, a flight beyond the Earth's atmosphere not only evokes the mystery of the unknown and the pleasure of discovery.[1] It also prefigures the realization of a possible utopia, as any architectural project, however small, should do. But if it is true that utopia has always been "an almost inescapable companion of architectural invention,"[2] it must also be said that its constructive role in this field is far from being unquestioned. In 1922, for instance, long before Paul Ricoeur's recognized that it not only could be a constitutive but also a pathological form of imagination,[3] Lewis Mumford had already written that utopias could be "of reconstruction," and thus constitutive and projective, or "of escape," inherently unrealizable and futile. And whereas he used a house to symbolically represent the first form, he used the expression "castle in the air" to exemplify the latter and its petty claims.[4] Therefore, it is not surprising that, in a matter of a few years, the term "starship" began to be used to highlight the unrealistic nature of some high-tech speculative experimentations.[5] Nor that, after the end of the Modern Movement, it ended up representing, from a compositional point of view, the epitome of the detachment and indifference to the sites that have been attributed to many contemporary projects. What is curious, by contrast, is that it has never symbolized what in literature, from Lucian of Samosata's voyage to the Moon to Jules Verne's one, has always materialized.[6] That is the most radical device of defamiliarization from common standards of living that one could imagine, and which, despite having been described thousands of times, has never found a better depiction than that given by Aleksandr Bogdanov in 1908.

Bogdanov was a peculiar man. A physician and a philosopher, he was also one of the founders of the Bolshevik faction of the Russian Social Democratic Labor Party, and while always being one of the most influential opponents of Vladimir Lenin's politics, he also found the time to work on the most disparate researches, such as the study of the possibility of human rejuvenation, or the development of a unified theory of organization. For his idea was that every biological phenomenon and every social process had to be considered as part of a natural and cultural continuum. Thus, he first proposed a general law of organization on materialistic and naturalistic bases, which long anticipated many of the ideas later expanded both by Cybernetics and the General Systems Theory.[7] However, the work for which he has probably been most remembered is a 1908 science fiction novel, titled *Red Star*, in which he precociously exposed his political and scientific beliefs, writing about an extraordinary travel to a socialist utopia based on Mars. The story, in this case, is that of Leonid, a mathematician and a revolutionary who, during the Russian Revolution of 1905, gets in touch with a technocratic, free, and egalitarian society, both classless and genderless, which represented the peak of human social order, by following a natural form of organization. But it is also the story of a starship, the Etheroneph, aboard of which the protagonist starts to get rid of all the normative conventions based on individual identity, gender included, to open up to this new vision of the world.[8] All this through a process of radical defamiliarization from the self that, in fact, could only have been directly and physically experienced almost a century later, through a particular architectural device, which oddly recalled the Etheroneph, both in terms of shape and mechanism.

This story began in 1998, when the organizing committee of the sixth Swiss national exposition, which should have taken place three years later, invited Elizabeth Diller and Ricardo Scofidio to work collaboratively, as part of a team led by West 8, on a proposal for one of its venues.[9] The general concept was in fact that of holding the art exhibition, which was aimed at questioning some inherent issues of the current model of development, not in a single place, but spread out over a whole region, three lakes, and five different sites. And for that at Yverdon-les-Bains, on the banks of Lake Neuchâtel, the idea was to

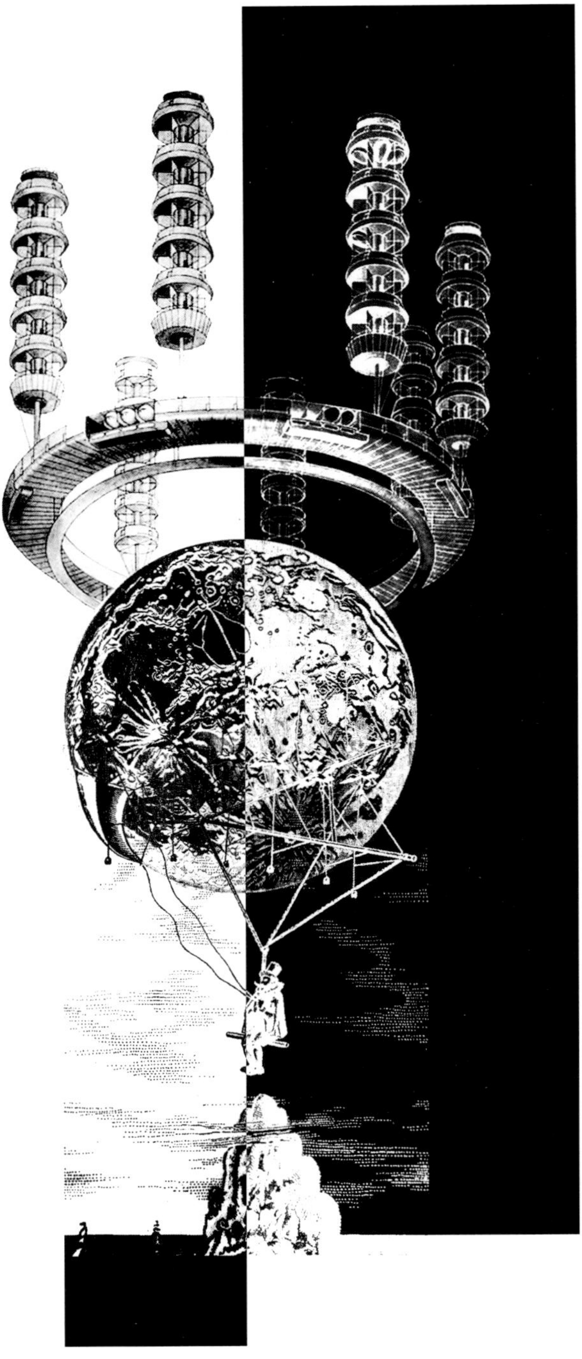

Utopias between escape and reconstruction. From Francis Goodwin's *Man in the Moone* to Georgij Krutikov's Flying City

have a new media landscape that could bring visitors to reflect on the relationship between "sensuality and sexuality," through an "immaterial [form of] design."[10] Then, due to economic reasons, the Expo was postponed to the following year, and Diller and Scofidio's intervention was brought ahead as a separate project for a temporary media pavilion, which had to focus on the theme called "Me and the Universe." And from a first proposal, which was imagined as a submerged restaurant, a completely different one emerged, to question the human position into the world, by erasing all the information traditionally associated with exhibitionary structures, and offering "a blank interpretive surface" for one's individual sensorial experience.[11] All this within a "featureless, depthless, scaleless, spaceless, massless, surfaceless, and contextless" building,[12] which would have taken the endlessly mutable shape of a vapor cloud floating over the lake. A piece of architecture, called *Blur*, made, according to the architects, out of nothing but "atmosphere," "water," and "the site itself."[13]

Yet, it must be said that the idea was not totally new at that age. In 1968, for instance, Coop Himmelb(l)au had used the concept of the cloud to propose an architecture that could be meant as a differentiated system rather than an individuated object.[14] And two years later, for the International Fair at Osaka, Fujiko Nakaya had already designed a pavilion consisting of a geodesic dome covered by artificial fog.[15] But both buildings, as different as they were, still adhered to the conventional norm of considering architecture as the definition of a shelter, through a tectonic that, however fanciful, responded to a logic of confinement. For Diller and Scofidio, on the contrary, architecture was not meant to create a space, but to interrogate it, by subverting a given spatial ecology and revealing the underlying social and political structure. Since they established their practice in 1981, their aim had in fact always been examining the relationship between a certain site and a situation taking place within its limits. And they had always used design, in its larger and processual meaning, to trigger this situation, by catalyzing reactions among human, natural, and artificial agents into new and unexpected combinations. Exactly as Walter De Maria had done, for example, with his *Lightning Field*, a one mile wide parcel of desert in New Mexico, which he covered, between 1973 and 1979, with four hundred sharpened steel poles, to attract the frequent lightning bolts of the region.[16] With the only difference that, at Yverdon, instead of simply relying on natural climatic conditions, Diller and Scofidio had to design a complex environmental solution that could meet the programmatic requirements.

For this reason, they began to work, with a real scale model, on an incredibly sophisticated system of pumps and filters, which could aspirate the water from the lake and inject it, once purified, into a network of pipes, pierced at regular intervals by a dense array of high-pressure spouts. These would have sprayed water as a fine mist that, accumulating at the periphery of the system, would have produced, through the contact with the ambient air, a thick cloud of fog. And with the help of a built-in weather station, a computer could have prevented the cloud from dissipating, by monitoring the atmospheric conditions and regulating the water flow accordingly. This, however, was only a part of the problem, as *Blur* had not only to represent a spectacular artistic installation but also a real "habitable medium" that could be physically accessible by visitors.[17] Thus, inspired by Richard Buckminster Fuller's work, while refining their responsive "fog machine," the architects designed an ovoid tensegrity system of rectilinear metallic struts and diagonal rods, which would have suspended two levels of platforms above the water, by means of four extremely thin tubular piles sunk into the lake bed. With the result of realizing an impressively light reticular structure, one hundred meters long by fifteen high, halfway between a heliport and an oil plant, only "cladded" by the jet of over thirty thousand nozzles.

At the Expo's opening, needless to say, the overall effect was breathtaking. Not only in terms of visual appearance but also for the multisensorial experience that, for six months, *Blur* offered its visitors in their progressive approach. For the pavilion was not directly accessible from the main parade of the exposition but was hidden behind the dunes of an artificial landscape designed by West 8. And only when crossing it, by following its winding paths, they could appreciate a first view of the constantly changing mass. The experience, however, did not end there. On the shore, they were in fact provided with raincoats and invited onto a ramped bridge, which brought them into the cloud. And in this passage, step by step, they could feel their auditory perception progressively obliterated by the white noise of the pulsing nozzles, while their whole optical field was entirely being filled by a soft blanket of vapor. In this way, when they were finally "deposited" at the center of the pavilion, onto a large open-air platform, their visual and acoustic references were completely erased. And only by ascending a stair to a superior deck at the summit, they could emerge from the "white-out" of the fog and regain, for a while, the view of the lake. All this through a processional path of sensorial deprivation and reacquisition that has never been interpreted in metaphorical terms, only because of Elizabeth Diller's denial, moreover written in bold type.[18]

This also explains why, despite the rich imagery mobilized by *Blur*'s construction, the ensuing critical debate ultimately revolved around some topics that were strictly linked to design disciplines. On the one hand, highlighting the innovative tectonics introduced by the architects, whose concept has been seen by Hubert Damisch as the most advanced and original interpretation of the "structuralist thought [...] [which] was first systematically expressed by Viollet-le-Duc."[19] And on the other, as Georges Teyssot did by reflecting on Peter Sloterdijk's study on spherology,[20] considering *Blur* as the purest materialization of a projective idea of architecture, for which the environment [...] [could be] designed in terms of the superimposition of various spheres" conceived "as an extension of the human being."[21] In any case, both readings substantially concurred in tracing its genealogy back to the conceptual space opened in 1969 by Reyner Banham, when he first wrote about architecture in terms

"To 'blur' is to make indistinct, to dim, to shroud, to cloud, to make vague, to obfuscate. […] For our visually obsessed, high-resolution/high-definition culture, blur is equated with loss. […] Our proposal […] offers little to see. It is an immersive environment in which the world is put out of focus."

Diller + Scofidio

0
3.00
6.00
12.00
18.00m

of an artificial environment characterized by its interior atmosphere.[22] That which Mark Wigley deemed as "the core of architecture […] that cannot simply be addressed or controlled,"[23] and which took shape, over the years, through a heterogeneous series of "pneumatic" realizations.[24] On the contrary, for the most of the public *Blur* represented little more than a simple divertissement, as clever and astonishing as it was, without any real speculative repercussion that exceeded the dimension of an ephemeral, however unseen, spectacle.[25] And even the architects' critique of the presence of media in contemporary society resulted someway unclear, when not apparently contradictory.[26]

Little attention, by contrast, has been devoted to the value of their design as an attempt of creating a complex apparatus for questioning the concept of subjective identity, with all its implications, from its very base. A fact that would have been even more evident if the project had entirely been accomplished as it was actually designed. Initially, in fact, the architectural project had to be complemented by a "media event," to be realized in collaboration with IDEO of Palo Alto, which was never realized because of the lack of a sponsor.[27] All *Blur*'s visitors, in the original plan, should have filled out a questionnaire at the entrance, and their personal profile should have been uploaded on a database. Then, they would have been given a "braincoat," a smart raincoat coupled with the imprint of their profile, which would have reacted to the proximity of other people, according to the different degrees of virtual affinity. By glowing in the fog, for instance, like an involuntary blush, by pulsing while approaching, like an accelerating heartbeat, or vibrating, in case of supposed physical attraction, like a thrill of pleasure. In this way, the visitors, temporary blinded by the white-out, and deafened and speechless because of the buzz of the nozzles, would have been able to interact with strangers in a spontaneous and emotional way, in "a condition of anonymous intimacy."[28] All this by simply being erased from all the superstructural traces of a predetermined individuality, to open up to others through a renewed and extended dimension of the self.

What is even more interesting, however, is the form through which this erasure should have taken shape. For while the extension of "the body's natural system of perception" should have been entrusted to a prosthetic technological skin connected to a data cloud,[29] the architects worked on its deconstruction in a very physical way. Exactly as they were doing to deconstruct the identity of the building from its very foundations, by questioning its need of formal definiteness. Using nature, in other words, not only as the raw material, but also, and for the first time, as the very agent of both visitor's experience and the whole architectural construction.[30] As though the possible return to a primary "state of nature," despite the complex technological apparatus involved, could effectively be implemented only by nature itself. And the task of design, by consequence, was simply to provide an infrastructure for its constructive agency to develop. For this reason, to create their estranging immersive environment, Diller and Scofidio did not recreate a cloud in picturesque terms, nor did they domesticate wind and water within the limits of a containing structure. On the contrary, they channeled all their force, flow, and mutability, to capture the moment in which they showed their natural ability of constantly escaping any human attempt to tame them. And in so doing, they renounced the final responsibility of the formalization process, to realize the first and most complete attempt ever made of building a piece of responsive architecture, in all its complexity.

Not that responsivity represented a novel theme for that age. Back in the late sixties, for instance, Nicholas Negroponte had already explored the topic when looking at spatial design problems through the lens of cybernetics in its relationship with architecture. And in 1975, he had first described it as the natural result of the integration of computing power into built spaces and structures, which would have allowed a given spatial arrangement to automatically adapt to changing environmental conditions.[31] The realized precedents, however, were few,[32] and none of them could match the complexity with which *Blur* in-

Blurred landscapes. Clouds on Lake Neuchâtel

"Certain dualisms have been persistent in Western traditions [...] self/other, mind/body, culture/nature, [...] agent/resource, maker/made, active/passive [...] High-tech culture challenges these dualisms in intriguing ways."

Donna J. Haraway

corporated reflexive and simulated responses, as well as operational and informational ones,[33] into the crystal-clear shape of a single and synthetic system. Moreover, the architects' approach presented two other striking unprecedented aspects, which steered the responsive theory towards unexplored fields. The first was that, in *Blur*, they did not use artificial intelligence to control the form of architecture in response to specific climatic conditions, but to serve as the activator of a reaction that had to be constantly shaped by natural elements, and only by them. And the second, which was probably a corollary of the former, was that, in so doing, they expressively ignored the implicit functionalism that had always been inherent in any form of user-centered design,[34] which the search for a responsive architecture belonged to. For *Blur* was not thought to adapt its space to meet people's needs and satisfy their desires in an automatic way. On the contrary, it was meant to question them, by means of a hybrid system, natural and artificial at the same time, which had not to substitute human agency for their comfort, but to dispute the supposed centrality of their role.

In this sense, in a certain way, one could even see *Blur* as a sort of "cyborg architecture," given also the architects' interest in the topic.[35] And not only because of the integration of two opposing terms,[36] which is however crucial, but mainly for its ability to challenge any form of predetermined identity, in favor of an ongoing process of definition, multilayered and interconnected, of people as well as of architecture. The only difference with the cyborg theory,[37] is that, in the end, in *Blur*, as it was effectively realized, there was no space for an affirmative action, or a form of reconstruction. More like a starship, it was only meant to transport people out of the existing reality, into a dimension that, without further inputs, would only represent an open field of possibilities, with no effective potentials for materialization.[38] It is not surprising, therefore, that the outcomes of Diller and Scofidio's work, as partially introduced by Fujiko Nakaya and Walter De Maria, have been developed almost exclusively in the field of the arts, where "thought-provoking hesitations in the routines of everyday life" do not require any form of reconciliation.[39] And here, in particular with the contemporary experimentations of Olafur Eliasson, they have begun to interrogate the human position into the world, not only from an individual standpoint, but also from a social one.[40] For what concerns architecture, things have instead evolved in a more utilitarian direction. And while responsive technologies have been called to face the issues posed by climate changes, the recognition of a formative natural agency has been interpreted mostly by confining means. Thus leaving to other attempts the task of defining the new limits of an intersubjective dimension that *Blur* just initiated to open.

Notes

1 Adam Roberts, *The History of Science Fiction* (London: Palgrave Macmillan, 2016).

2 Nathaniel Coleman, *Utopias and Architecture* (London-New York: Routledge, 2005), 48.

3 Paul Ricoeur, "Ideology and Utopia as Cultural Imagination," *Philosophic Exchange* 7, no. 1 (1976): 17-28.

4 Lewis Mumford, *The Story of Utopias* (Gloucester MA: Peter Smith, 1959), 15.

5 Especially after the publication of Georgij Krutikov's project for a Flying City (1928). In this regard, see Selim Omarovich Khan-Magomedov, *Georgii Krutikov: The Flying City and Beyond* (Barcelona: Editorial Tenov, 2015).

6 Lucian, *Ἀληθῆ διηγήματα* (175 AD ca), or *The True History*, trans. Paul Turner (Bloomington: Indiana University Press, 1958); Jules Verne, *De la Terre à la Lune, trajet direct en 97 heures 20 minutes* (Paris: Pierre-Jules Hetzel, 1865).

7 Aleksandr Bogdanov, *Tektologiya: Vseobschaya Organizatsionnaya Nauka* (Berlin-Petrograd-Moscow, 1922). Indeed, there are some evidences that both Norbert Wiener and Karl Ludwig von Bertalanffy might have read the German edition of *Tektology*, the name that Bogadnov gave to his theory, which was published in Berlin in 1928.

8 Id., *Red Star: The First Bolshevik Utopia*, edited by Loren Graham and Richard Stites (Bloomington: Indiana University Press, 1984), 36-56.

9 The whole story is reported in the book Diller + Scofidio, *Blur: The Making of Nothing* (New York: Harry N. Abrams, 2002).

10 Charles Renfro, "Blur Building," *A+U* 428 (2006): 67.

11 Diller + Scofidio, *Blur*, 325. "To 'blur' is to make indistinct, to dim, to shroud, to cloud, to make vague, to obfuscate. [...] For our visually obsessed, high-resolution/high-definition culture, blur is equated with loss. [...] Our proposal [...] offers little to see. It is an immersive environment in which the world is put out of focus." Ibid., 195.

12 Ibid., 162.

13 Renfro, "Blur Building," 67.

14 Frank Werner, *Covering + Exposing: The Architecture of Coop Himmelb(l)au* (Basel-Berlin-Boston: Birkhäuser, 2000) 67.

15 Billy Kluver, Julie Martin, and Barbara Rose, eds., *Pavilion: Experiments in Art and Technology* (New York: Dutton, 1972).

16 Jeffrey L. Kosky, *Arts of Wonder: Enchanting Secularity* (Chicago-London: The University of Chicago Press, 2012), 15-58.

17 Elizabeth Diller and Ricardo Scofidio, "Architecture as a Habitable Medium," in *Disappearing Architecture*, eds. Georg Flachbart and Peter Weibel (Basel-Boston-Berlin: Birkhäuser, 2005), 184-195.

18 "The media project must be liberated from all immediate and obvious metaphoric associations such as clouds, god, angels, ascension, dreams, Greek mythology, or any other kitsch relationships. [...] *Blur* is a spectacle with nothing to see." Diller + Scofidio, *Blur*, 325.

19 Hubert Damisch, *Noah's Ark: Essays on Architecture* (Cambridge MA: The MIT Press, 2016), 205.

20 Peter Sloterdijk, *Sphären. I. Blasen* (Frankfurt: Suhrkamp Verlag, 1998). Indeed, Sloterdijk himself took in consideration *Blur* in the third volume of

Spherology, to then deepen the topic in a dedicated essay. Peter Sloterdijk, "Foam City: About Urban Multitudes," *New Geographies* 0 (2007): 151.

21 Georges Teyssot, *A Topology of Everyday Constellations* (Cambridge MA: The MIT Press, 2013), 239.

22 Reyner Banham, *The Architecture of the Well-tempered Environment* (Oxford: Architectural Press, 1969). In this regard, see also the drawing by François Dallegret that illustrated Banham's article, titled "A Home Is Not a House," *Art in America* 2 (1965): 58-77.

23 Mark Wigley, "The Architecture of Atmosphere," *Daidalos* 68 (1998): 27.

24 From Archigram's Cushicle (1960) to Mark Rakowitz's Parasite (1998), the list is very long. In this regard, see Vincenzo Latina and Marco Navarra, eds., *Air fundamental: Collision between Inflatable and Architecture* (Siracusa: LetteraVentidue, 2018).

25 Notably, a Swiss newspaper reviewer, Roger Anderegg, wrote in the opening report: "What a crazy, idiosyncratic thing! How deliciously without purpose!" Quoted in Diller + Scofidio, *Blur*, 372.

26 On the one hand, the cloud can be seen as a device though to deprive people of the visual clarity and immediacy that mass media attempt to give its consumers. While on the other, it can be meant as a metaphorical representation of "the electronic ether that people nowadays inhabit like a medium." In this regard, see Cary Wolfe, "Lose the Building: Systems Theory, Architecture, and Diller+Scofidio's Blur," *Postmodern Culture* 16, no. 3 (2006).

27 Diller and Scofidio, "Architecture as a Habitable Medium," 190-195.

28 Ibid., 192.

29 Ibid.

30 Although in the history there have been many precedents of architectures activated in some way by natural elements, from ancient mills to Jean Nouvel's Institut du Monde Arabe (1987), *Blur* was the first case in which architecture was actually made of and by nature.

31 Nicholas Negroponte, *Soft Architecture Machines* (Cambridge MA: The MIT Press, 1975), 130.

32 Besides Jean Nouvel's already mentioned project, in fact, the other only possible reference was the Fresh Water Pavilion, a programmable audio–visual interior, designed by NOX in 1996.

33 These are the four classes according to which Negroponte categorized responsive architectures. Negroponte, *Soft Architecture Machines*, 143-145.

34 Jonathan Hill, *Actions of Architecture: Architects and Creative Users* (London: Routledge, 2003).

35 Elizabeth Diller and Ricardo Scofidio, *Flesh: Architectural Probes* (New York, Princeton Architectural Press, 1994)

36 The word cyborg is in fact a portmanteau of "cybernetic organism," which was coined in 1960 during a research conducted to identify new survival structures for deep space missions. Manfred E. Clynes and Nathan S. Kline, "Cyborgs and Space," *Astronautics Journal of the American Rocket Society* 9 (1960): 26-27; 74-76.

37 "Certain dualisms have been persistent in Western traditions; they have all been systemic to the logics and practices of domination [...]. Chief among these troubling dualisms are self/other, mind/body, culture/nature, male/female, civilized/primitive, reality/appearance, whole/part, agent/resource, maker/made, active/passive, right/wrong, truth/illusion, total/partial, God/man. [...] High-tech culture challenges these dualisms in intriguing ways."

Donna J. Haraway, "A Cyborg Manifesto: Science, Technology, and Socialist-Feminism in the Late Twentieth Century (1985)," in *Simians, Cyborgs and Women: The Reinvention of Nature* (New York: Routledge, 1991), 177.

38 "Potential means indeterminate yet capable of determination." Charles S. Peirce, *Philosophy of Mathematics: Selected Writings* (Bloomington: Indiana University Press, 2010), 185.

39 Beatriz Colomina and Mark Wigley, *Are We Human?* (Zürich: Lars Müller, 2016), 162-163.

40 "The world is trying to grasp these causal contracts with the climate. Here, we first have to acknowledge that the climate is in fact relative. When I was young, we all still assumed that the climate was a constant, that it was something outside of human reach. Now, we understand that the climate is not something natural but something cultural; we are co-responsible for it." Olafur Eliasson in Christian Borch ed., *Architectural Atmospheres: On the Experience and Politics of Architecture* (Basel: Birkhäuser, 2014), 100.

Visual atlas (following spread)

1 "A Home Is Not a House," Reyner Banham, 1965
2 Cushicle and Suitaloon, Michael Webb, 1967
3 Yellow Heart, Haus Rucker, 1968
4 The Cloud, Coop Himmelb(l)au, 1968
5 Pepsi Pavilion, Fujiko Nakaya, 1970
6 *Lightning Field*, Walter De Maria, 1973
7 Institut du Monde Arabe, Jean Nouvel, 1987
8 Heliotrope House, Rolf Disch, 1994
9 Fresh Water Pavilion, NOX, 1996
10 Auerworld Palace, Marcel Kalberer and Sanfte Strukturen Team, 1997
11 *Ice Pavilion*, Olafur Eliasson, 1998
12 Icelandic Pavilion, Ámi Páll Jóhansson, 2000
13 Milwaukee Art Museum, Santiago Calatrava, 2001
14 Media-TIC, Enric Ruiz Geli, 2011
15 Syddansk Universitet, Henning Larsen, 2014
16 Fab Tree Hab, Terreform One, 2007
17 Dune, Magnus Larsson, 2010
18 Iceberg Living Station, Map Architects and David Garcia, 2013
19 Amphibious Architecture, The Living and Natalie Jeremijenko, 2009
20 Living Light Pavilion, The Living, 2009
21 Bloom, DOSU architecture, 2013
22 Water Pavilion, Daniel Valle Architects, 2012
23 *Fog Assembly*, Olafur Eliasson, 2016
24 Shiver House, NEON, 2019

pneumatic starships

1 1A

2 2A

3 3A

visualatlas clouds

4 4A

5 5A

6 6A

softarchitecture machines

7 7A

8 8A

9 9A

natureshaped solutions

10 10A

11 11A

12 12A

responsive systems

13 13A

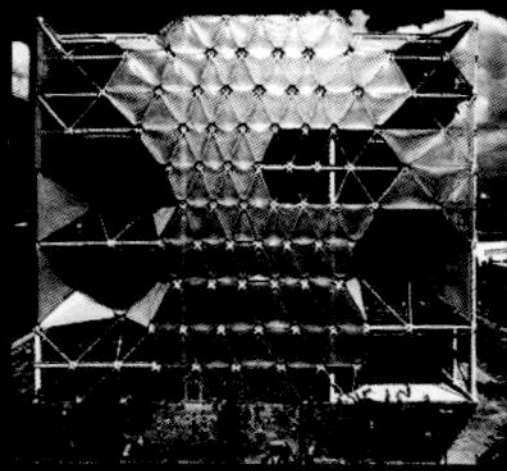

14 14A

15 15A

new metabolisms

16 16A

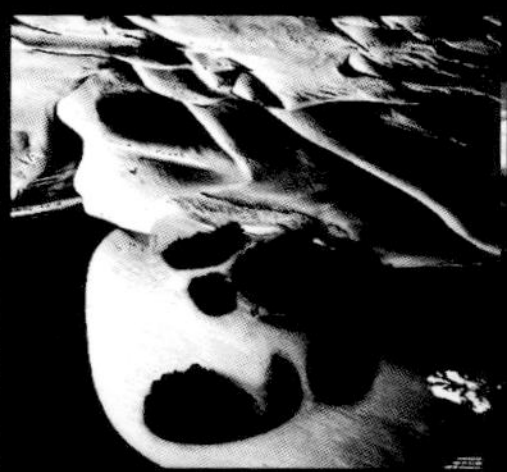

17 17A

18 18A

human-nature interfaces

19 19A

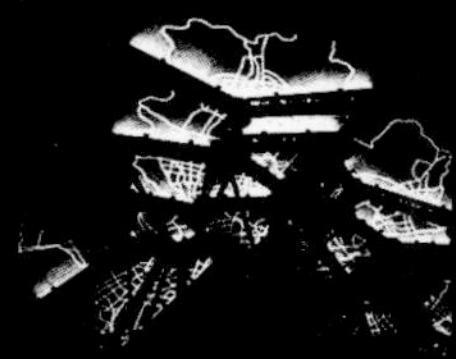

20 20A

21 21A

analogic cyborgs

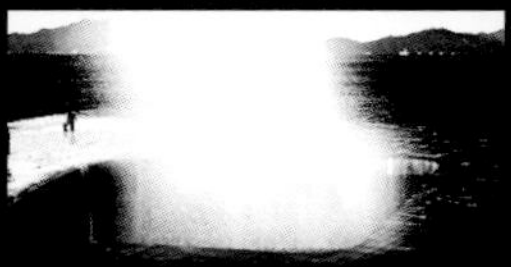

22 22A

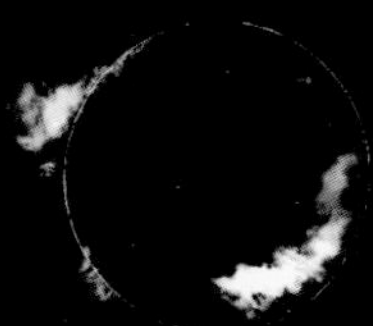

23 23A

24 24A

A colony

Matali Crasset
Caudry, FR
50.129329, 3.399900
2002-2003

"Companion species infect each other all the time. [...] [So] why tell stories like my pigeon tales, when there are only more and more openings and no bottom lines? Because there are quite definite response-abilities that are strengthened in such stories."

Donna J. Haraway, *Staying with the Trouble: Making Kin in the Chthulucene* (Durham-London: Duke University Press, 2016), 29.

Whereas starships have always represented the clearest archetype of a utopia "of escape," it cannot be said that speculative fiction has been ungenerous in offering also models "of reconstruction."[1] In particular, since the seventeenth century, when the invention of the telescope hastened the popular acceptance of the idea that outer space could be eventually colonized by humans. In 1638, for example, eighteen years after the establishment of Plymouth Colony, John Wilkins published a broadly circulated book, in which he predicted that also the Moon would have been inhabited in the future.[2] And from that moment, a flight beyond the Earth's atmosphere, which had previously been used as the essential plot device to question the role of humanity, has been increasingly described as a way to expand control over the unknown.[3] All this by borrowing the characters, the scenes, and the tropes from the literature of earthly colonization, without even doubting the legitimacy of the act.[4] To the point that, at the beginning of twentieth century, as visions of spaceflight advanced towards reality, the rhetoric of space colonization, promoted by the likes of Konstantin Tsiolkovsky and Wernher von Braun, continued to draw on the same mythology of the frontier to be conquered. Not only for the survival of human civilization, as Olaf Stapledon candidly wrote in 1948, but mainly to exploit the resources of other planets to the earth's benefit.[5] And although in the seventies, writers and scientists tried to point out its underlying imperialistic view,[6] the idea of space colonization continued to thrive, nurtured by a cultural narrative of "pioneering, continual progress, manifest destiny, free enterprise, rugged individualism, and a right to life without limits."[7]

Not all the colonies that have been recently imagined, however, can be attributed to this kind of ideology. Over the last hundred years, humans have in fact also planned other types of colonization that, as few as they have been, instead of representing a form of appropriation, have finally worked as a sort of restitution. Like in the case, for instance, of the reintroduction projects used to repopulate particularly deprived areas with extirpated or extinct species, which curiously have first been initiated in the same years in which the pioneers of spaceflight advocacy were starting devising their outer colonies.[8] For even though humans had moved animals from one place to another for millennia, the early history of repopulations invariably followed the need of providing new food resources, as in game reserves.[9] While the reintroduction of species for restoring or preserving biodiversity only developed with the increasing awareness of the interdependence of all the components of a certain ecosystem.[10] At first by simply releasing wild or specifically bred individuals within their historical ranges, and then through the definition of physical infrastructures that could attract and accommodate species otherwise hard to be implanted. And even though, in this regard, the history of "non-pedigreed" design offers a huge variety of references, from beehives to bat houses,[11] none is more revealing than the *Capsule* realized in 2003 by Matali Crasset, which would have served as a facilitator for what Donna Haraway some years later deemed, quite surprisingly, as one of the most interesting experiments of interdependent colonization of the last two decades.[12]

Its story, from conception to realization, is in fact very simple and someway ordinary in its development. It began in 1993, when an association of communes for the development of tourism in Val du Riot, in Northern France, decided to found a thirty-acre leisure park between Caudry and Beauvois in the form of an ecological reserve. The idea was to try to restore part of the rich environment that had disappeared due to intensive farming with an educational green space that could recover more balanced customs of territorial anthropization. A mission that moved Raymond Balembois, head of the Beauvois pigeon fanciers' association, to plan the reintroduction of those birds in the area, by building a public dovecote amidst the park, both as a measure to increase biodiversity and to revive a traditional form of care for animals that was slowly fading.[13] The problem, however, was that, even though park authorities were interested in the idea of realizing a breeding structure that could also

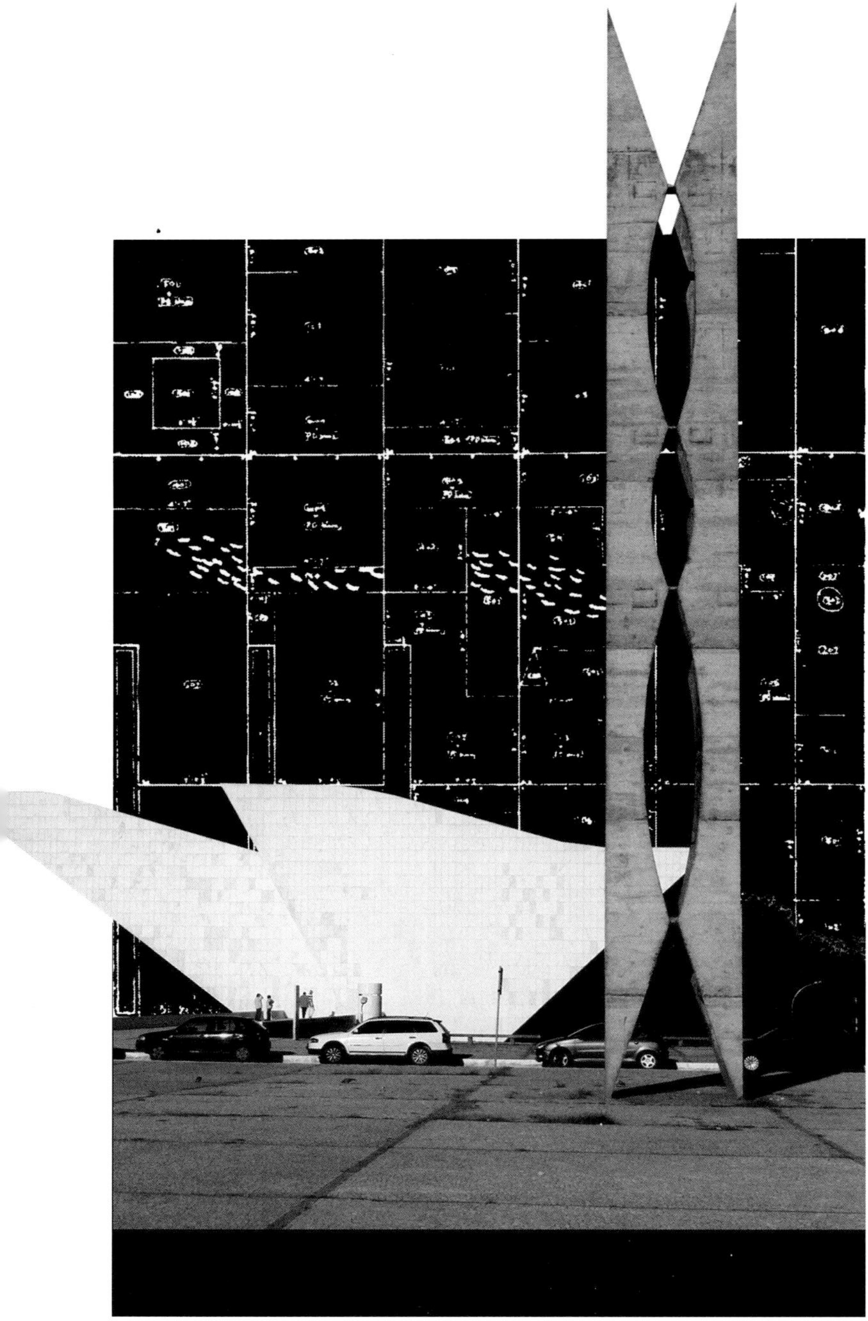

Architectures and pigeons. From Le Corbusier to Oscar Niemeyer

serve as a pedagogic facility, they were quite disappointed by the projects presented. Until the moment when, some years later, Balembois talked about his idea to a young photographer, who introduced him to Bruno Dupont, director of an association devoted to the promotion of public art projects. And with his help, in 2002, he finally got access to a national cultural program that gave him the possibility to commission and follow the development of an artwork for the community.[14] With a grant that allowed him to hire Matali Crasset, one of Dupont's acquaintances, who ended up conferring on the project an unexpected resonance, in terms both of popular engagement and critical reception.

Obviously, such a clamor for a simple device like a dovecote may appear surprising, especially when looking for new archetypes of coexistence. Nevertheless, as David Gissen noted, there are no subjects like pigeons to appreciate the mutable approach of architectural design towards nature. For they have been bearers of "one of the longest and most unique conceptualizations within" the field, through a relationship that dates back to ancient times.[15] As in fact testified by the decorative patterns on the moldings of classical temples, from Egypt to Greece, pigeons were often welcomed to roost in their nooks to use their eggs for sacrifices.[16] And the custom of making them breed inside buildings, to have constant supply of food or a means for distant communication, inspired the definition of a clear architectural type that was so diffused in Europe during the Middle Ages to appear also in the first architectural studies of the age. In the mid-fifteenth century, for instance, Leon Battista Alberti dedicated a part of his treatise to instruct readers on how to design suitable buildings for pigeons.[17] And three centuries later, Jean-Jacques Lequeu drew a section of this kind of construction,[18] called *pigeonnier*, which after some years would have been included with few variations in Viollet-le-Duc's *Dictionnaire*.[19] It was only, however, at the end of the nineteenth century that pigeons became a subject and not only an object of architectural design, by representing, for the newborn metropolitan culture, the symbol of an untamed form of nature which could have prospered within the city, while escaping, for better or for worse, the laws of urbanization. A change that, whereas had already been stressed by John Ruskin and Le Corbusier's respective praises of the animals' esthetic ability to counterpoint architecture with a movable and variable pattern,[20] had to wait for the contribution of Oscar Niemeyer to unfold in all its political relevance.

The story in this case is that of a sculpture named *Pombal*, located in the Square of the Three Powers in Brasilia, and designed by the Brazilian architect in 1961, a year after the city's inauguration, upon the First Lady's request. In her vision the square would in fact have not been complete without a monument to underline its newly acquired role. And even though Niemeyer was initially reluctant to please her, he decided to take that opportunity to realize a tribute to decolonization, which could contemporarily work both as an ironic counter-monument to the country's colonialist oppressors and as a symbolic memorial to informal reappropriation.[21] All this in the shape of a sort of a concave obelisk made of two concrete blocks, twenty-five meters high each, arranged as in a clothespin, one facing the other, and pierced by several ovoid openings, in order to encourage pigeons to roost inside. Not for any functional reason, however, or any actual use, but for their intrinsic symbolic power. Or better, for their being considered an infesting species in the eyes of the urban law, which Niemeyer turned into an act of subversion against the colonial rule. As if their appropriation of the new capital's core would represent the restitution of the nation to a natural process of self-determination finally freed from any form of external imposition. And the architecture of Pombal was meant to complement the three institutional powers with a living symbol of the popular one.

In Matali Crasset's project, however, there is even more than this. Sure, as in Niemeyer's one, pigeons are neither a pest to be controlled nor livestock to be bred. But unlike him, the designer did not consider them a mere symbol of something else.

On the contrary, she considered them as one of the subjects of a complex ecosystem relationship, which had to be revived by means of a new colonization. And by consequence she began to work on the project as she were facing the problem of a real "living … place" for the birds.[22] Not only by visiting other pigeon lofts and talking with local fanciers, but also by studying and taking detailed notes about the birds' habits, in order to understand which habitat could suit them best.[23] All this while also complying with the funding program guidelines, which required the loft to be open to the public. For this reason, after a first attempt, which consisted in the superimposition of two upscaled flowerpots, one dedicated to the pigeons and the other to the people, Crasset worked on a totally different solution, which could represent an integrated expression of this twofold role. And she ended up designing a bright colored and inhabitable capsule, in between the head of a rocket and an Egyptian dovecote, seemingly tangled in a stylized metallic tree, which in turn pierced its smooth surface with perfectly rounded holes. As to solve through an iconic form the ambivalence between permeability and confinement that the structure had ultimately to materialize.

In this regard, it must be said that Crasset's choice of a capsular approach did not come up unprecedented. Not only because capsules, by implicitly referring to an idea of mobility, had traditionally represented, for the history of architecture, the archetypal device for imagining new forms of colonization.[24] But also because, due to this character, they had also interpreted the perfect combination of the search for interior habitability and outer receptivity in a clear and synthetic shape. At least since the end of the Second World War, when the term began to substitute "cell" to indicate the module of a mass housing production that could finally overcome standardization.[25] And then during the seventies, when the investigation on capsular architecture monopolized the debate about the "new domestic landscapes" that were emerging at that time.[26] On the one hand by drawing designers' attention onto the study of the actual ges-

"Pigeons have very old histories of becoming-with human beings. [...] They are treasured kin and despised pests, subjects of rescue and of invective, [...] food and neighbor, targets of extermination and of biotechnological breeding and multiplication."

Donna J. Haraway

0 0.55 1.10 2.20 3.30m

tures of living and their productive value,[27] and on the other by translating the concept of habitability into unexplored territories and subjects.[28] Each time, however, with a specific formalization that recalled a sort of independent "monad open to its surroundings." Exactly like the proposal presented by Crasset to its patrons.[29] A nuclear but porous structure that, unexpectedly, was immediately welcomed with great enthusiasm by both park authorities and local fanciers, and approved without hesitation, thus leaving the designer to study the details of the realization phase.

Despite the clarity of the solution, in fact, there were many aspects that still needed to be solved. The location, for instance, had to be distant from large trees that could house raptors, while however being shielded from prevailing winds. And the construction needed to obey a few rules for pigeons' comfort and safety. Being well ventilated and protected from the damp, or having a smooth external surface, to prevent the access of climbing predators, and suitably sized openings, to enable the pigeons to freely circulate were some of the conditions required. Moreover, in Crasset's intentions, the capsule had also to be easily accessible both for visitors, especially school groups, pigeon fanciers, who would have taken care of the daily maintenance, and local farmers, who would have collected the guano from the birds as fertilizer. Therefore, to realize the loft, she opted for a simple and essential structure, made of only three components. A prefabricated mast in galvanized steel, articulated in a series of branches that supported two landing platforms and a quarantine box hanging from a pulley. An umbrella-like frame in laminated wood, suspended from the mast. And a five meter dome in polyester resin as a protecting cover, all dotted by scattered portholes, and painted orange to stand out against the green landscape. While for the inside she left part of the interior surface empty, to be lined with educational posters, and part covered by small bended shelves, to work as *boulins* for pigeons, thus reiterating the role of contact zone that she meant for the loft to interpret.

For, unlike most of the structures designed to facilitate projects for wildlife reintroduction, Crasset's *Capsule* was not aimed at giving some animals a shelter to survive in a hostile territory. Nor its purpose, on the other hand, was providing fanciers with an efficient farming facility. On the contrary, as highlighted by Vinciane Despret, one of the foundational thinkers in the field of animal studies, the project was meant to recuperate a mutual relationship between two former companion species that needed to activate a new form of kin to coexist again. Not for any utilitarian reason, but to open unexpected possibilities of becoming together, beyond the limits of given social norms or cultural habits.[30] A subject that Crasset assumed, by simply working on the intersection of two opposite figurative elements, the dome and the tree, reduced to their iconic form and combined with no apparent hierarchy. One artificial and one natural, one confining and one defining, one enclosing and one projecting, one suspended and one rooted. Both grafted into each other with no tensions, to produce an interstitial space that was not meant for the animals alone, but "for both the carrier pigeons and their people, past, present and yet to come." For "neither the critters nor the people could have existed or could endure without each other in ongoing, curious practices,"[31] and the loft had just to represent the room for these practices to develop with the most absolute liberty.

What Crasset did, in other terms, to capture this relationship in its open-ended potential, was to work on the definition of a polyvalent space that could be meaningfully for and freely appropriated by both subjects. While contemporarily studying an archetypal shape that, by recalling both a starship and an ancient breeding structure, could engage them on the edge of misunderstanding and disjunction. It is not surprising, therefore, that, from an architectural point of view, her design resulted in an evident tribute to the typical *folies* that characterized the eighteenth-century French landscape gardening.[32] For they had historically represented upscaled and accessible objects, both hermetic and responsive, designed, to borrow the words from

An interpsecies interface. Matali Crasset's *Capsule*

"What is commemorated ... is not the animal alone, nor the practice alone, but the activation of two "becomings-with" [...]. What is brought into existence are the relations by which pigeons transform men into talented pigeon fanciers and by which the fanciers transform the pigeons into reliable racing pigeons."

Vinciane Despret

Bernard Tschumi, as a sort of insurrection in the landscape, for no specific purpose but to leave place to the spontaneous and unexpected event.[33] With the only difference that the event, in this case, had to be generated by the interaction between different species, involved in an act of disinterested care. An idea that clashed not only with most of the later analyses in this regard, which have focused on the designer's ability of realizing an effective "instrument of management," by enabling "pigeons to become a functioning aspect of the local agricultural economy."[34] But also with the character of many subsequent projects developed for the sake of returning wildlife to cities, which have ultimately been aimed at managing urban pests through a "natural" answer to the problem.[35] Thus leaving Crasset's prototype partially unparalleled, despite the abundance of attempts in this direction, which have flourished in the last few years.

Since 2003, in fact, projects for animal colonization of anthropized contexts have multiplied many times over. With a growth rate, moreover, that has been unmatched by other researches in the field of posthuman design. Not only through a variegated landscape of fanciful hybrid typologies, like hotels for insects, bat towers, and birds' monasteries, but also with new ingenious technological solutions, like modular façade components for nesting butterflies, or assembly kits for building urban beehives.[36] All following Crasset's modal strategies and the objectual dimension in which she worked, while however ignoring the final principles materialized by Caudry's *Capsule*. Considering animals, in other words, as they could not escape the traditional tropes that see them either glorified as a representation of an unleashed nature, or treated like an object of spatial management. But never, in any case, as part of a natural and cultural relationship that exceeds the functionalist limits of an ecosystem exchange. As though design approach towards them, from a conceptual point of view, was still constitutionally "stuck between a Victorian clean-up effort and a vitalist search for ways to transcend existing socionatural representations."[37] Whereas, from an operative one, it could not easily abandon the strict functionalist perspective that prevents designers from seeing interspecies coexistence without a specific purpose other than living well together. A possibility that, although Crasset had already hinted at it, would probably need dwelling models other than colonies, without all their intrinsic cultural connotations, to unfold in all their potential.

Notes

1 Lewis Mumford, *The Story of Utopias* (Gloucester MA: Peter Smith, 1959), 15.

2 John Wilkins, *The Discovery of a World in the Moone* (London, 1638). Notably, in that year Francis Goodwin's utopian fantasy titled *The Man in the Moone: or a Discourse of a Voyage thither by Domingo Gonsales* (London, 1638) was also published.

3 The best example is Edward Everett Hale's fictional tale about a first inhabited artificial satellite, significantly titled "Brick Moon." *Atlantic Monthly* 24 (1869).

4 Fredric Jameson, "Progress Versus Utopia: Or, Can We Imagine the Future?," *Science- Fiction Studies* 9 (1982): 147-158.

5 Olaf Stapledon, "Interplanetary Man," *Journal of the British Interplanetary Society* 7 (1948): 213-233.

6 In this regard, see respectively Ursula K. Le Guin, *The Word for World is Forest* (New York: Berkley Publishing, 1976); and Gerard K. O'Neill, *The High Frontier: Human Colonies in Space* (New York: William Morrow, 1977).

7 Linda Billings, "Ideology, Advocacy, and Space Flight: Evolution of a Cultural Narrative," in *Societal Impacts of Space Flight*, eds. Steven J. Dick and Roger D. Launius (Washington DC: NASA, 2007), 483.

8 With all probability, in fact, the first actual reintroduction project, consisting in the release of fifteen American bison into a newly established reserve in Oklahoma, dates back to 1907, few years after Tsiolkovsky had first pictured greenhouses built and crops raised in space. In this regard, see respectively Devra G. Kleiman, "Reintroduction of captive mammals for conservation," *BioScience* 39 (1989): 152-161; and Konstantin Tsiolkovsky, *Beyond the Planet Earth* (1900), trans. Kenneth Syers (London: Pergamon Press, 1960).

9 Indeed, this attitude lasted long after the early history of reintroduction. See, in this regard, *Aldo Leopold, Game Management* (New York: Scribner's, 1933).

10 The reference, again, is to the early studies on the relationships among organisms and their biophysical environment dating back to the mid-nineteenth century, from Charles Darwin's to Ernst Haeckel's one. For a complete overview on the theme of reintroductions, see John G. Ewen, et al., *Reintroduction Biology: Integrating Science and Management* (London: Wiley-Blackwell, 2012).

11 See, for instance, the chimney swifts' towers invented by ornithologist Althea Sherman in 1915, designed specifically for chimney swift nesting.

12 Donna J. Haraway, *Staying with the Trouble: Making Kin in the Chthulucene* (Durham-London: Duke University Press, 2016), 25-26.

13 The story is briefly narrated in Matali Crasset, *Le Pigeonnier/The Pigeon Loft* (Paris: Pyramid NTCV, 2004).

14 More precisely, the New Patrons program (*Les nouveaux commanditaires*), funded by Fondation de France.

15 David Gissen, *Subnature: Architecture's Other Environments* (New York: Princeton Architectural Press, 2009), 180. "Pigeons have very old histories of becoming-with human beings. [...] They are treasured kin and despised pests, subjects of rescue and of invective, [...] targets of extermination and of biotechnological breeding and multiplication, companions in work and play and carriers of disease'" Haraway, *Staying with the Trouble*, 15.

16 George Hersey, *The Lost Meaning of Classical Architecture: Speculations on Ornament from Vitruvius to Venturi* (Cambridge MA: The MIT Press, 1988),

34. For a complete overview on this particular typology, see Arthur Cooke, *A Book of Dovecotes* (London: T. N. Foulis, 1920).

17 Leon Battista Alberti, *Della Architettura: Libri Dieci*, trans. Cosimo Bartoli (Milan, 1833) 168.

18 Bibliothèque nationale de France, département Estampes et photographie, Reserve Fol-Ha-80 (B, 6).

19 Eugène Emmanuel Viollet-le-Duc, *Dictionnaire raisonné de l'architecture française du XIe au XVIe siècle*, tome III (Paris: Édition Bance, 1856), 482.

20 "St. Mark's porches are full of doves that nestle among the marble foliage, and mingle the soft iridescence of their living plumes." John Ruskin, *The Stones of Venice*, second volume (London: Smith, Elder and Co., 1873), 67. About the same Venetian piazza Le Corbusier wrote that "the pigeons of St. Mark's themselves add their own uniform module, providing a varied and effective note in the scheme." Le Corbusier, *The City of Tomorrow and Its Planning* (New York: Dover, 1987), 69. In this regard, see also Catherine Ingraham, *Architecture, Animal, Human: The Asymmetric Condition* (London-New York: Routledge, 2006).

21 The monument's name is in fact a play on words that refers to the Portuguese term for pigeons, *os pombos*, and the name of Portugal's interior minister Marquês de Pombal, who in the mid-eighteenth century expanded the land privileges in colonial Brazil. See, in this regard, the interpretation of Justin Read in "Alternative Functions: Oscar Niemeyer and the Poetics of Modernity," *Modernism/modernity* 12, no. 2 (2005): 253-272.

22 Crasset, *Le Pigeonnier*, 6.

23 Ruth Slavid, *Micro: Very Small Buildings* (New York: Laurence King Publishing, 2009), 86.

24 See, for instance, Wenzel Hablik's vision of a Discoverer's Colony (1920) or the already mentioned project by Georgij Krutikov for a Flying City (1928). Wenzel Hablik, *Hablik, Designer, Utopian, Architect, Expressionist, Artist, 1881-1934* (London: Architectural Association, 1980); Selim Omarovich Khan-Magomedov, *Georgii Krutikov: The Flying City and Beyond* (Barcelona: Editorial Tenov, 2015).

25 See, in this regard, the description of Richard Buckminster Fuller's Wichita House (1948). Federico Neder, *Fuller Houses: R. Buckminster Fuller's Dymaxion Dwellings and Other Domestic Adventures* (Zürich: Lars Müller Publishers, 2008).

26 The term refers to MoMA's seminal exhibition *Italy: The New Domestic Landscape*, which first showcased this approach to the general public. Emilio Ambasz, *Italy: The New Domestic Landscape* (New York: The Museum of Modern Art, 1972). The topic was however being developed also in the United Kingdom, by Archigram, in Japan, by Metabolists, and in Austria, by collectives like Coop Himmelb(l)au and Haus Rucker.

27 The approach that Antti Lovag, one of the fathers of capsular approach, named *habitologie*. Pierre Roche, *Antti Lovag Habitologie* (Paris: France Europe Editions 2010).

28 Exactly like Ant Farm did when they designed their Dolphin Embassy (1974), the first extraordinary architecture for interspecies encounters ever planned. Constance Lewallen, Steve Seid, and Chip Lord, *Ant Farm, 1968-1978* (Berkeley: University of California Press, 2004), 142-144.

29 Alexandra Midal in Crasset, *Le Pigeonnier*, 22.

30 "Without the lover of pigeons, [...] what then would remain would be pigeons, but not homing pigeons, not voyageurs. What is commemorated,

then, is not the animal alone, nor the practice alone, but the activation of two "becomings-with" [...]. Otherwise said, what is brought into existence are the relations by which pigeons transform men into talented pigeon fanciers and by which the fanciers transform the pigeons into reliable racing pigeons." Vinciane Despret, "Ceux qui insistent: Les nouveaux commanditaires," in *Faire art comme on fait société*, ed. Didier Debaise et al. (Dijon: Les Presses du Réel, 2013), 133-146.

31 Haraway, *Staying with the Trouble*, 133.

32 The history of architectural *folies* and their enduring value within French design culture is too long to be narrated here. In this regard, see Patrick Broquet, and Evelyne Malnic, *Folies de jardin: Art et architecture des fabriques de jardin du XVIIIe siècle à nos jours* (Paris: Éditions du Chêne, 1996).

33 This is the meaning that the French architect attributed to *folies*, when he updated the topic for the project of Parc de la Villette (1983). See Bernard Tschumi, Jacques Derrida, and Anthony Vidler, *Parc de la Villette* (London: Artifice, 2014).

34 Gissen, *Subnature*, 186-187.

35 See, for instance, Fritz Haeg,'s *Animal Estates*, by which, since 2008, he has proposed the reintroduction of hawks and other predators within cities, to reduce the number of pigeons.

36 The list would be too long to be mentioned here. For a partial catalogue, see the atlas of references on the following pages.

37 Gissen, *Subnature*, 187.

Visual atlas (following spread)

1 Tower of Silence, mid-5th century BCE
2 Dovecote at Karanis, 1st century BCE
3 Chimney Swift Towers, Althea Sherman, 1915
4 Dymaxion "Wichita" House, Richard Buckminster Fuller, 1948
5 Living Pod, David Greene, 1966
6 Dolphin Embassy, Ant Farm, 1974
7 *Land(e)scape*, Marco Casagrande and Sami Rintala, 1999
8 Jellyfish House, Lab Zero, 2004
9 *Animal Estates*, Fritz Haeg, 2008
10 Insect Hotel, Arup Associates, 2010
11 Bat Tower, Joyce Hwang, 2010
12 Habitat for Urban Wildlife, Ifat Finkelman_Ofer Bilik Architects, 2011
13 *I'm lost in Paris*, R&Sie(n), 2008
14 Mellor Primary School, Sarah Wigglesworth Architects, 2015
15 Habitat Wall, Ants of the Prairie, 2015
16 Bat Cloud, Ants of the Prairie, 2012
17 Bower, Joyce Hwang and Ellen Driscoll, 2016
18 Orientation, Carpenter | Lowings, 2017
19 Nomadic Shelter, SALT Siida Workshop, 2014
20 Grooming Retreat, Gartnerfuglen and Mariana de Delás, 2014
21 Bird Hide, Biotope, 2014
22 Wildhomes for Wildlife, IKEA and eight Artists, 2019
23 *Hidden in Plain Sight*, Double Happiness, 2019
24 Bee Home, IKEA and Space 10 and Bakken & Bæck and Tanita Klein, 2020

historical dovecotes

1 1A

2 2A

3 3A

capsular logics

4 4A

5 5A

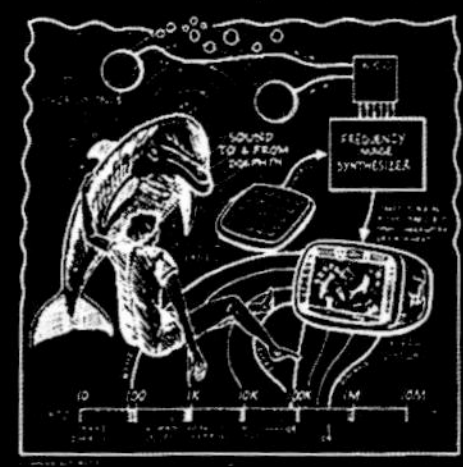

6 6A

critical graftings

7 7A

8 8A

9 9A

human-made nests

10 10A

11 11A

12 12A

b i o p h i l i c m o d u l e s

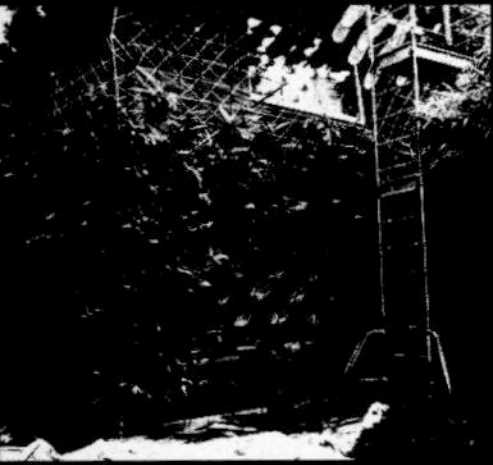

13 13A

14 14A

15 15A

a n i m a l d w e l l i n g s

16 16A

17 17A

18 18A

h y b r i d c a p s u l e s

19 19A

20 20A

21 21A

f u r n i t u r e s o l u t i o n s

22 22A

23 23A

24 24A

A reserve

William Harrison Jr., Nam Il, et al.
P'anmunjŏm, KR
37.966667, 126.55
1953-2011

"Like winds and sunsets, wild things were taken for granted until progress began to do away with them. Now we face the question whether a still higher "standard of living" is worth its cost in things natural, wild, and free. For us of the minority, the opportunity to see geese is more important than television, and the chance to find a pasque-flower is a right as inalienable as free speech."

Aldo Leopold, *A Sand County Almanac: And Sketches Here and There* (Oxford: Oxford University Press, 1949), vii.

Although reintroduction projects have constituted a relevant share of the relatively recent attempts to restore or preserve biodiversity, it cannot be said that, traditionally, they have represented the preeminent strategy to pursue this objective. And not even the first, when seen in a longer historical perspective. For the establishment of any new colony has always been preceded by the creation of an enclosed and protected area, or a reserve,[1] that could guarantee the future sustainability of the reintroduction. Even when the aim of repopulation was just to provide constant food supply. The origin of modern nature reserves in fact dates back to medieval times, when landowners began to protect their hunting grounds from poachers by means of enclosure. And later, when the idea of protecting animals simply to keep them from dying out first emerged, reserves continued to follow the same logic. Like in the case, for instance, of the first modern reserve ever realized, established in 1821 by pioneering conservationist Charles Waterton for his researches, around his estate in West Yorkshire.[2] A scientific arcadia surrounded by a three-mile long wall, three meters high, which, unlike a garden, was not meant to keep animals inside its borders, but to prevent humans from entering. And if in a first moment the creation of this kind of reserve was still based on the artificial recreation of a natural environment within a certain perimeter, during the course of the eighteenth century it finally opened up to the preservation of wild areas.[3] Not only because of a growing ecological awareness, but mainly thanks to the American invention of a new cultural myth, that of wilderness,[4] which ultimately represented one of the key drivers for the development of the modern policies concerning global environmental protection.

The history of this myth, as richly depicted in a 1967 celebrated book by Roderick Nash, approximately began in the same years in which Charles Waterton founded his reserve, but it took some time to consolidate, in that proclivity towards wilderness was not intrinsic to American character.[5] Initially, in fact, the Pilgrim Fathers, like their European coevals, tended to see wild areas as dangerous, uncivilized, and thus inherently evil and ungodly. Then, however, as forests were being rapidly cleared and Romantic tastes imported from the continent,[6] East Coast elites started finding more and more positive virtues in wilderness.[7] To the point that, in the second half of the century, a sort of "cult," indirectly nurtured by the paintings of Thomas Cole and David Henry Thoreau's words,[8] almost fanatically advocated the contact with nature as a cure for the problems of the modern society.[9] A vision contested, on the one hand, by the already established conservation movement, as led by Gifford Pinchot, which meant the protection of wilderness only as a strategy for prolonging access to vital natural resources,[10] and, on the other, by the newborn preservation one, represented by co-founder of Sierra Club John Muir, who saw nature as possessing intrinsic worth to be safeguarded from any kind of human use but contemplation.[11] As though any possible relationship with nature, resulting in a sort of voluntary exclusion, lied someway between the recognition of a self-sufficient biotic community and the observation of a secular form of transcendentalism. A value that resisted over time thanks to the efforts of scientists like Aldo Leopold, who first used the term wilderness to describe this kind of selfless preservation,[12] and artists like Ansel Adams.[13] And which ultimately informed, the drafting of one of the most extraordinary legal documents of all time, the Wilderness Act, signed by Lyndon Johnson in 1964.[14] Just over ten years after the same American government had already unconsciously promoted what would have turned out to be the most radical and complete, however unintentional, experiment of natural preservation ever realized.

The exact date was 27 July 1953, when Generals William Harrison Jr., representing the United Nations Command, and Nam Il, for the Korean People's and the Chinese Volunteer Armies, signed an armistice to "ensure a complete cessation of hostilities" between North and South Korea after three years of war.[15] The armistice in fact established that each side had to move their troops back two thousand meters from the front

American wilderness. From Yellowstone National Park to the Wilderness Act

"A wilderness [...] is ... recognized as an area where the earth and its community of life are untrammeled by man, where man himself is a visitor who does not remain."

Wilderness Act

line, which was then intersecting the former border of the thirty-eighth parallel north. And here, as a preventive containment measure, to create a demilitarized buffer zone between the two republics, spanning a length of two hundred and fifty kilometers, and crossed by a frontier in one single point, which had to be maintained by a small contingent of civilian police from both sides.[16] Immediately after signing, however, things took a different turn, and while almost all the local residents were not allowed to return home, military personnel were simply redesignated as "civilian police." And as tension between the Koreas remained high, since 1963, after a partial escalation, both parties began to build fortifications and plant hundreds of thousands of land mines, until the area became the most highly militarized strip in the world. A huge territory not only uninhabitable but also inaccessible to anyone, with the exception of the few hundred residents of two villages protected by the United Nations Command,[17] and the one thousand "police" persons allowed to enter to patrol their respective sides of the front line. And even though in 2018, as part of a strategy to reduce tension, the two parties agreed to dismantle the major guard posts across the area, it still remains the widest and strictest exclusion zone in the world.[18]

Even today, in fact, driving from Seoul, halfway to the border, one would first encounter a large uninhabited area, from five to twenty kilometers wide, established some months after the end of hostilities to prevent farmers from settling near a possible field of conflict. And only at its end the actual frontline could be accessed, by entering through the forward edge of the battle area, until the northern limit of the general outpost line. Even if arriving there, however, one would still be outside the actual Demilitarized Zone. For this array of garrisons, which is constantly operated for control and observation by three regiments, only introduce to its southern limit line. A border spanning the peninsula from coast to coast, surrounded by threefold barbed-wire fences, and equipped at periodic intervals, in coincidence with the supply routes, with reinforced gates guarded

ARTICLE V

MISCE

61. Amendments and ad must be mutually agreed to b sides.

62. The Articles and Agreement shall remain in either by mutually acceptabl provision in an appropriate a at a political level between bo

63. All of the provisions than Paragraph 12, shall becc on 27 JULY 195

Done at Panmunjom, K 27th day of JULY , Chinese, all texts being equal

KIM IL SUNG	PENG TEH-HUAI	MARK W. CLARK
Marshal, Democratic People's Republic of Korea Supreme Commander, Korean People's Army	Commander, Chinese People's Volunteers	General, United States Army Commander-in-Chief, United Nations Command

HARRISON, JR.

by military forces, unmanned cameras, and infrared sensors. All marking the boundary of a totally different landscape, which opens up and unfold for four kilometers until the northern limit line. One made of untouched forests and swamps, deserts and screes, nests and burrows, known as the reconnaissance area, where only small units of "civilians," for a short time, are allowed to carry out intelligence operations. A stretched territory occasionally dotted by the ruining strongholds informally built on the tops of the mountains, with a profusion of cast concrete, often painted camouflage, concentric circles of barbed-wire fences, and anti-personnel mines scattered across the area. But without anything else of artificial, nor a real demarcation line between the two Koreas. As to testify the permanent absence of any human trace that has eventually resisted for more than half a century, and which has made room, from the very beginning, to other kinds of life to settle.

For although the place has represented a deadly place to humans for more than half a century, its natural isolation and its particular geography, which in its length crosses prairies and mountains, as well as lakes and tidal marshes, have soon proved an involuntary but extraordinary biological resource. In 1966, for instance, in response to a sudden upsurge of violence following President Johnson's Korean visit, it was proposed to transform the area into a natural park, "where the unique profusion of plant and animal life that has grown up there relatively undisturbed ... might be enjoyed and subjected to scientific inquiry."[19] And in 1997, after some first partial surveys confirmed it as one of the world's most well-preserved areas of temperate habitat, housing more than two thirds of the peninsula's biodiversity, two Korean-Americans, namely Kim Ke Chung and Lee Seung-ho, founded an international non-governmental organization, named DMZ Forum, to support, as a means for peace-seeking, the conservation of this unique biological richness. An impressive and spontaneous resurgence of primary habitats, which has seen the return not only of endangered species, like the red-crowned crane, the Korean fox, and the Asiatic black bear,

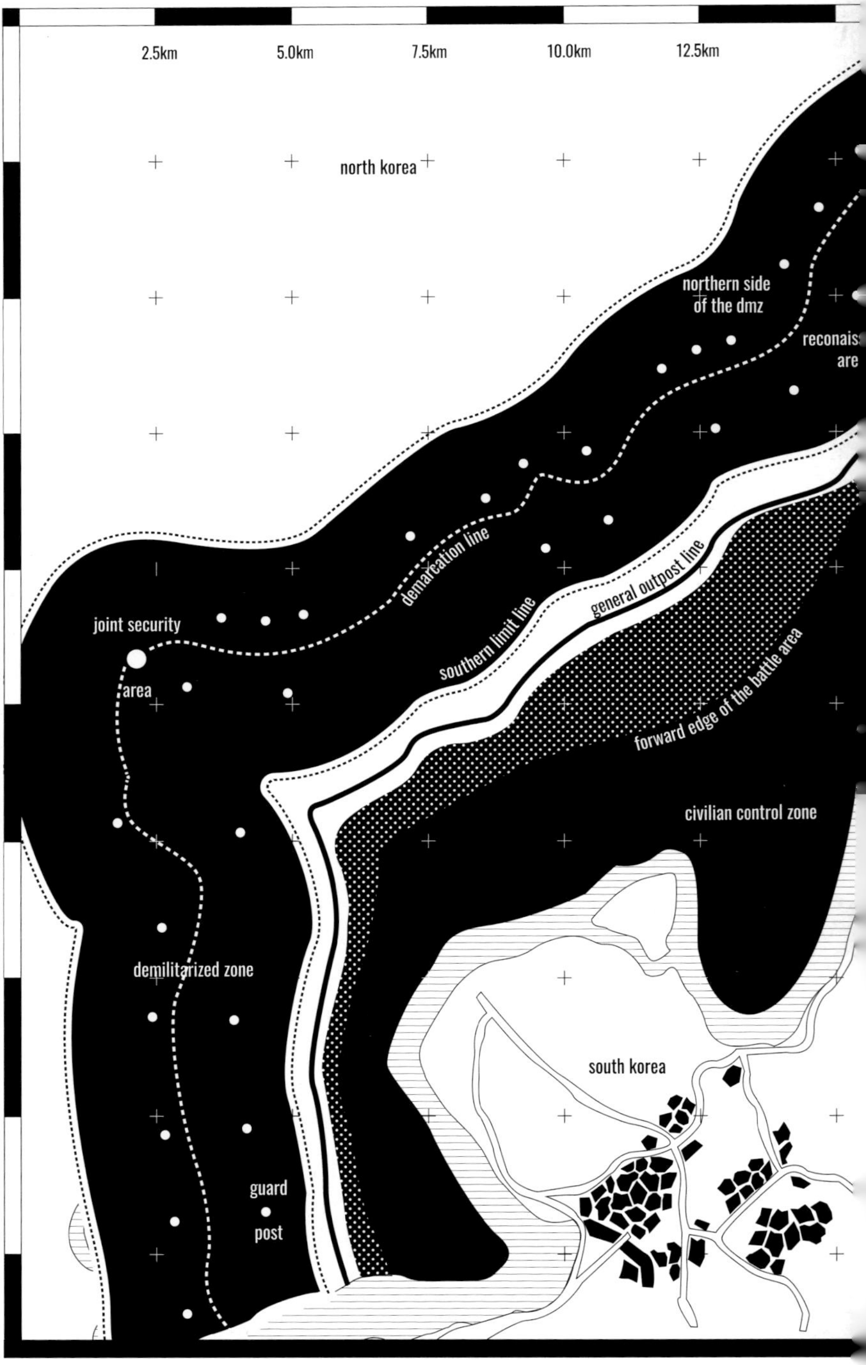

2.5km
5.0km
7.5km
10.0km
12.5km
north korea
northern side of the dmz
reconais are
demarcation line
joint security area
southern limit line
general outpost line
forward edge of the battle area
civilian control zone
demilitarized zone
south korea
guard post

A reserve

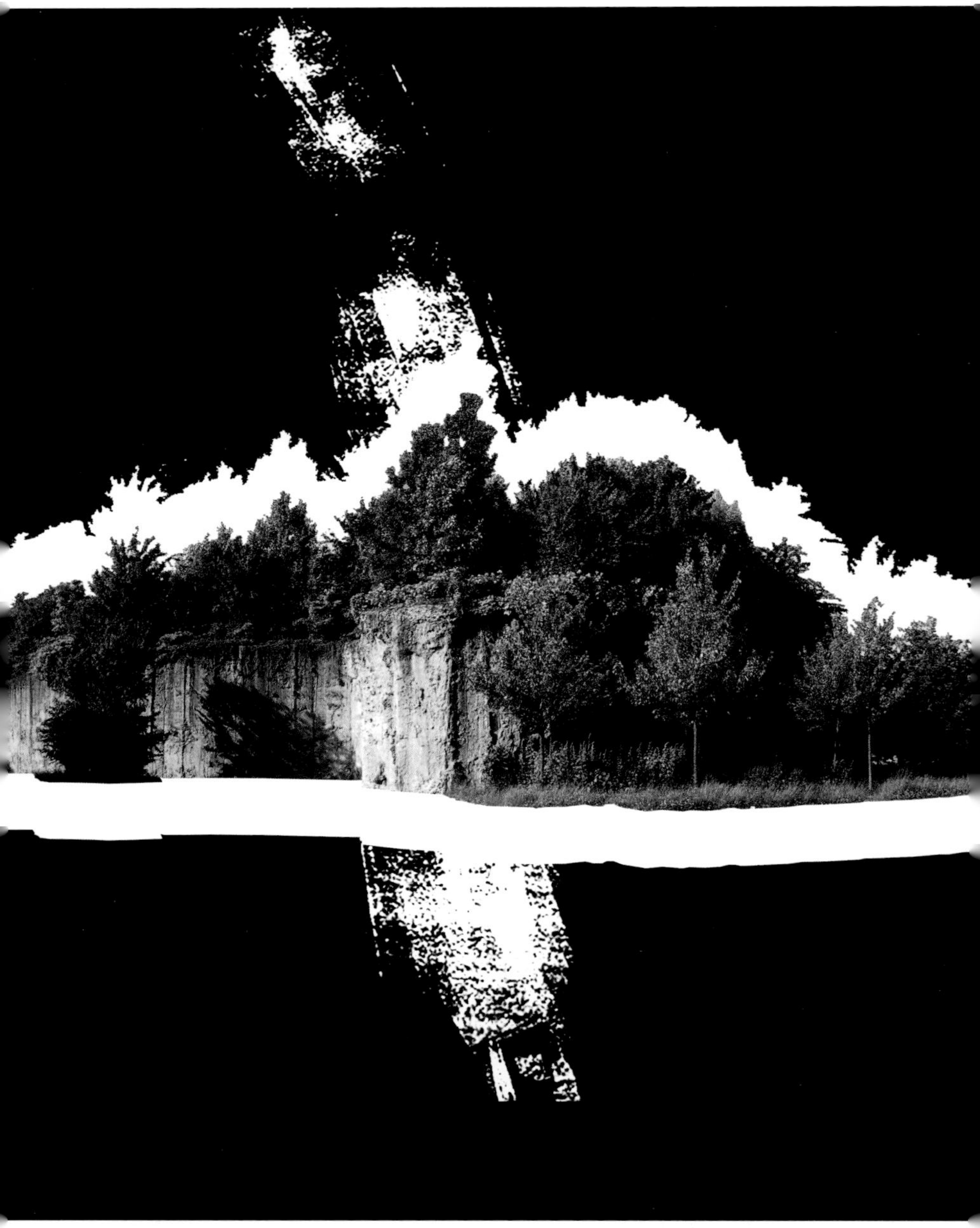

Reserves of wilderness. Gilles Clément's Île Derborence

but also of some animals that had been considered long disappeared, like the Amur leopard and, allegedly, the Siberian tiger.[20] All data that were first announced to the world in 2003, on the occasion of the fiftieth anniversary of the armistice, by a highly impactful CNN's story,[21] and which were finally documented six years later by a magnificent photographic report by Park Jong-woo, the first civilian who had obtained such a permission since the war outbreak.[22] Thus reinforcing the proposal of a formal project of preservation and development, like that presented in 2007 by DMZ Forum,[23] which could eventually sanction what had already spontaneously emerged and managed to thrive with such a power.

The idea, in other words, was to attribute a new value to that which Gilles Clément, just in 2003, called "Third Landscape," to designate the sum of the spaces left over by humans to nature alone and its spontaneous evolution, which had previously been looked upon as completely negligible. Unattended and residual areas like abandoned sites, transitional spaces, or neglected lands, but also those simply set aside, like inaccessible places, non-cultivatable areas, or reserves themselves. All spaces that, if compared to the territories subdued to human control, formed a privileged area of receptivity to biological diversity, thus ending up representing the genetic reservoir of the planet, or, in Clément's view, the space of the possible future, out of the logic of binary identities.[24] Undecided, in constant evolution, and open to heterogeneous forms of cross-fertilization. Determined, on the one hand, by unconstrained patterns of natural growth and, on the other, by a precise political recognition concerning their biological necessity. A recognition that, according to Clément's Manifesto, had to require planners and designers not only to designate as public amenity unattended areas created, voluntarily or not, by the absence of a functional destination, but also to include in their new projects some unorganized spaces for this third landscape to develop. Exactly as he already did from 1996 to 2000 for the Parc Henri Matisse in Lille, where he planted an inaccessible but monitored forest on a central rock mass, seven meters above ground, to serve both as a matrix and a guideline for the ecological management of the park.[25] Or again in 2011, when he realized a *Jardin du Tiers-Paysage* to regenerate by re-naturalization the concrete roof of an abandoned submarine base in Saint Nazaire, by making use of the natural capacities of some native species.[26]

Even Clement's idea, however, was not totally new, at least from a design standpoint. For something similar, also in terms of location, in reality had already been attempted by Cedric Price in 1989, when he started devising the first conscious, although unrealized, architectural project of "restitution" ever imagined. The one he planned for regenerating the Hamburg Docklands through what he referred to as a particular form of "relief from development."[27] At that time, in fact, the city of Hamburg was seeking new opportunities for its redundant historical harbor, and for this reason, urban authorities organized an architectural masterclass with sixteen design teams invited, among which the one led by Price. Instead of defining a masterplan for redevelopment, his team listed a series of questions for citizens and authorities to ask what growth exactly meant. And after two years of work, they presented to the public a project, called Ducklands Experiment, that instead of repurposing the docklands through housing, offices, and other tertiary functions, it proposed the creation of a river marshland in the center of Hamburg, to become a resting place for migratory birds.[28] At first by demolishing the existing buildings and structures, with the exception of key railway links and some listed constructions, and later by leaving the site to be gradually submerged by the Elbe River. All this by making use of adjustable gantries that would have served, initially, to remove soil from the riverbed, then for planting and husbandry, and finally as adaptable walkways for visitors who, as in his Snowdon Aviary, would have remained only occasional spectators of an environmental setting, or a third habitat, "constructed" exclusively for birds, with nothing but water, sand, and plants. And through both a final principle and a modal strategy that in the following years would have often been replicated, though never fully realized.

What, on the contrary, is extraordinary about the resurgence of life in the Korean Demilitarized Zone, despite the lack of any direct intention, as those orienting designers' recent speculative proposals, is actually its existence. A living and flourishing "reserve" that testifies with facts that a different way of conceiving the human constructive role is not only imaginable but also realizable. And thus that it can retrospectively be taken as a reference for similar projects, starting from the results and not from the aims, as if it were the outcome of an additive and tentative form of landscape design that inexplicably managed to function. In this way, for instance, one would notice that the emergence of such a natural ecosystem did not simply depend on the total absence of human presence, but specifically on the interdiction of any form of territorial domestication. And that this interdiction was carried out through a strategy of spatial definition implemented not by enclosure but, so to say, by exclosure, in both functional and figurative terms. For the area was not "designed" through a projective form of confinement, like gardens or traditional reserves were. On the contrary, its perimeter was molded, on the one hand, by a really peculiar act of strategic retreat, or a setback, which resulted, from a formal standpoint, in the territorial offset of the landscape's morphological features intersecting the frontline. And on the other, by the multiplication of this offset in a series of contour lines, which transformed the linear limit into an expanded threshold made of different environmental settings and architectural elements, corresponding to as many levels of restriction. As to provide effective zones and vectors of mutual separation and contact among diverse subjects and opposed uses.

Common narratives on the DMZ, however, tend to ignore such specific design features, only focusing on it being a "reminder of nature's tremendous resilience."[29] To the point that the recent proposals concerning its preservation have paradoxically represented different attempts of transforming the involuntary effect of a process of retreat into the object of a deliberate project of confinement. Or better, to turn the spon-

Designed to decay. Marco Casagrande's Ruin Academy

taneous reserve, on the one hand, into a living laboratory for studying nature's adaptability, human ecology, and sustainability. And on the other, into a natural park that could constitute both a primary asset for economic development, and a strategic driver to peace-keeping, or even reunification.[30] This was, for instance, the strategic perspective through which, in 2011, South Korea submitted a nomination for the designation of the southern part of the area as a biosphere reserve to UNESCO's Man and the Biosphere Programme.[31] But it was also the same ideological basis that, however through a more refined conceptualization, formed some design proposals concerning DMZ's ecological preservation and its future development. Like the collaborative project initiated in 2015 by artist Jae-Eun Choi in collaboration with architect Shigeru Ban, titled *Dreaming of Earth*, which proposed a comprehensive intervention to both protect and celebrate the untouched reserve, by creating a space for contemplation. In the form of a sprawling floating garden, metaphorically reconnecting the two fronts, which included a series of traditional Korean pavilions and observation towers designed, among the others, by Lee Ufan, Studio Mumbai, and Olafur Eliasson.[32]

On the contrary, the formal and authorial interventions that most recall DMZ's informal and anonymous creation, besides some heterogeneous artistic installations, are those recently developed, through a new form of shamanism, by Finnish architect Marco Casagrande, to create an ecologically sustainable transition towards what he refers to as the "Third Generation City." In particular that represented by his Ruin Academy, an independent architectural research center started in Taipei, in 2010, as a sample of that possible city. Or better, a piece of the industrial one, transformed into the "compost" of a new form urbanization, which has to grow from the ruins of the former sanitized, specialized, and hierarchical complex, in the form of a hybrid organism.[33] An organism realized by occupying an abandoned apartment building of the city center, then taken back to its basic construction, by removing all the windows and the interior walls, and piercing the outer ones from the roof to the basement, to let the rain fall inside and water the new plantations of trees, bamboos and vegetables throughout its rooms. The same rooms where professors and students, who call themselves "constructor-gardeners," sleep and work in wooden structures, to find possible ways of "farming" the city towards an organic state and "growing" a new one. All this through a particular kind of acupuncture that can find a balance between the official industrialism and the anarchy of the jungle. As the Third Generation City, like any other form of Third Landscape, has to emerge not from a binary logic, but from the inclusive, interconnected, and evolving acceptance of any biological diversity that, in the same way, has marked the evolution of the DMZ since its inception.

There is even more than this, however, that the comparison with Casagrande's project suggests. Not only, in other words, that what has long been considered as the perfect spatial archetype of exclusion, in a sublime depiction of "a universe without us,"[34] can indeed make room for the most radical form of inclusion that one may imagine.[35] But even that a retreat, rather than merely representing a surrender of any constructive strategy, can be meant as a clear design action. Both formal, as ideally shown by the impressive infrastructural shape of the Demilitarized Zone that, as a seismic crack, has let a new and unknown landscape emerge from the ground, and environmental, as its biological evolution has widely demonstrated over the years. All this through a particular kind of project that while refusing any form of predetermination, does not exclude humanity and its formative role, even in spite of a different original intentionality. For as anthropologist Anna Tsing demonstrated, when dealing with another kind of ruin, nature's resurgence often needs a human act of "disturbance to enhance diversity and the healthy functioning of ecosystems."[36] An act that can be both deliberate in its intentions and unintentional in its effects, but which nonetheless remains, in many instances, strictly necessary to its initiation and development.

Notes

1 For a synthetic definition of reserves, see Gilles Clément, *Manifeste du Tiers paysage* (Paris: Éditions Sujet/Objet, 2003).

2 Brian W. Edginton, *Charles Waterton: A Biography* (Cambridge: James Clarke & Co., 1996).

3 Bernhard Gissibl, Sabine Höhler, and Patrick Kupper, eds., *Civilizing Nature: National Parks in Global Historical Perspective* (Oxford-New York: Berghahn Books, 2012).

4 Michael Lewis, *American Wilderness: A New History* (Oxford-New York: Oxford University Press, 2007).

5 Roderick Frazier Nash, *Wilderness and the American Mind* (New Haven-London: Yale University Press, 1967).

6 "In Europe people talk a great deal of the wilds of America, but the Americans themselves never think about them; they are insensible to the wonders of inanimate nature." Alexis de Tocqueville, *Journey to America 1831-1832*, trans. George Lawrence (New Haven: Yale University Press, 1960), 335.

7 This vision of nature culminated in 1872 in the creation of the Yellowstone National Park, established by the U.S. Congress and signed into law by President Ulysses Grant, as the first national park in the world.

8 "In wildness is the preservation of the world." Henry David Thoreau, "Walking," in *The Norton Book of Nature Writing*, eds. Robert Finch and John Elder (New York: W. W. Norton, 2002), 192.

9 "West Cure" was the name of a therapeutic strategy designed in the 1860s to treat neurasthenia, which consisted in encouraging young men to engage in vigorous physical activity out West. Among the men treated were poet Walt Whitman, and future President Theodore Roosevelt. In this regard, see Barbara Will, "The Nervous Origins of the American Western," *American Literature* 70, no. 2 (1998): 293-316.

10 Nash, *Wilderness and the American Mind*, 130-134.

11 John Muir, *Our National Parks* (Boston: Houghton Mifflin, 1901).

12 Aldo Leopold, *A Sand County Almanac: And Sketches Here and There* (Oxford: Oxford University Press, 1949). Besides being an extraordinary writer and naturalist, in 1935 Leopold contributed to found the Wilderness Society, dedicated to expanding and protecting nation's wild areas.

13 Ansel Adams, *This is the American Earth* (San Francisco: Sierra Club, 1960).

14 According to the Act, in fact, "a wilderness, in contrast with those areas where man and his own works dominate the landscape, is ... recognized as an area where the earth and its community of life are untrammeled by man, where man himself is a visitor who does not remain." Howard Zahniser, Pub.L. 88-577.

15 Text of the Korean War Armistice Agreement, July 27, 1953.

16 The frontier is in P'anmunjŏm, home of the Joint Security Area, where the armistice itself was signed.

17 Namely Daeseong-dong in the southern side, and Kijŏng-dong in the northern.

18 Robert Koehler, *The DMZ: Dividing the Two Koreas* (Seoul: Seoul Selection, 2010).

19 Glenn D. Paige, "1966: Korea Creates the Future," *Asian Survey* 7, no. 1 (1967): 27.

20 Hall Healy, "Korean Demilitarized Zone: Peace and Nature Park," *International Journal on World Peace* 24, no. 4 (2007): 61-83.

21 Nick Easen, *Korea's DMZ: The thin green line*, CNN, 2003. In the same year the DMZ Forum organized a conference in New York City on the importance of preserving the DMZ for the world, notably sponsored, among the others, by Sierra Club.

22 Park Jongwoo, *DMZ: Demilitarized Zone of Korea* (Göttingen: Steidl, 2017).

23 Hall Healy, "Korean Demilitarized Zone." In this regard, see also Kim Kwi-Gon, *The Demilitarized Zone (DMZ) of Korea: Protection, Conservation and Restoration of a Unique Ecosystem* (New York-Dordrecht-London: Springer Science & Business Media, 2013).

24 Clément, *Manifeste du Tiers paysage*. A similar concept was proposed few years later by Bruno Latour, in the form of a "manifesto." The idea was that once the two organizing principles of nature and society were gone, one of the remaining solutions was to "compose" the common world. Bruno Latour, "Steps Toward the Writing of a Compositionist Manifesto," *New Literary History* 41 (2010): 471-490.

25 "A primary and impregnable relic [...] a forest for the future." Gilles Clément in Giuseppe Marinoni, "Parc Henri Matisse," *Lotus Navigator* 122 (2004): 113-117. For an overview of Clément's early landscape projects, see Alessandro Rocca, *Planetary Gardens: The Landscape Architecture of Gilles Clément* (Berlin: Walter de Gruyter, 2008).

26 Gilles Clément and Coloco, "Jardin du Tiers-Paysage," *Area* 152 (2017): 84-87.

27 Cedric Price Architects, memorandum 13th July 1990, Canadian Centre for Architecture (File 153: Duck Land, folder DR2004:0876).

28 Cedric Price, *Building Design 1071* (January 11, 1991): 18-21. Through his friend, the ornithologist Peter Scott, whom he met while working on the Snowdon aviary, Price knew that this was a stopping route for migrating birds. In a talk at the Architectural Association in 1990, he had already claimed: "Have Ducklands, never mind Docklands! Ducklands. In the middle of Hamburg. You know. A wonderful new link, a new lung! What a wonderful generosity of the city – hasn't cost a thing! Saved us a fortune!" In Samantha Hardingham, *Cedric Price Works 1952-2003, A Forward-Minded retrospective*, Volume 2 (London: Architectural Association, 2016), 432.

29 Hall Healy, "Korean Demilitarized Zone," 61.

30 In an explicit reference to American national parks, Yellowstone in particular, and the income they annually generate in terms of eco-tourism and related activities. Ibid. 70.

31 An attempt turned down one year later, due to the opposition of Pyongyang, which considered the proposal a violation of the armistice agreement. See the report from the 24th Session of the International Co-ordinating Council (ICC) of the Man and the Biosphere (MAB) Programme, UNESCO, July 2012 (SC-12/CONF.224/15).

32 The concept was first presented at the 2016 Venice Architecture Biennale, curated by Alejandro Aravena.

33 Ariane Lourie Harrison, ed., *Architectural Theories of the Environment: Posthuman Territory* (New York-Abingdon: Routledge, 2013), 304-314.

34 Matthew A. Taylor, *Universes without Us: Posthuman Cosmologies in American Literature* (Minneapolis: University of Minnesota Press, 2013).

35 In this regard, for instance, see also the extraordinary natural resurgence of the Chernobyl Exclusion Zone, and its adaptation, also in evolutionary

and biological terms, to the site's extreme conditions. T. G. Deryabina, et al., "Long-term census data reveal abundant wildlife populations at Chernobyl," *Current Biology* 25, no. 19 (2015): R824-R826.

36 Anna Lowenhaupt Tsing, *The Mushroom at the End of the World: On the Possibility of Life in Capitalist Ruins* (Princeton: Princeton University Press, 2015), 152. "This idiom has allowed me to consider how landscapes more generally are products of unintentional design, that is, the overlapping world-making activities of many agents, human and not human. The design is clear in the landscape's ecosystem. But none of the agents have planned this effect. Humans join others in making landscapes of unintentional design." Ibid.

Visual atlas (following spread)

1 Walton Hall, Charles Waterton, 1821
2 Hampstead Heath Act, 1871
3 *The Wild Garden*, William Robinson, 1883
4 Yosemite National Park, John Muir, 1890
5 *A Sand County Almanac*, Aldo Leopold, 1949
6 *Wilderness and the American Mind*, Roderick Frazier Nash, 1967
7 *A Tour of the Monument of Passaic, New Jersey*, Robert Smithson, 1967
8 Gas Work Park, Richard Haag, 1975
9 Duisburg Nord Landscape Park, Peter Latz, 1991
10 Ducklands Experiment, Cedric Price, 1991
11 Adlershof Nature Reserve, Gabriele Kiefer, 1996
12 Derborence Island, Gilles Clement, 2000
13 *Manifeste du Tiers paysage*, Gilles Clément, 2003
14 *Compositionist Manifesto*, Bruno Latour, 2010
15 *Milano Animal City*, Stefano Boeri and Michele Brunello, 2016
16 European Green Belt initiative, 2003
17 Natuurbrug Zanderij Crailoo, 2006
18 Norway's Bee Highway, Bybi, 2015
19 *Dreaming of Earth*, Jae-Eun Choi and Shigeru Ban, 2016
20 *Condensation Pavilion*, Olafur Eliasson, 2017
21 Bird's Monastery, Seung H-Sang, 2017
22 Wasit Natural Reserve Visitor Centre, X Architects, 2016
23 Shanghai Yangtze River Estuary Nature Preserve, Ennead Architects, 2019
24 The Whale, Dorte Mandrup, 2019

wild gardens

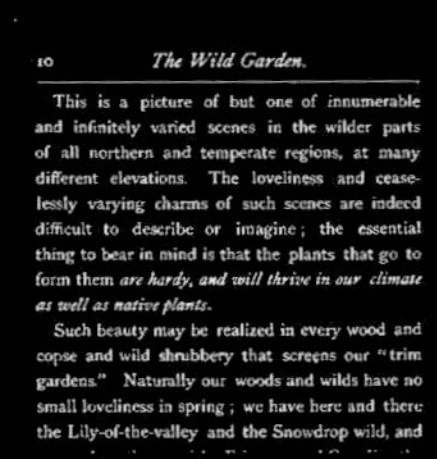

10 *The Wild Garden.*

This is a picture of but one of innumerable and infinitely varied scenes in the wilder parts of all northern and temperate regions, at many different elevations. The loveliness and ceaselessly varying charms of such scenes are indeed difficult to describe or imagine; the essential thing to bear in mind is that the plants that go to form them *are hardy, and will thrive in our climate as well as native plants.*

Such beauty may be realized in every wood and copse and wild shrubbery that screens our "trim gardens." Naturally our woods and wilds have no small loveliness in spring; we have here and there the Lily-of-the-valley and the Snowdrop wild, and

1 1A 2 2A 3 3A

wilderness culture

4 4A 5 5A 6 6A

post-industrial sublime

7 7A 8 8A 9 9A

urban reserves

10 10A 11 11A 12 12A

n e w c o h a b i t a t i o n s

An Attempt at a «Compositionist Manifesto»

Bruno Latour

13 13A

14 14A

15 15A

w i l d l i f e c o r r i d o r s

16 16A

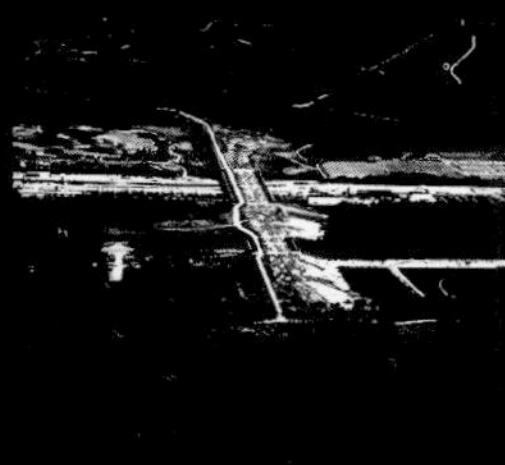

17 17A

18 18A

w i l d e r n e s s m o n u m e n t a l i z a t i o n

19 19A

20 20A

21 21A

h u m a n g r a f t i n g s

22 22A

23 23A

24 24A

A biotope

Junya Ishigami
Nasu, Tochigi, JP
37.059076, 139.978298
2013-2018

"Working with forest managers in Japan changed how I thought about the role of disturbance in forests. Deliberate disturbance to revitalize forests surprised me. Kato-san was not planting a garden. The forest he hoped for would have to grow itself. But he wanted to help it along by creating a certain kind of mess."

Anna Lowenhaupt Tsing, *The Mushroom at the End of the World: On the Possibility of Life in Capitalist Ruins* (Princeton: Princeton University Press, 2015), 152.

KramerAllrad

What is interesting about the term "disturbance," at least as Anna Tsing used it when describing interspecies relationships in Japanese forests, is that it not only reframes perfectly the range of human agency in the process of shaping landscapes, by both decentering and valorizing its role. But even that, from her perspective, it also represents a precise strategy of "collaborative survival," as she called it, in the spreading ruins of our traditional model of growth. Or better, a new way to imagine different forms of living together among different subjects, "by making world together," be they humans, pines, or even fungi. For the ability of doing that, in her view, "is not limited to humans," but belongs to "all organisms [that] make ecological living places."[1] Through projects that often overlap and leave room for other subjects, in what can be interpreted as a complex process, sometimes unconscious or unintentional, of multispecies world-making.[2] The same process also documented by other contemporary studies in this field, like those by Isabelle Stengers, Donna Haraway or Vinciane Despret,[3] who, in the same years, by looking at the world in terms of connections rather than divisions, have shown how it is co-inhabited and built by a myriad of entangled and "sympoietic" existences.[4] All this by mobilizing a truly extraordinary collection of stories of mutual survival and ecological animism, involving characters like bacteria, pigeons, or octopuses, which have not only called for studying humans as part of multispecies and symbiotic communities, but also asked to reconsider the world as designed "by" and "for" these communities. Thus challenging the traditional idea of "habitat" that consolidated over the years and, with it, one of the most crucial ecological concepts for describing the relationship between species and their environment.

In reality, it must be said that the consistency of the term to describe such complex relationships had already been brought into question in 1959 by Miklos Udvardy, one of the fathers of biogeography, but the story is even longer. At that time, in fact, the word habitat, which had been in use since the mid-eighteenth century, was such a commonly accepted term that few ecology textbooks, above the elementary level, bothered with a clear definition. And, by consequence, they used it in a very generic way, often as being a synonymous with others, like "niche" or "biotope," with no clear distinctions. Udvardy, on the contrary, traced back the history of their development to define the limits of a proper use.[5] Describing, on the one hand, a habitat as the sum of the physical and biotic resources of a locality that allows the survival and reproduction of a particular species. And a biotope, on the other, as the habitat not of a specific population, but of a whole biotic community.[6] A concept already introduced in 1908 by zoologist Friedrich Dahl, which in the second half of the twentieth century, with the increasing awareness of the ecosystem interconnectivity, would have taken more and more relevance.[7] By being distinguished not only for what concerned an expanded subject of reference, but also according to a specific scale, local instead of territorial, a high level of mutual connections among different biotopes, the human presence within them, and, consequently, a certain degree of artificialization that would often have been of great importance for their regeneration. All features that perfectly matched with Tsing's observations, and which would have been realized from scratch, in a Japanese forest and in the same period of the publication of her book, through the first conscious attempt of designing and building a biotope in all its complexity, not only as a habitat for a biotic community, but also as a form of art.

Everything began in 2013, in a wooded and verdant area at the foot of Mount Nasu, in Tochigi, a prefecture north of Tokyo, where a local artist residence surrounded by nature, significantly named Art Biotop, was planning an expansion. The initial idea was in fact to provide the resort with a shared space in which visitors could have planted crops, to complement the services and courses in pottery, glass making, and other artistic activities already offered, with another way of exploring one own creativity in relation with nature.[8] By growing something, in other words, that could become part of the existing landscape and live on its own accordingly. All this thanks to the transfor-

A hybrid model. Between a farm and a *tsubo-niwa*

mation of a former paddy field close to the residence, which had earlier been a forest overgrown with moss, into a garden that could work as a new form of rental farm. A task that fell, quite naturally, to the young architect Junya Ishigami, who, despite his age, had already shown an extraordinary ability to treat with the same finesse the materials of landscape and those of architecture. Not only for his considering the two as part of a unique set of tools for making worlds, but also because of his effortless mastery in attracting them onto a scale that had always been commensurable with human gestures, perceptions, and sensations. As he had previously done, for instance, when he had turned a garden into a pavilion, made a building in the shape of a forest, or brought nature inside a house, as if it were part of the furniture.[9] But also when he had written marvelous books in the language of clouds, woods, and rain, to explain his own vision of architecture.[10] The same spirit with which he faced the commission to design the new farm garden, through an unprecedented conceptualization of its agricultural role.

The intention of the artist residence to bring patrons in direct contact with nature, in fact, partially clashed with the fact that, traditionally, since the introduction of intensive agriculture, the landscape created by farming activities had been much more artificial than that of any city in the world. As the efficiency required to increase crop yields had entailed a form of layout standardization, determined by the operating space reserved for machines, which had been so far a priority for farmers.[11] Ishigami, by contrast, since the beginning of his practice, had promoted an architecture of "freeness" from any predetermined function, format, and scale of design, which could respond to an existing reality that he felt "irregular, unstable, uncertain, and continue to diversify rapidly an excessively."[12] For this reason, given also the relative smallness of the available area and the agricultural diversity expected, instead of developing a plan dictated by certain conditions of production, he focused on a specific spatial setting, the Japanese *tsubo-niwa* courtyard garden, which incorporated in an organic and synthetic shape all the features he was looking for. And he worked on the adaptation of this domestic model by multiplying it, in a combination of single and diverse patches, which would have covered the whole extension of the field, through "a geometric pattern conceived as a complicated arrangement of curvatures, like the repetition of puzzle pieces."[13] Each one characterized not only by a different variety of plants, but also by the excavation of a small and shallow water pond, roughly circular, which had to be fed, at continuously varying rates, by water drawn from the existing sluice gate, and connected to the others through the existing irrigation system. Something that, in his view, would have transformed the space of the farm garden into "a landscape [...] in a state of ever-changing flux, like a kaleidoscope."[14]

Soon, however, things became even more complex in their development, as the plan for realizing also a restaurant, a library, a health center, and fifteen cottages entered the scene. The foreseen site of these new structures in fact was a dense forest near the paddy field, where many trees would have been cut down owing to the construction. And since the total area of the woodland and the meadows were approximately the same, Ishigami began to think to relocate the entire population of trees to the adjacent field, in order not only to save them, but also to create a new kind of living landscape, derived by the superimpositions of different layers. Thus, he started listing an accurate catalogue of all the three hundred trees of the small forest, including their species, their size, and their possible interactions, to plan a second digging campaign, comprising an impressive series of deep pits to lodge the already mature plants among the one hundred and sixty already designed ponds.[15] And then, by means of excavators, he moved them all, one by one, in a layout studied to trigger unexpected biological and aesthetic interactions, through a close density and a variety that would have never been traceable in nature. Bringing together, for example, species like oaks and beech trees, which could have not theoretically coexisted in such a proximity with water, by applying a waterproofing system in the ponds in order to create the conditions for new relationships of interdependence. And thus turning what was imagined as a productive facility into "a dream-like landscape" of contemplation,[16] through the artificial re-composition of the natural elements that used to exist there, like trees, moss, stones, water, and soil, in an entirely new way.

New in terms of arrangement, obviously, yet not entirely for what concerned the design process. In that Ishigami's attempt to create a new environment relied on the idea that landscape could be considered as a piece of architecture, which had been underlying Japanese gardening for ages, at least since the first diffusion of Tachibana no Toshitsuna's *Sakuteiki*, in the late eleventh century.[17] That which intended gardens not as an interpretation of architectural typologies realized by natural means, as in many coeval models, but, on the contrary, as the reconstruction, by design, of a miniature and idealized view of the natural world.[18] The same that filtered in Europe through Fischer von Erlach's drawings, to inform a great part of French and British landscape architecture from the late eighteenth and early nineteenth century, although only in picturesque terms.[19] Without deciphering, in other words, the incredible vocabulary of signs and meanings that the Japanese art of gardening refined over time, and which Ishigami renewed and brought to its extreme limits and respectful synthesis, as probably only Mirei Shigemori had done before.[20] All this while also showing both the same bravery in manipulating topographies with which the "landscape urbanists" from the nineties had updated the approach to nature of the avant-garde projects by Emilio Ambasz, Hans Hollein, or Raimund Abraham, among the others, and the poetic imagination of artists like Robert Smithson and Eduardo Chillida in working with the same material.[21] Not to mention his intimate awareness of being a "planetary gardener" who was not only dealing with spaces, objects, and shapes, but also with ecological niches, living organisms, and interspecies relationships, which made his operation of "landforming" also a real action of "terraforming."[22]

0 3.55 7.10 14.20 21.30m

stepping stone
discrete concrete
N° P4- Lv 532.90
stepping stone
foundation stone
levelling concrete
root ball
A93 - h. 13m - ø 270mm - p 990mm
field soil covering
root ball
N81 - h. 16m - ø 260mm - p 980mm
rubber band
N° P99- Lv 532.60
filed soil covering
bentonite waterproofing shhet
communication pipe
siphon type ø 100mm
trickle pipe ø 100mm
N° P100- Lv 532.65
filed soil covering
bentonite waterproofing shhet
N82 - h. 16m - ø 260mm - p 980mm
A32 - h. 14m - ø 300mm - p 1100mm
improved soil
N° P106 - Lv 532.80
assorted moss
drainage pipe
(overflow wastewater)
N° P106 - Lv 532.80
filed soil covering
bentonite waterproofing shhet
0
0.80
1.60
3.20
4.80m

An artificial laboratory. From a rice field to a water garden

"It is clear that we cannot satisfy the needs of human activity in the coming era by explicitly distinguishing between nature and artifice."

Junya Ishigami

Partly a rice field and partly a forest, Ishigami's water garden in fact questions the boundaries between architecture, landscape design, art, and ecology.[23] By being at once a highly artificial environment, finely fashioned by means of invasive processes and technological artefacts, and an undisputable natural and living ecosystem, growing over time according to its own inherent dynamics. Those of a collection of one hundred and sixty different biotopes, both autonomous and interconnected, representing as many worlds for a myriad of possible biotic communities, emerging from the inedited conditions there established. As though ponds were thought as incubators of a living laboratory for a new form of nature to develop, as an extension of the existing one. Through a design approach that not only showed no hesitations about its formative role in complying with such a delicate task, but which was also materialized in a spatial composition that perfectly reflected this innovative vision of nature and human "disturbance." For even though it can recall a traditional stroll garden,[24] Ishigami's project was not configured as a sequence of carefully designed scenes to be discovered by walking along a predetermined path.[25] On the contrary, despite the huge excavations involved, it was drawn, as an essentially bidimensional surface in which everything had to be visible at a first sight. As if the position of the spectator was no longer at the center of the environmental construction, but belonged to a greater whole that followed different and more complex logics. And nature, instead of being an enchanting mystery to be unveiled through immersion, was a community of living organisms, to be experienced and contemplated as a real ecosystem.

Ishigami's idea of creating a new form of nature, in other words, can be seen both as an attempt of preservation and an experimental kind of grafting, by which he tried to improve and condense variety and diversity into one place, to enhance its affordance for spontaneous forms of world-making. All this, however, while using the resources and tools of architecture, although released from traditional normative categories.[26] And

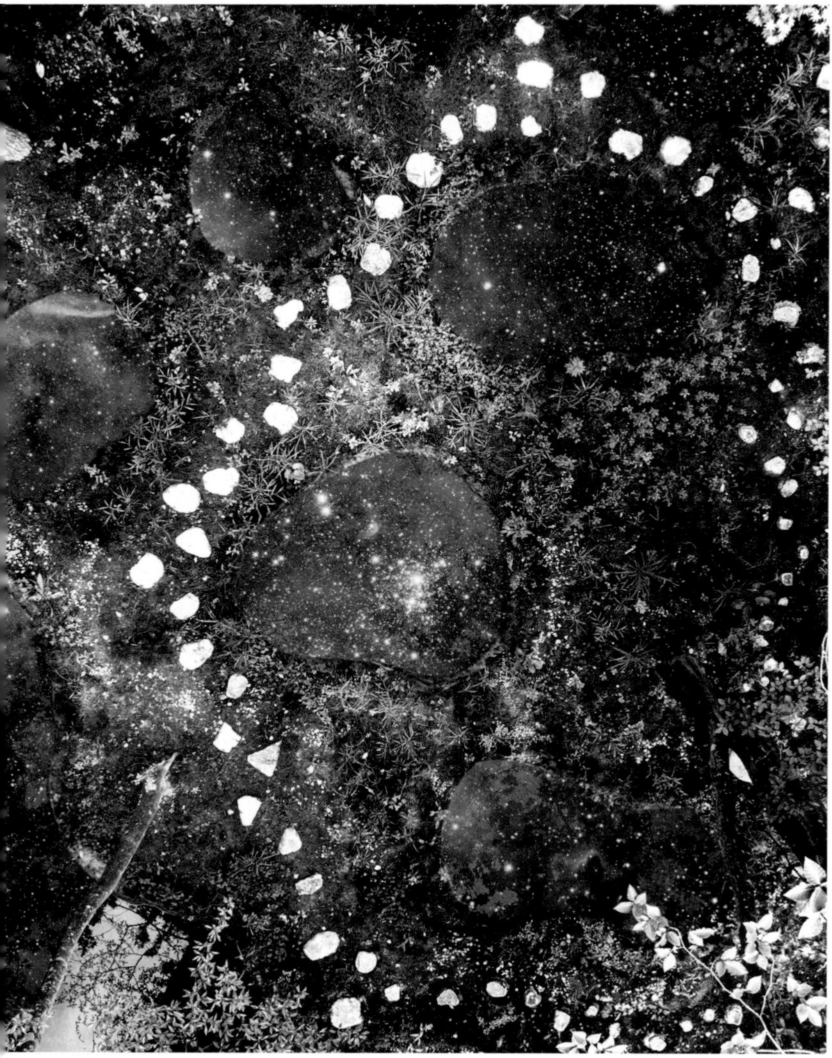

A living incubator. Ishigami's Art Biotop

"We architects today must comprehend architecture on a planetary scale."

Junya Ishigami

working on a composition of different natural elements, temporal layers, and environmental conditions, neither mimetic nor idealized, but reduced to an essential vocabulary, and interpreted through an extremely refined exercise of calligraphy. It is not surprising, therefore, that much of its remarkable resonance, instead of relying on its ecological depth, is due to its unique spatial features and figurative power, which indeed know few equals. For the result of this process is an extraordinary place pervaded by a subtle sense of "magical realism," at once peaceful and uncanny, unfolding along a sinuous maze of white pebble stones across a sea of downy moss. One dotted with the mirroring surface of an incredibly dense archipelago of ponds, and pierced by the black thin trunks of an ordered mass of trees. A vast landscape in the limited space of a small field, designed as a sort of "cartographic ground,"[27] in which planetary relations can be brought within human reach. Or better, in an almost domestic form of possible interaction with nature, freed from any potential symbolism and predetermined value, and turned into a new source of poetic expression. A feature that, ultimately, has made Ishigami's project quite a unique example on approaching the theme, on such many diverse and profound levels of meaning.

In this regard, however, it must be said that its uniqueness can also represent a certain limit to its exemplariness. It is not surprising, therefore, that current approaches to building possible biotopes consider very different forms of living laboratories as a source of reference, as well as different kinds of grafting to activate them. Like that initiated in 2018 in Berlin, by Benjamin Foerster-Baldenius and Florian Stirnemann of Raumlabor Architects, for example, as a continuation on their previous educational experiments, though implemented in a very dissimilar place. The story, in this case, is in fact that of a nineteenth century retention basin, which had been used to store rainwater drawn from the runways of the Tempelhof Airport, before it was definitively transformed into a public park in 2010. A large, contaminated concrete pool, immersed in a thick and

Third landscapes. Raumlabor's Floating University

wild wood, whose area had been restricted for over sixty years, leaving space, in its muddy waters, for a new biotic community to emerge, through a rich variety of plants, insects, amphibians, and birds. A fact that persuaded the architects, once granted with the funds from the German Federal Cultural Foundation, as part of the Bauhaus centenary celebrations, to think about its reactivation in quite a peculiar way. Not through its reform into a garden, in other words, or as a piece of the public park, but by building a temporary laboratory for collective, experimental learning, and the formation of trans-disciplinary networks. To study what had happened there and, as a consequence, to answer more suitably to some urgent questions about contemporary cities, involving themes like global warming, the shortage of resources, and ecologically aware modes of living. All this in the strange shape of an ephemeral and self-built offshore structure, named Floating University, which would have occupied the center of the basin for six months, with a free composition of scaffolding volumes and floating platforms with inflatable rooftops. In order to "broaden the often-rigid or exclusionary nature of education"[28] to comprise both a new public and a totally different and more inclusive concept of "urban" environment.

To this purpose, Raumlabor called students and their teachers from Berlin, Europe and elsewhere, to collaborate on building the campus, through a model that was "part-pirate ship and part-Princeton, part-Archigram and part-Burning Man."[29] Provided, for instance, with adaptable learning spaces, public workshops, and a one hundred seat auditorium, with a separate floating floor. But also with a bar, a modular kitchen, and a laboratory tower for experimental water filtration systems, designed by artist in residence Katherine Bell, drawing the ditch water through a series of interconnected bathtubs "containing biological filters, such as sand-biofilm, mushroom mycelium, and zebra mussels."[30] All spaces that, over the whole period from April to September, attracted students and scientists from more than twenty international universities, attending lectures, seminars, hot tub talks, concerts, and performances, along with local experts, architects, and various artists. To investigate and build, in a participated way, new possibilities of being together and "becoming-with," which could extend the idea of community to a larger subject of reference. And through a structure whose lightness, openness, and ephemerality represented one of the most interesting interpretations of how humans can join, in a conscious and respectful way, an already existing biotic community, without renouncing their transformative ability. By first observing a certain place, and then discussing, testing, and eventually reformulating the possibilities of dwelling, without a preconceived idea in mind, but considering the fact that a grafting, sometimes, can also be unfruitful.

That said, however, it must be recognized that in Ishigami's project there is even more than this, at least from a design point of view. Not only owing to the fact that it suggests a possible method to actually build a biotope, rather than simply inhabiting it, but also because it challenges the contemporary architectural theory that Raumlabor instead supports. And precisely the theory emphasizing an eco-scientific approach on systems and metabolisms, and questioning the idea of architecture as a historically constituted symbolic system. For Ishigami's water garden, on the contrary, as any other reconstructive reading of nature, "complicates the claim that contemporary ecological, bio-mimetic, and geo-mimetic work operates in a post-representational regime."[31] By offering an architectural interpretation that, while taking into account all the metabolic processes and exchanges involved, de-emphasizes physical interrelations, to focus on a specific imagery and its symbolic power. And thus shows the project, in its poetic expression, not only as a set of instructions to live differently from common standards, but mainly as a true and realizable "promise of happiness." A fact that is even more important than its actual realization, from a political point of view. Both to provide a historically grounded framework for future explorations of nature in architecture and, more importantly, to promote a posthuman vision of the world that could be socially accepted.

Notes

1 Anna Lowenhaupt Tsing, *The Mushroom at the End of the World: On the Possibility of Life in Capitalist Ruins* (Princeton: Princeton University Press, 2015), 22.

2 "Pines, with their associated fungal partners, often flourish in landscapes burned by humans; pines and fungi work together to take advantage of bright open spaces and exposed mineral soils. Humans, pines, and fungi make living arrangements simultaneously for themselves and for others: multispecies worlds." Ibid.

3 In this regard, as an example, see respectively Isabelle Stengers, *Au temps des catastrophes: Résister à la barbarie qui vient* (Paris: Editions La Découverte, 2009); Donna J. Haraway, *Staying with the Trouble: Making Kin in the Chthulucene* (Durham-London: Duke University Press, 2016); and Vinciane Despret, *What Would Animals Say if We Asked the Right Questions?* (Minneapolis: University of Minnesota Press, 2016).

4 "Sympoiesis is a simple word; it means 'making-with.' Nothing makes itself; nothing is really autopoietic or self-organizing. [...] Sympoiesis is a word proper to complex, dynamic, responsive, situated, historical systems. It is a word for worlding-with, in company." Haraway, *Staying with the Trouble*, 58.

5 Miklos F. D. Udvardy, "Notes on the Ecological Concepts of Habitat, Biotope and Niche," *Ecology* 40, no. 4 (1959): 725-728.

6 "In other words, the species has a habitat but it does not have a biotope. The biotope harbours instead, a biotic community." Ibid, 726.

7 For a complete overview about the topic, see Georg Toepfer, "Biotop," in *Historisches Wörterbuch der Biologie* (Berlin-Heidelberg: Springer Verlag, 2011), 305-319.

8 Junya Ishigami, *El Croquis* 182 (2015): 256-261.

9 The reference is respectively to the projects for the Japan Pavilion at 11th Venice Biennale (2008), the KAIT Workshop in Kanagawa (2004-2008), and the House with Plants in Tokyo (2010-2012). Ibid., 178-241.

10 Junya Ishigami, *Another Scale of Architecture* (Kyoto: Seigensha Art Publishing, 2010).

11 The literature in this regard is of course huge. For the most recent overview of the topic, see AMO/Rem Koolhaas, *Countryside: A Report* (Köln: Taschen, 2020).

12 Junya Ishigami, *El Croquis*, 157.

13 Ibid., 259.

14 Ibid.

15 For a complete background, see Id., "Artificial Landscape Poetry," *Domus* 1036 (2019): 664-673; and Matteo Zambelli, "Artificial Natures," *Abitare* 580 (2018): 40-51. Given the novelty of the project, however, critical readings in this regard are still lacking.

16 Junya Ishigami, *El Croquis*, 259.

17 *Sakuteiki* (Records of Garden Making) is the oldest published Japanese text on gardening and probably the oldest garden planning one in the world. Jiro Takei and Marc P. Keane, *Sakuteiki Visions of the Japanese Garden: A Modern Translation of Japan's Gardening Classic* (Boston: Tuttle Publishing, 2001).

18 Tashiro Inaji, *The Garden as Architecture: Form and Spirit in the Gardens of Japan, China, and Korea* (Tokyo-New York-London: Kodansha International, 1998).

19 Johann Bernhard Fischer von Erlach, *Entwurff Einer Historischen Architectur* (Leipzig, 1725).

20 Christian Tschumi, *Mirei Shigemori, Rebel in the Garden: Modern Japanese Landscape Architecture* (Basel-Boston-Berlin: Birkhäuser, 2007).

21 For an overview, see Stan Allen and Marc McQuade, eds., *Landform Building: Architecture's New Terrain* (Zürich: Lars Müller, 2011).

22 As Ishigami said, during his acceptance speech of the Obel Award 2019, assigned to his project, "the effects of human activities are beyond the scale of cities and are getting so vast that they are affecting the natural environments of the entire globe. I therefore believe that we architects today must comprehend architecture on a planetary scale, or rather on a natural scale, in contrast to the architects of yesterday who comprehended architecture on a city scale." For a comparison, see also the already mentioned text by Gilles Clément, *Thomas et le Voyageur* (Paris: Albin Michel, 1997).

23 "It is no longer possible for us to consider architecture in ways that distinguish between the natural and the artificial environment. [...] It is clear that we cannot satisfy the needs of human activity in the coming era by explicitly distinguishing between nature and artifice." Junya Ishigami, *El Croquis*, 163.

24 The term stroll garden, or *kaiyushiki-teien*, emerged during the Tokugawa regime (1603-1868) and its strict social hierarchy, to indicate the spacious gardens built on the private properties of feudal lords. Tashiro Inaji, *The Garden as Architecture*, 74.

25 The word *miegakure* (hide-and-reveal), one of the first principles of Japanese stroll gardens, refers to a number of kinetic and multifaceted compositional techniques created in accord with human motion and sense of discovery. "The term was first used in regard to the techniques employed in the small, rustic walkways, known as *roji*, that lead to teahouses." Ibid, 61.

26 "The image of architecture as shelter is unsuited to the new environment that is gradually been conceived. Architecture should not be regarded as shelter but rather as the environment that surrounds us. If we can do this, architecture will cease to be a device that separates us as human beings from the existing environment." Junya Ishigami, *El Croquis*, 165.

27 Jil Desimini, Charles Waldheim, and Mohsen Mostafavi, *Cartographic Grounds: Projecting the Landscape Imaginary* (New York: Princeton Architectural Press, 2016).

28 George Kafka, "What Is a School if not a Promise?," in *Archifutures. Volume 5: Apocalypse. A Field Guide to Surviving the Future of Architecture*, eds. George Kafka, Sophie Lovell, and Fiona Shipwright (Barcelona: dpr-barcelona, 2018), 100.

29 Ibid.

30 Ibid., 104.

31 David Gissen, "The Architectural Reconstruction of Nature," in *Landform Building: Architecture's New Terrain*, eds. Stan Allen and Marc McQuade (Zürich: Lars Müller, 2011), 456.

Visual atlas (following spread)

1 *Sakuteiki*, Tachibana no Toshitsuna, 11th century
2 *Entwurff Einer Historischen Architectur*, Johann Bernhard Fischer von Erlach, 1725
3 Gardens at Tôfuku-ji's main hall, Mirei Shigemori, 1939
4 Universal City, Raimund Abraham, 1966
5 Museum im Mönchsberg, Hans Hollein, 1989
6 *Montaña Tindaya*, Eduardo Chillida, 1993
7 San Antonio Botanical Garden, Emilio Ambasz, 1982
8 The Garden of Cosmic Speculation, Charles Jencks, 1989
9 Barcelona Botanical Garden, Carlos Ferrater, 1999
10 Engineered Biotopes, Anthi Grapsa and Konstantinos Chalaris, 2010
11 Oyster-tecture, Scape Studio, 2011
12 WTP campus, 3deluxe, 2021
13 The Soul of Nørrebro, SLA - Stig L. Andersson, 2016
14 BUGA Heilbronn 2019, Sinai, 2019
15 Lakeside Garden, Ramboll Studio Dreiseitl, 2019
16 Booster, SHJWORKS and Silas Inoue, 2017
17 Biotope, SHJWORKS, 2018
18 Dutch pavilion at EXPO 2020, V8 Architects, 2021
19 Vac-Library, Farming Architects, 2018
20 Return of the Hill, Atelier Scale, 2019
21 The Biotope, Henning Larsen, 2020
22 Observatory in the Scheelhoek Nature Reserve, RAU Architects and RO&AD Architecten, 2019
23 Denmark's NATURKRAFT, Thøgersen & Stouby and SLA, 2020

nature reconstructed

1 1A

2 2A

3 3A

excavated architecture

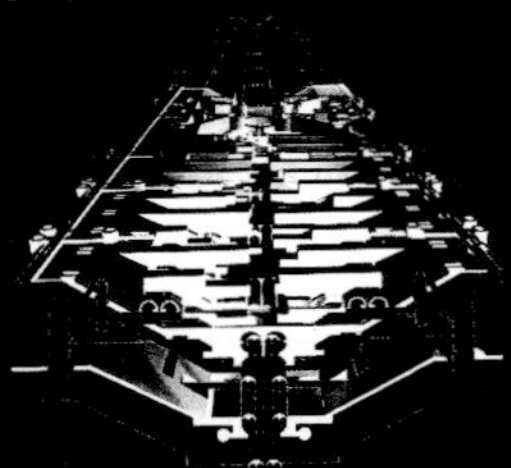

4 4A

5 5A

6 6A

landform gardening

7 7A

8 8A

9 9A

urban biotopes

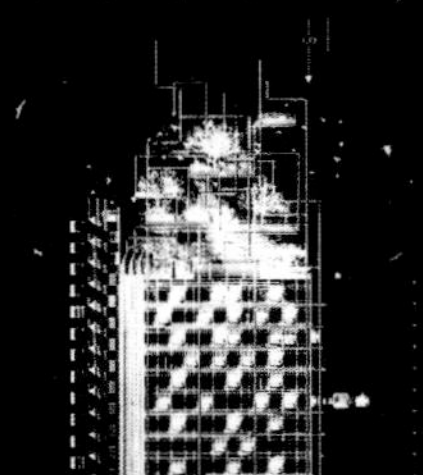

10 10A

11 11A

12 12A

new parks

13 13A

14 14A

15 15A

biophilic design

16 16A

17 17A

18 18A

collaborative buildings

19 19A

20 20A

21 21A

human graftings

22 22A

23 23A

A catalogue of resonance chambers

"Je voudrais pas mourir
Sans qu'on ait inventé
[...]
Tant de trucs ...
Qui dorment dans les crânes
Des géniaux ingénieurs
Des jardiniers joviaux
Des soucieux socialistes
Des urbains urbanistes
Et des pensifs penseurs."

Boris Vian, *Je voudrais pas crever* (Paris: J.J. Pauvert, 1962), 7-14.

At the end of the tour, when closing the catalogue, things can still look a bit confused. Because, even at this point, one may legitimately question whether the archetypes presented here can represent working solutions for building real posthuman habitats. But that question would be essentially misleading since, as Isabelle Stengers wrote in 2015, the present historical moment is characterized by the impossibility of finding solutions for what she named the "intrusion of Gaia."[1] The myth of progress has in fact been debunked, and whereas existing social practices and imaginaries no longer produce the outcomes they once did, no new ones have been created yet. At the same time, however, "progress ... continues to impose itself as the only conceivable horizon,"[2] as institutional solutions keep offering a choice between two bad alternatives. That, for instance, between doing nothing about climate change or geo-engineering the climate. Or again, that between ignoring deforestation or trading forests as commodities in order to maintain their value. Stengers, by contrast, instead of solutions, proposed to imagine a new form of "objectors" to escape the logic of growth and the consequential exploitation of labor and nature, to create "a life [...] that explores connections with new powers of acting, feeling, imagining, and thinking."[3] All this, by means of political experimentations that, in her view, must not happen through direct production, but through the "production of repercussions." Or better, through building "resonance chambers" that support the struggle to break free from the dominant narratives, by letting those experiments be shared, so that "what happens to one group makes others think and act." For the problem is not to invent new solutions, but to build consensus upon already practicable different ways of living.[4]

This is the most relevant thing that architectural design can do, if meant as a critical tool, when dealing with the emergence of posthuman condition. Not simply building working habitats for "other" subjects, but rather creating resonance chambers that challenge, step by step, the centrality of human position in the present and future pictures of the planet. Because, historically, architecture's task has been not only that of making spaces, but mainly giving them a meaning, through a shape that could be conceptualized. And good design, besides making things work, has always had the ability of turning these things, however new or unconventional, into parts of a formal discourse that could enter and have a weight in the ongoing cultural and political debate. This is why, even in this moment, within the limits of a post-representational regime, looking at architecture and its symbolic system is still crucial. For architecture can be capable of de-naturalizing the anthropocentric perspective of the world, by proposing visions of alternative futures, radical yet transmissible. In that architects, but also landscape, and industrial designers, can offer not only sets of instructions to live differently, but also stories, interpretations, and expectations on how to be in the world differently as humans, both functionally and symbolically. And in so doing they can challenge the current model of development in ways that could be increasingly culturally perceived. By showing how, for instance, a house may be a means to adapt oneself to the natural order rather than a tool to transform it. Or how a biotope, just to consider the two extremes of the book, besides being a scientific concept, may also represent the most beautiful way of relating to landscape that one may imagine.

The aim, in other words, when looking for resonance chambers that support a posthuman vision of the world, is not the definition of new architectural typologies to serve unwonted needs. On the contrary, it is to question the traditional typological catalog to which the project of dwelling is usually reduced, according to the reconsideration of the subjectivity at its center. By thinking, for instance, at architecture in terms of interconnection rather than division, of openness rather than segregation, and of indeterminacy instead of specialization. But even by looking at the project of dwelling as a different form of extended cohabitation or collaborative survival, involving diverse and heterogeneous subjects. Which is precisely the reason why this catalogue, instead of dealing with a given type of space or a particular dimension, focuses on a specific topological condition,[5] which is that of its affordance, concrete or symbolic, to expanded forms of inhabitability. Because building a posthuman habitat, as any other "chamber," means not only to make space for some sort of function, but also to define the relationship between spaces and inhabitants that are capable of creating a qualitative and relational condition, beyond any kind of typological or scalar distinction.[6] And then to turn these relationships into characterizing features of a design, aimed at creating a novel understanding of conventional categories, through a peculiar operative approach that, despite being liable to very different interpretations, shows an underlying recurring principle. Whether it refers to infrastructures thought as communities of living things, or to factories drawn as hybrid homeostatic systems.

Across the pages, the years, and the territories, in fact, the design theories produced in this catalogue are among the most diverse that one could encounter, ranging from expressive functionalism, mutualism, and responsivity on the one hand, to redundancy, vagueness, and disjunction on the other. Yet, each of them seems to respond, in some way, to the same approach briefly sketched by Henry David Thoreau, going "from within" outwards, in a defining rather than confining process of formalization. The approach emerging from a logical system of organization built on the features, the actions and the relationships of its inhabitants, which is inherent the very idea of "creative user" and the search for personal inhabitability.[7] With the only difference that, in these cases, the inhabitants are not individuals, but heterogeneous communities, not always conscious or intentional, whose dynamics are even harder to be determined. For this reason, in most of these projects, whereas design emerges from certain practices and relationships, it often develops to make space for new and unpredicted ones, by focusing more on the potential effects of the intervention than on the causes that determined it. More on the use and interpretation of a space, in other words, than on its function and shape. Within a field that, obviously, remains that of the project, but a project meant as a proposal rather than predetermination. And through an operational attitude towards habitability which, thanks to its topological nature, is not limited to a single type, but can bridge landscapes of very different nature, spanning from the scale of a continent to a transistor.

In the end, in summary, the resonance of these architectures does not simply rely on their being a medium for some sort of conceptual content. On the contrary, it mainly depends on their capacity of representing complex and dynamic devices, meant to generate unexpected relationships and unprecedented tensions. In space and with space. All this thanks to some extraordinary "place-makers," be they professional or accidental practitioners, who have dismantled, willingly or not, the historically constituted vocabulary of architecture, to recompose it into an unconventional system of construction and expression. One speaking the language of wires and clouds, metabolic exchanges and arcadian imageries, to reflect the programmatic openness and the sense of freeness that have made room for surprising stories of cohabitation among diverse species and technologies. By invariably working on their interconnection rather than on their specificity, and sometimes renouncing the final responsibility of the formalization process in favor of other forms of agency. As though the affirmative idea of radical inclusion that is implicit in a posthuman vision of the world could affect any facet of the design process. And in so doing, besides opening unknown paths to future inhabited landscapes, it could prefigure a different way of thinking architecture to support that vision and that way of dwelling.

Notes

1 Isabelle Stengers, *In Catastrophic Times: Resisting the Coming Barbarism* (Lüneburg: Open Humanities Press, 2015), 41. The intrusion of Gaia, for Stengers, marks the end of any possibility of ignoring the damage done to the planet's biosphere, as well as the end of progress as a guiding myth of contemporary society. It is something very similar to what Michel Serres exemplified with Francisco Goya's painting mentioned in the first chapter. Michel Serres, *Le Contrat naturel* (Paris: Flammarion, 1992).

2 Isabelle Stengers, *In Catastrophic Times*, 20.

3 Ibid., 24.

4 "It is not a question of making things better, but of experimenting [...]. However precarious or small it might be each achievement matters. None will suffice to appease Gaia, but all will contribute to responding to the trials that are coming." Ibid., 152-153.

5 Unlike typology, the term topology refers to one of the most important branches of modern mathematics, the motivating insight behind which is that some geometric problems depend not on the exact shape of the objects involved, but rather on the way in which they are connected. For a complete discussion, see John L. Kelley, *General Topology* (Berlin: Springer, 1975). About its application in architecture, see Giuseppa Di Cristina, "The Topological Tendency in Architecture," in *Architecture and Science*, ed. Giuseppa Di Cristina (New York: Wiley, 2001), 7-13.

6 Jacopo Leveratto, *From Within: Between Interior Architecture and Design* (Siracusa: LetteraVentidue, 2020).

7 Jonathan Hill, *Actions of Architecture: Architects and Creative Users* (London-New York: Routledge, 2003.

Bibliography

- Aben, Rob, and Saskia de Wit. *The Enclosed Garden: History and Development of the Hortus Conclusus and its Reintroduction into the Present-day Urban Landscape*. Rotterdam: 010 Publisher, 1999.
- Adams, Ansel. *This is the American Earth*. San Francisco: Sierra Club, 1960.
- Adorno, Theodor W. *Minima Moralia: Reflections on a Damaged Life*. Translated by E. F. N. Jephcott. London-New York: Verso, 2005.
- Agamben, Giorgio. *The Open: Man and Animal*. Stanford: Stanford University Press, 2004.
- Alberti, Leon Battista. *Della Architettura: Libri Dieci*. Translated by Cosimo Bartoli. Milan, 1833.
- Allen, John. *Biosphere 2: The Human Experiment*. New York: Penguin Books, 1991.
- Allen, John. *Me and the Biospheres: A Memoir by the Inventor of Biosphere 2*. Santa Fe: Synergetic Press, 2009.
- Allen, Stan, and Marc McQuade, eds. *Landform Building: Architecture's New Terrain*. Zürich: Lars Müller, 2011.
- Althusser, Louis. *Pour Marx*. Paris: Maspero, 1965.
- Ambasz, Emilio. *Italy: The New Domestic Landscape*. New York: The Museum of Modern Art, 1972.
- AMO, and Rem Koolhaas. *Countryside: A Report*. Köln: Taschen, 2020.
- Antonelli, Paola, and Ala Tannir, eds. *Broken Nature: Design Takes on Human Survival*. Milan: Electa, 2019.
- Arnheim, Rudolf. *The Dynamics of Architectural Form*. Berkeley: University of California Press, 1977.
- Bachelard, Gaston. *La poétique de l'espace*. Paris: Presses Universitaires de France, 1957.
- Banham, Reyner. "A Home Is Not a House." *Art in America* 2 (1965): 58-77.
- Banham, Reyner. "Aviary, London Zoological Gardens." *The Architectural Review* 138 (1965): 186.
- Banham, Reyner. *The Architecture of the Well-Tempered Environment*. London: The Architectural Press, 1969.
- Banham, Reyner. *Buffalo Architecture: A Guide*. Cambridge MA: The MIT Press, 1981.
- Banham, Reyner. "Art and Necessity: Inmos and the Persistence of Functionalism." *The Architectural Review* 172, no. 1030 (1982): 34-38.
- Baratay, Eric, and Elisabeth Hardouin-Fugier. *Zoo: A History of Zoological Gardens in the West*. London: Reaktion Books, 2002.
- Barksdale, Maynard W. "Thoreau's House at Walden." *The Art Bulletin* 81, no. 2 (1999): 303-325.
- Barton, Gregory A. *Empire Forestry and the Origins of Environmentalism*. Cambridge: Cambridge University Press, 2004.
- Bentham, Jeremy. *An Introduction to the Principles of Morals and Legislation*. London, 1780.
- Berrahmouni, Nora, Pedro Regato, and Marc Parfondry. *Global Guidelines for the Restoration of Degraded Forests and Landscapes in Drylands: Building Resilience and Benefiting Livelihoods*. Rome: FAO, 2015.
- Billings, Linda. "Ideology, Advocacy, and Space Flight: Evolution of a Cultural Narrative." In *Societal Impacts of Space Flight*, edited by Steven J. Dick and Roger D. Launius, 483-499. Washington DC: NASA, 2007.

- Blondel, Jacques-François. "Architecture." In *Encyclopédie, ou Dictionnaire raisonné des sciences, des arts et des métiers*, vol. 1, edited by Denis Diderot and Jean Le Rond d'Alembert, 617. Paris, 1751.
- Bogdanov, Aleksandr. *Tektologiya: Vseobschaya Organizatsionnaya Nauka*. Berlin-Petrograd-Moscow, 1922.
- Bogdanov, Aleksandr. *Red Star: The First Bolshevik Utopia*. Edited by Loren Graham and Richard Stites. Bloomington: Indiana University Press, 1984.
- Borch, Christian, ed. *Architectural Atmospheres: On the Experience and Politics of Architecture*. Basel: Birkhäuser, 2014.
- Borges, Jorge Luis. "The Analytical Language of John Wilkins." In *Other inquisitions 1937-1952*. Translated by Ruth L. C. Simms, 101-105. Austin-London: University of Texas Press, 1964.
- Braidotti, Rosi. *The Posthuman*. Cambridge: Polity, 2013.
- Braidotti, Rosi, and Maria Hlavajova, eds. *Posthuman Glossary*. London: Bloomsbury, 2018.
- Brain, Stephen. "The Great Stalin Plan for the Transformation of Nature." *Environmental History* 15, no. 4 (2010): 670-700.
- Brand, Stewart. *Whole Earth Catalog*. Santa Cruz, 1968.
- Broquet, Patrick, and Evelyne Malnic. *Folies de jardin: Art et architecture des fabriques de jardin du XVIIIe siècle à nos jours*. Paris: Éditions du Chêne, 1996.
- Brown, John Croumbie. *French Forest Ordinance of 1669 with Historical Sketch of Previous Treatment of Forests in France*. Edinburgh: Oliver and Boyd, 1883.
- Buckminster Fuller, Richard. "Tensegrity." *Portfolio and Art News Annual*, no.4 (1961).
- Buckminster Fuller, Richard. *Operating Manual for Spaceship Earth*. New York: Simon & Schuster, 1969.
- Buckminster Fuller, Richard. *Your Private Sky: Discourse*. New York: Springer, 2001.
- Buell, Lawrence. *The Environmental Imagination: Thoreau Nature Writing and the Formation of American Culture*. Cambridge MA: Harvard University Press, 1995.
- Butler, Judith. *Gender Trouble: Feminism and the Subversion of Identity*. New York: Routledge, 1990.
- Calvino, Italo. *Il barone rampante*. Turin: Einaudi, 1957.
- Carboni, Milco, and Barbara Radice, eds. *Ettore Sottsass, Metafore*. Milan: Skira, 2002.
- Carson, Rachel. *Silent Spring*. Boston: Houghton Mifflin, 1962.
- Chambers, William. *A Treatise on Civil Architecture*. London: J. Haberkorn, 1759.
- Clément, Gilles. *Le Jardin en mouvement*. Paris: Pandora, 1991.
- Clément, Gilles. *Thomas et le Voyageur*. Paris: Albin Michel, 1997.
- Clément, Gilles. *Manifeste du Tiers paysage*. Paris: Éditions Sujet/Objet, 2003.
- Clément, Gilles. *Une brève histoire du jardin*. Paris: Editions du 81, 2011.
- Clément, Gilles, and Coloco. "Jardin du Tiers-Paysage." *Area* 152 (2017): 84-87.
- Clynes, Manfred E., and Nathan S. Kline. "Cyborgs and Space." *Astronautics Journal of the American Rocket Society* 9 (1960): 26-27; 74-76.
- Coccia, Emanuele. *The Life of Plants: A Metaphysics of Mixture*. Cambridge-Malden: Polity Press, 2018.
- Coleman, Nathaniel. *Utopias and Architecture*. London-New York: Routledge, 2005.
- Colomina, Beatriz, and Mark Wigley. *Are We Human?* Zürich: Lars Müller, 2016.
- Connell, Raewyn. *Gender: In World Perspective*. Cambridge-Malden: Polity Press, 2002.

- Cooke, Arthur. *A Book of Dovecotes*. London: T. N. Foulis, 1920.
- Copley, Frank Barkley. *Frederick W. Taylor, Father of Scientific Management*, vol. 2. New York: Harper and Brothers, 1923.
- Crasset, Matali. *Le Pigeonnier/The Pigeon Loft*. Paris: Pyramid NTCV, 2004.
- Crutzen, Paul J. "Geology of Mankind." *Nature* 415, no. 23 (2002): 23.
- Damisch, Hubert. *Noah's Ark: Essays on Architecture*. Cambridge MA: The MIT Press, 2016.
- Darwin, Charles. *On the Origin of Species by Means of Natural Selection, or the Preservation of Favoured Races in the Struggle for Life*. London: John Murray, 1859.
- Davidson, Robert. *Genesis 1-11: Commentary by R. Davidson*. Cambridge: Cambridge University Press, 1973.
- Davies, Colin. *High Tech Architecture*. New York: Rizzoli, 1988.
- Davis, Heather, and Etienne Turpin, eds. *Art in the Anthropocene*. London: Open Humanities Press, 2015.
- Davis, Mike. "Who Will Build the Ark." *New Left Review* 61, no. 1 (2010): 29-46.
- De Brincken, Baron. *Mémoire descriptif sur la foret impériale de Bialowieza en Lituanie*. Warsaw: Glucksberg, 1826.
- Deleuze, Gilles, and Felix Guattari. *Mille Plateaux: Capitalisme et Schizophrénie*. Paris: Minuit, 1980.
- Deryabina, T. G., S. V. Kuchmel, L. L. Nagorskaya, T. G. Hinton, J. C. Beasley, A. Lerebours, and J. T. Smith. "Long-term Census Data Reveal Abundant Wildlife Populations at Chernobyl." *Current Biology* 25, no. 19 (2015): R824-R826.
- Derrida, Jacques. "The Animal That Therefore I Am (More to Follow)." *Critical Inquiry* 28, no. 2 (2002), 369-418.
- Desimini, Jil, Charles Waldheim, and Mohsen Mostafavi. *Cartographic Grounds: Projecting the Landscape Imaginary*. New York: Princeton Architectural Press, 2016.
- Despret, Vinciane. "Ceux qui insistent: Les nouveaux commanditaires." In *Faire art comme on fait société*, edited by Didier Debaise et al., 133-146. Dijon: Les Presses du Réel, 2013.
- Despret, Vinciane. *What Would Animals Say if We Asked the Right Questions?* Minneapolis: University of Minnesota Press, 2016.
- de Tocqueville, Alexis. *Journey to America 1831-1832*. Translated by George Lawrence. New Haven: Yale University Press, 1960.
- Díaz, Eva. "Dome Culture in the Twenty-first Century." *Grey Room* 42 (2011): 80-105.
- Di Cristina, Giuseppa, ed. *Architecture and Science*. New York: Wiley, 2001.
- Diller + Scofidio. *Blur: The Making of Nothing*. New York: Harry N. Abrams, 2002.
- Diller, Elizabeth, and Ricardo Scofidio. *Flesh: Architectural Probes*. New York, Princeton Architectural Press, 1994.
- Diller, Elizabeth, and Ricardo Scofidio. "Architecture as a Habitable Medium." In *Disappearing Architecture*, edited by Georg Flachbart and Peter Weibel, 184-195. Basel-Boston-Berlin: Birkhäuser, 2005.
- Downing, Andrew Jackson. *Architecture of Country Houses; Including Designs for Cottages, Farm-Houses, and Villas, with Remarks on Interiors, Furniture, and the Best Modes of Warming and Ventilating*. New York: Wiley and Putnam, 1841.
- Edelman, Bernard. *La maison de Kant*. Paris: Payot, 1984.
- Edginton, Brian W. *Charles Waterton: A Biography*. Cambridge: James Clarke & Co., 1996.
- Ellis, Cristin. *Antebellum Posthuman: Race and Materiality in the Mid-Nineteenth Century*. New York: Fordham University, 2018.

- Ellis, Erle. *Anthropocene: A Very Short Introduction.* Oxford: Oxford UP, 2018.
- Emerson, Ralph Waldo. *Nature.* Boston: James Munroe and Company, 1836.
- Evelyn, John. *Silva, or a Discourse of Forest-Trees and the Propagation of Timber in His Majesty's Dominions.* London: John Martin, 1664.
- Ewen, John G., Doug P. Armstrong, Kevin A. Parker, and Philip J. Seddon, eds. *Reintroduction Biology: Integrating Science and Management.* London: Wiley-Blackwell, 2012.
- Ferguson, Adam. *Essay on the History of Civil Society* (1767). Philadelphia: A. Finlay, 1819.
- Fernow, Bernhard E. *A Brief History of Forestry.* Toronto: Toronto University Press, 1907.
- Ferriss, Hugh. *The Metropolis of Tomorrow.* New York: Princeton Architectural Press, 1929.
- Fischer von Erlach, Johann Bernhard. *Entwurff Einer Historischen Architectur.* Leipzig, 1725.
- Flückiger, Urs Peter. *How Much House: Thoreau, Le Corbusier and the Sustainable Cabin.* Basel: Birkhäuser, 2016.
- Foucault, Michel. *Les mots e les choses.* Paris: Gallimard, 1966.
- Foucault, Michel. *Surveiller et punir: Naissance de la prison.* Paris: Alcan, 1975.
- Foucault, Michel. *Power/Knowledge.* Edited by Colin Gordon. New York: Pantheon Books, 1980.
- Fowler, Cary. *Seeds on Ice: Svalbard and the Global Seed Vault.* Westport CT: Easton Studio Press, 2016.
- Galison, Peter. *Image and Logic: The Material Culture of Twentieth Century Physics.* Chicago: University of Chicago Press, 1997.
- Galison, Peter, and Caroline A. Jones. "Factory, Laboratory, Studio: Dispersing Sites of Production." In *The Architecture of Science*, edited by Peter Galison and Emily Thompson, 497-540. Cambridge MA: The MIT Press, 1999.
- Giedion, Sigfried. *Mechanization Takes Command: A Contribution to Anonymous History.* Minneapolis: University of Minnesota Press, 2013.
- Giono, Jean. *The Man Who Planted Trees.* White River Junction: Chelsea Green Publishing, 1985.
- Gissen, David. *Subnature: Architecture's Other Environments.* New York: Princeton Architectural Press, 2009.
- Gissibl, Bernhard, Sabine Höhler, and Patrick Kupper, eds. *Civilizing Nature: National Parks in Global Historical Perspective.* Oxford-New York: Berghahn Books, 2012.
- Godel, Addison. "When Windows Were Wires: The Projection of Network Invulnerability and the Architecture of the AT&T Long Lines." *Grey Room* 61 (2015): 34-65.
- Goffner, Deborah, Hannah Sinare, and Line J. Gordon. "The Great Green Wall for the Sahara and the Sahel Initiative as an Opportunity to Enhance Resilience in Sahelian Landscapes and Livelihoods." *Reg Environ Change* 19 (2019), 1417-1428.
- Goldberger, Paul. "When Building for Future Means a Step Backwards." *New York Times* (6 December 1975): 33.
- Gomez-Luque, Mariano, and Ghazal Jafari, eds. *New Geographies 09: Posthuman.* Cambridge MA: Harvard GSD, 2018.
- Goodwin, Francis. *The Man in the Moone: or a Discourse of a Voyage thither by Domingo Gonsales.* London, 1638.
- Greenough, Horatio. *Form and Function: Remarks on Art.* Berkeley: University of California Press, 1947.

- Gridley, Karen, ed. *Man of the Trees: Selected Writings of Richard St. Barbe Baker.* Willits CA: Ecology Action, 1989.
- Grimal, Pierre. *L'art des jardins.* Paris: PUF, 1974.
- Günther, Hanns (Walter de Haas). *In hundert Jahren: Die künftige Energieversorgung der Welt.* Stuttgart: Kosmos, 1931.
- Hablik, Wenzel. *Hablik, Designer, Utopian, Architect, Expressionist, Artist, 1881-1934.* London: Architectural Association, 1980.
- Haeckel, Ernst. *Generelle Morphologie der Organismen.* Berlin, 1866.
- Hale, Edward Everett. "Brick Moon." *Atlantic Monthly* 24 (1869).
- Handlin, David P. *The American Home: Architecture and Society,* 1815-1915. Boston-Toronto: Little, Brown & Co., 1979.
- Haraway, Donna J. "A Cyborg Manifesto: Science, Technology, and Socialist-Feminism in the Late Twentieth Century (1985)." In *Simians, Cyborgs and Women: The Reinvention of Nature,* 149-181. New York: Routledge, 1991.
- Haraway, Donna J. "Sowing Worlds: A Seed Bag for Terraforming with Earth Others." In *Beyond the Cyborg: Adventures with Donna Haraway,* edited by Margret Grebowicz and Helen Merrick, 137-146. New York: Columbia University Press, 2013.
- Haraway, Donna J. *Staying with the Trouble: Making Kin in the Chthulucene.* Chicago: Duke University Press Books, 2016.
- Harding Davis, Rebecca. *Bits of Gossip.* Boston: Houghton Mifflin, 1904.
- Hardingham, Samantha. *Cedric Price Opera.* London: Wiley, 2003.
- Hardingham, Samantha. *Cedric Price Works 1952–2013: A Forward-Minded Retrospective.* London: AA Publications, 2016.
- Hardingham, Samantha, and Kester Rattenbury. *Richard Rogers: The Pompidou Center.* Abingdon: Routledge, 2012.
- Harrison, Ariane Lourie, ed. *Architectural Theories of the Environment: Posthuman Territory.* New York-Abingdon: Routledge, 2013.
- Harrison, Robert Pogue. *Forests: The Shadow of Civilization.* Chicago: The University of Chicago Press, 1992.
- Healy, Hall. "Korean Demilitarized Zone: Peace and Nature Park." *International Journal on World Peace* 24, no. 4 (2007): 61-83.
- Heidegger, Martin. *Brief über den Humanismus.* Frankfurt am Main: Klostermann, 1947.
- Hersey, George. *The Lost Meaning of Classical Architecture: Speculations on Ornament from Vitruvius to Venturi.* Cambridge MA: The MIT Press, 1988.
- Hill, Jonathan. *Actions of Architecture: Architects and Creative Users.* London: Routledge, 2003.
- Hoffmann, E. T. A. "Rat Krespel." In *Die Serapionsbrüder.* Berlin: G. Reimer, 1819.
- Inaji, Tashiro. *The Garden as Architecture: Form and Spirit in the Gardens of Japan, China, and Korea.* Tokyo-New York-London: Kodansha International, 1998.
- Ingraham, Catherine. *Architecture, Animal, Human: The Asymmetric Condition.* London-New York: Routledge, 2006.
- Irigaray, Luce. *This Sex Which Is Not One.* Ithaca NY: Cornell University Press, 1985.
- Ishigami, Junya. *Another Scale of Architecture.* Kyoto: Seigensha Art Publishing, 2010.
- Ishigami, Junya. *El Croquis* 182 (2015).
- Itard, Jean Marc Gaspard, *De l'éducation d'un homme sauvage ou des premieres developpements physiques et moraux de jeune sauvage de l'Aveyron.* Paris: Goujon Imprimeur-Libraire, 1801.

- Jameson, Fredric. "Progress Versus Utopia: Or, Can We Imagine the Future?" *Science- Fiction Studies* 9 (1982): 147-158.
- Jencks, Charles. *Modern Movements in Architecture.* London: Penguin, 1985.
- Jencks, Charles. *Post-Modernism: The New Classicism in Art and Architecture.* New York: Rizzoli, 1987.
- John, Richard D. *Network Nation: Inventing American Telecommunications.* Cambridge MA: Belknap Press, 2010.
- Kadinsky, Sergey. *Hidden Waters of New York City: A History and Guide to 101 Forgotten Lakes, Ponds, Creeks, and Streams in the Five Boroughs.* Woodstock: Countryman Press, 2016.
- Kafka, George, Sophie Lovell, and Fiona Shipwright, eds. *Archifutures. Volume 5: Apocalypse. A Field Guide to Surviving the Future of Architecture.* Barcelona: dpr-barcelona, 2018.
- Kelley, John L. *General Topology.* Berlin: Springer, 1975.
- Khan-Magomedov, Selim Omarovich. *Georgii Krutikov: The Flying City and Beyond.* Barcelona: Editorial Tenov, 2015.
- Kim, Kwi-Gon. *The Demilitarized Zone (DMZ) of Korea: Protection, Conservation and Restoration of a Unique Ecosystem.* New York-Dordrecht-London: Springer Science & Business Media, 2013.
- Kircher, Athanasius. *Arca Noë.* Amsterdam: Johannes van Waesbergen, 1675.
- Kleiman, Devra G. "Reintroduction of captive mammals for conservation." *BioScience* 39 (1989): 152-161.
- Kluver, Billy, Julie Martin, and Barbara Rose, eds. *Pavilion: Experiments in Art and Technology.* New York: Dutton, 1972.
- Knobel, Lance. "Rogers Quimper: factory." *The Architectural Review* 171, no. 1020 (1982) 23-30.
- Koehler, Robert. *The DMZ: Dividing the Two Koreas.* Seoul: Seoul Selection, 2010.
- Kohn, Eduardo. *How Forests Think: Toward an Anthropology Beyond the Human.* Berkeley: University of California Press, 2013.
- Kosky, Jeffrey L. *Arts of Wonder: Enchanting Secularity.* Chicago-London: The University of Chicago Press, 2012.
- Kvanvig, Helge. *Primeval History: Babylonian, Biblical, and Enochic: An Intertextual Reading.* Leiden: Brill, 2011.
- Lambert, Phyllis. *Building Seagram.* New Haven and London: Yale University Press, 2013.
- Landau, Roy. *New Directions in British Architecture.* London: Studio Vista, 1968.
- Landau, Roy. "Engineers and Architects: Newby + Price." *AA Files* 27 (1994): 25-32.
- Latina, Vincenzo, and Marco Navarra, eds. *Air fundamental: Collision between Inflatable and Architecture.* Siracusa: LetteraVentidue, 2018.
- Latour, Bruno. "Steps Toward the Writing of a Compositionist Manifesto." *New Literary History* 41 (2010): 471-490.
- Laugier, Marc-Antoine. *Essai sur l'architecture.* Paris, 1753.
- Le Corbusier. *The City of Tomorrow and Its Planning.* New York: Dover, 1987.
- Le Guin, Ursula K. *The Word for World is Forest.* New York: Berkley Publishing, 1976.
- Leopold, Aldo. *Game Management.* New York: Scribner's, 1933.
- Leopold, Aldo. *A Sand County Almanac: And Sketches Here and There.* Oxford: Oxford University Press, 1949.
- Leveratto, Jacopo. *From Within: Between Interior Architecture and Design.* Siracusa: LetteraVentidue, 2020.

- Lewallen, Constance, Steve Seid, and Chip Lord. *Ant Farm*, 1968-1978. Berkeley: University of California Press, 2004.
- Lewis, Michael. *American Wilderness: A New History*. Oxford-New York: Oxford University Press, 2007.
- Linnaeus, Carolus. *Systema naturae, sive, Regna tria naturae systematice proposita per classes, ordines, genera, & species*. Haak: Lugduni Batavorum, 1735.
- Loisel, Gustave. *Histoire des Menageries: De l'antiquité à nos jours*. Paris: Doin et Fils, 1912.
- Lovelock, James E. "Gaia as Seen through the Atmosphere." *Atmospheric Environment* 6, no. 8 (1972): 579-580.
- Lowenhaupt Tsing, Anna, *The Mushroom at the End of the World: On the Possibility of Life in Capitalist Ruins*. Princeton: Princeton University Press, 2015.
- Lucian. *The True History*. Translated by Paul Turner. Bloomington: Indiana University Press, 1958.
- Macdonald, Angus, ed. *Anthony Hunt*. London: Thomas Telford, 2000.
- Malafouris, Lambros, and Carl Knappett, eds. *Material Agency: Towards a Non-Anthropocentric Approach*. New York: Springer, 2008.
- Mallet, Abbé Edme-François. "Arche." In *Encyclopédie, ou Dictionnaire raisonné des sciences, des arts et des métiers*, vol. 1, edited by Denis Diderot and Jean Le Rond d'Alembert, 607. Paris, 1751.
- Mann, William N. *Wild Animals In and Out of the Zoos*. Washington: Smithsonian Institution, 1930.
- Marcuse, Herbert. "Philosophy and Critical Theory (1937)." In *Negations: Essays in Critical Theory*, translated by Jeremy J. Shapiro, 99-118. London: MayFlyBooks, 2009.
- Marinoni, Giuseppe. "Parc Henri Matisse." *Lotus Navigator* 122 (2004): 113-117.
- Massey, Jonathan. "Buckminster Fuller's Reflexive Modernism." *Design and Culture* 4, no. 3 (2012): 325-344.
- Masteller, Richard N., and Jean Carwile Masteller. "Rural Architecture in Andrew Jackson Downing and Henry David Thoreau: Pattern Book Parody in Walden." *New England Quarterly* 57, no.4 (December 1984): 483-510.
- Mathews, Stanley. *From Agit-Prop to Free Space: The Architecture of Cedric Price*. London: Black Dog Publishing, 2007.
- Maturana, Umberto, and Francisco J. Varela. *Autopoiesis and Cognition*. Dordrecht: Reidel, 1980.
- Matuz, Roger. *Albert Kahn: Builder of Detroit*. Detroit: Wayne State University Press, 2002.
- McHarg, Ian. *Design with Nature*. New York: Doubleday, 1969.
- McLean, Mick, and Tom Rowland eds. *The Inmos Saga: A Triumph of National Enterprise?* London: Pinter, 1985.
- Meadows, Donella H., Dennis L. Meadows, Jørgen Randers, and William W. Behrens III. *The Limits to Growth*. New York: Universe Books, 1972.
- Morton, Timothy. *Dark Ecology: For a Logic of Future Coexistence*. New York: Columbia University Press, 2016.
- Morton, Timothy. *Being Ecological*. Cambridge MA: The MIT Press, 2018.
- Muir, John. *Our National Parks*. Boston: Houghton Mifflin, 1901.
- Mullin, Stephen. "Cedric Price: 1934-2003." *Arq* 7, no. 2 (2003): 113-118.
- Mumford, Lewis. *The Story of Utopias*. Gloucester MA: Peter Smith, 1959.
- Mumford, Lewis. *Roots of Contemporary American Architecture*. New York: Dover Publications, 1972.
- Muschamp, Herbert. "Living Boldly on the Event Horizon." *The New York Times* (19 November 1998).

- Næss, Arne. *Ecology, Community and Lifestyle*. Cambridge: Cambridge University Press, 1989.
- Nash, Roderick Frazier. *Wilderness and the American Mind*. New Haven-London: Yale University Press, 1967.
- National Zoological Park. *Records: 1887-1966*. Washington DC: Smithsonian Institution Archives, 1966.
- Neder, Federico. *Fuller Houses: R. Buckminster Fuller's Dymaxion Dwellings and Other Domestic Adventures*. Zürich: Lars Müller Publishers, 2008.
- Negroponte, Nicholas. *Soft Architecture Machines*. Cambridge MA: The MIT Press, 1975.
- Nelson, Mark. *Pushing Our Limits: Insights from Biosphere 2*. Tucson: The University of Arizona Press, 2018.
- Noll, A. Michael. *Introduction to Telephones and Telephone Systems, 3rd ed.* Boston: Artech House, 1998.
- Nye, David. *Electrifying America: Social Meanings of a New Technology*. Cambridge MA: MIT Press, 1999.
- Obrist, Hans Ulrich. *Re: CP*. Basel: Birkhäuser, 2003.
- O'Neill, Gerard K. *The High Frontier: Human Colonies in Space*. New York: William Morrow, 1977.
- Owen, Robert. *A New View of Society*. London: Richard and Arthur Taylor, 1814.
- Paige, Glenn D. "1966: Korea Creates the Future." *Asian Survey* 7, no. 1 (1967): 21-30.
- Park, Jongwoo. *DMZ: Demilitarized Zone of Korea*. Göttingen: Steidl, 2017.
- Pask, Gordon. "The Architectural Relevance of Cybernetics." *Architectural Design* 9 (1969): 494-496.
- Paul, Sherman. *The Shores of America: Thoreau's inward Exploration*. Urbana: University of Illinois Press, 1958.
- Peirce, Charles S. *Philosophy of Mathematics: Selected Writings*. Bloomington: Indiana University Press, 2010.
- Pevsner, Nikolaus. *A History of Building Types*. Princeton: Princeton University Press, 1979.
- Price, Cedric. *Building Design* 1071 (January 11, 1991): 18-21.
- Qvenild, Marte. "Svalbard Global Seed Vault: a 'Noah's Ark' for the World's Seeds." *Development in Practice* 18, no. 1 (2008): 110-116.
- Radkau, Joachim. *Wood: A History*. Cambridge: Polity, 2011.
- Read, Justin. "Alternative Functions: Oscar Niemeyer and the Poetics of Modernity." *Modernism/modernity* 12, no. 2 (2005): 253-272.
- Reich, Wilhelm. *Die Sexualität im Kulturkampf*. Copenhagen: Sexpol, 1936.
- Renfro, Charles. "Blur Building." *A+U* 428 (2006): 67.
- Revell, Keith D. "Law Makes Order: The Search for Ensemble in the Skyscraper City, 1890-1930." In *The American Skyscraper: Cultural Histories*, edited by R. Moudry, 38-59. Cambridge MA-New York: Cambridge University Press, 2005.
- Ricoeur, Paul. "Ideology and Utopia as Cultural Imagination." *Philosophic Exchange* 7, no. 1 (1976): 17-28.
- Robbins, Roland Wells. *Discovery at Walden*. Somerville MA: Thoreau Foundation, 1970.
- Roberts, Adam. *The History of Science Fiction*. London: Palgrave Macmillan, 2016.
- Robinson, Sarah. *Nesting: Body, Dwelling, Mind*. San Francisco: William Stout Publishers, 2011.
- Rocca, Alessandro. *Planetary Gardens: The Landscape Architecture of Gilles Clément*. Berlin: Walter de Gruyter, 2008.

- Rocca, Alessandro, and Jacopo Leveratto. "Thoreau and Kaczynski, the Media Cabin: Building a Manifesto." *Vesper* 3 (2020): 36-48.
- Roche, Pierre. *Antti Lovag Habitologie*. Paris: France Europe Editions 2010.
- Rogers, Richard. "Inmos in Gwent." *The Architectural Review* 172, no. 1030 (1982): 26-33.
- Rogers, Richard. "Una macchina leggera e flessibile." *Casabella* 61, no. 651/652 (1997/1998): 132-139.
- Rogers, Richard. *A place for All People: Life, Architecture and the Fair Society*. Edinburgh: Canongate Books, 2017.
- Rohan, Timothy M. "From Microcosm to Macrocosm: The Surface of Fuller and Sadao's US Pavilion at Montreal Expo 67." *Architectural Design* 73, no. 2 (2003): 50-56.
- Rousseau, Jean-Jacques. *Discours sur l'origine et les fondements de l'inégalité parmi les hommes*. Paris: Marc-Michel Rey, 1755.
- Rousseau, Jean-Jacques. *Émile ou De l'éducation*. Paris: Jean Néaulme, 1762.
- Ruskin, John. *The Stones of Venice*, second volume. London: Smith, Elder and Co., 1873.
- Ryker, Lori. *Off the Grid Homes: Case Studies for Sustainable Living*. Layton UT: Gibbs Smith, 2007.
- Rykwert, Joseph. *On Adam's House in Paradise: The Idea of Primitive Hut in Architectural History*. New York: The Museum of Modern Art, 1972.
- Schleiden, Matthias Jacob. *The Plant: A Biography*. Translated by Arthur Henfrey. London, Hippolyte Bailliere, 1848.
- Schmarsow, August. *Das Wesen der architektonischen Schöpfung*. Leipzig: Hiersemann, 1894.
- Scully, Vincent. *Louis I. Kahn*. New York: George Braziller, 1962.
- Semper, Gottfried. *Der Stil in den technischen und tektonischen Künsten oder praktische Aesthetik*. Frankfurt, 1860.
- Serres, Michel. *Le Contrat naturel*. Paris: Flammarion, 1992.
- Shaw, Debra Benita. *Posthuman Urbanism: Mapping Bodies in Contemporary City Space*. London: Rowman & Littlefield, 2018.
- Slavid, Ruth. *Micro: Very Small Buildings*. New York: Laurence King Publishing, 2009.
- Sloterdijk, Peter. *Sphären. I. Blasen*. Frankfurt: Suhrkamp Verlag, 1998.
- Sloterdijk, Peter. "Foam City: About Urban Multitudes." *New Geographies* 0 (2007): 151.
- Sörgel, Herman. *Atlantropa*. Zurich: Fretz & Wasmuth; Munich: Piloty & Loehle, 1932.
- Stapledon, Olaf. "Interplanetary Man." *Journal of the British Interplanetary Society* 7 (1948): 213-233.
- St. Barbe Baker, Richard. *Men of Trees: In the Mahogany Forests of Kenya and Nigeria*. New York: The Dial Press, 1931.
- St. Barbe Baker, Richard. *Green Glory*. New York: A.A. Wyn, Inc., 1949.
- St. Barbe Baker, Richard. *Sahara Challenge*. London: Lutterworth Press, 1954.
- St. Barbe Baker, Richard. *Dance of the Trees*. London: Oldbourne Press, 1956.
- St. Barbe Baker, Richard. *Land of Tane*. London: Lutterworth Press, 1956.
- St. Barbe Baker, Richard. *My Life, My Trees*. London: Lutterworth Press, 1970.
- Steiner, Hadas A. "For the Birds." *Grey Room* 13 (2003): 5-31.
- Stengers, Isabelle. *In Catastrophic Times: Resisting the Coming Barbarism*. Lüneburg: Open Humanities Press, 2015.
- Stern, Robert. *New York 1960: Architecture and Urbanism between the Second World War and the Bicentennial*. New York: Monacelli Press, 1995.

- Stocchi, Attilio. *Vittoriano Vigano: Etica brutalista.* Turin: Testo & Immagine, 1999.
- Stoppani, Antonio. *Corso di geologia: Geologia stratigrafica*, Vol. 2. Milan, 1873.
- Sudjic, Deyan, *The Architecture of Richard Rogers.* New York: Harry N. Abrams, 1995.
- Takei, Jiro, and Marc P. Keane. *Sakuteiki Visions of the Japanese Garden: A Modern Translation of Japan's Gardening Classic.* Boston: Tuttle Publishing, 2001.
- Tansley, Arthur George. "The Use and Abuse of Vegetational Terms and Concepts." *Ecology* 16, no. 3 (1935): 284-307.
- Taylor, Frederick Winslow. *The Principles of Scientific Management.* New York: Harper & Brothers, 1911.
- Taylor, Matthew A. *Universes without Us: Posthuman Cosmologies in American Literature.* Minneapolis: University of Minnesota Press, 2013.
- Temko, Allan. "The Humanist Architecture of John Carl Warnecke." *Architectural Forum* 113 (1960): 97-98.
- Tempany, Andrew, and Tom Armour. *Nature of the City: Green Infrastructures from the Ground Up.* London: RIBA-Taylor and Francis, 2020.
- Teyssot, Georges, *A Topology of Everyday Constellations.* Cambridge MA: The MIT Press, 2013.
- Thomas, William L., ed. *Man's Role in Changing the Face of the Earth.* Chicago: University of Chicago Press, 1956.
- Thomas Karle, Sarah, and David Karle. *Conserving the Dust Bowl: The New Deal's Prairie States Forestry Project.* Baton Rouge: LSU Press, 2017.
- Thoreau, Henry David. "Walking." In *The Norton Book of Nature Writing*, edited by Robert Finch and John Elder, 180-205. New York: W. W. Norton, 2002.
- Thoreau, Henry David. *Walden: Or Life in the Woods* (1854). New Haven: Yale University Press, 2004.
- Toepfer, Georg. *Historisches Wörterbuch der Biologie.* Berlin-Heidelberg: Springer Verlag, 2011.
- Tschumi, Bernard, Jacques Derrida, and Anthony Vidler. *Parc de la Villette.* London: Artifice, 2014.
- Tschumi, Christian. *Mirei Shigemori, Rebel in the Garden: Modern Japanese Landscape Architecture.* Basel-Boston-Berlin: Birkhäuser, 2007.
- Tsiolkovsky, Konstantin. *Beyond the Planet Earth* (1900). Translated by Kenneth Syers. London: Pergamon Press, 1960.
- Udvardy, Miklos F. D. "Notes on the Ecological Concepts of Habitat, Biotope and Niche." *Ecology* 40, no. 4 (1959): 725-728.
- van Lengen, Johan. *Manual del Arquitecto Descalzo.* Mexico: Editorial Concepto, 1980.
- Vannini, Phillip, and Jonathan Taggart. *Off the Grid: Re-Assembling Domestic Life.* London-New York: Routledge, 2014.
- Vernadsky, Vladimir I. *The Biosphere.* New York: Springer-Verlag, 1998.
- Verne, Jules. *De la Terre à la Lune, trajet direct en 97 heures 20 minutes.* Paris: Pierre-Jules Hetzel, 1865.
- Vian, Boris. *Je ne voudrais pas crever.* Paris: J.J. Pauvert, 1962.
- Viollet-le-Duc, Eugène Emmanuel. *Dictionnaire raisonné de l'architecture française du XIe au XVIe siècle*, tome III. Paris: Édition Bance, 1856.
- von Carlowitz, Hans Carl. *Sylvicultura Oeconomica, oder haußwirthliche Nachricht und Naturmäßige Anweisung zur wilden Baum-Zucht.* Leipzig: Johan Friedrich Braun, 1713.
- von Uexküll, Jakob, and Georg Kriszat. *Streifzüge durch die Umwelten von Tieren und Menschen: Ein Bilderbuch unsichtbarer Welten.* Berlin: Springer, 1934.

- Werner, Frank. *Covering + Exposing: The Architecture of Coop Himmelb(l)au.* Basel-Berlin-Boston: Birkhäuser, 2000.
- White, Frank. *The Overview Effect: Space Exploration and Human Evolution.* Boston: Houghton-Mifflin, 1987.
- White, Lynn. "The Historical Roots of Our Ecological Crisis." *Science* 155 (1967): 1203-1207.
- Whyte, William. *City: Rediscovering the Center.* New York: Anchor Books, 1988.
- Wiener, Norbert. *Cybernetics: Or Control and Communication in the Animal and the Machine.* Cambridge Ma: The MIT Press, 1948.
- Wigley, Mark. "The Architecture of Atmosphere." *Daidalos* 68 (1998): 27.
- Wigley, Mark. "Cabin Fever." *Perspecta* 30 (1999): 122-125.
- Wilkins, John. *The Discovery of a World in the Moone.* London, 1638.
- Will, Barbara. "The Nervous Origins of the American Western." *American Literature* 70, no. 2 (1998): 293-316.
- Wittgenstein, Ludwig. *Culture and Value.* Chicago: University of Chicago Press, 1980.
- Worster, Donald. *Nature's Economy: A History of Ecological Ideas.* Cambridge: Cambridge University Press, 1995.
- Young, Liam. *Machine Landscapes: Architectures of the Post Anthropocene.* London: Wiley, 2019.
- Zabel, Bernd, Phil Hawes, Hewitt Stuart, and Bruno D.V. Marino. "Construction and Engineering of a Created Environment: Overview of the Biosphere 2 Closed System." *Ecological Engineering* 13 (1999): 43-63.
- Zambelli, Matteo. "Artificial Natures." *Abitare* 580 (2018): 40-51.
- Zimmer, Jeanne M. "A History of Thoreau's Hut and Hut Site." *Concord Saunterer*, Supplement no. 3 (1973).

Index